D1287474

ROBERTS' ILLUSTRATED MILLWORK CATALOG

A Sourcebook of Turn-of-the-Century Architectural Woodwork

E. L. ROBERTS & CO.

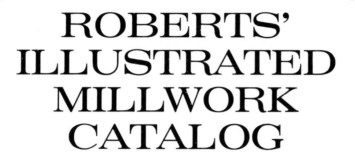

DOVER PUBLICATIONS, INC.
NEW YORK

NOTE

The page numbering in this Dover edition follows that of the original 1903 catalog volume in beginning with page 49 (page opposite to this one). The earlier 48 pages contained the separate Price Supplement mentioned at the bottom of page 49, and are not included here. Cross references to these pages are to be disregarded.

Published in Canada by General Publishing Company, Ltd., 30 Lesmill Road, Don Mills, Toronto, Ontario.

Published in the United Kingdom by Constable and Company, Ltd.

This Dover edition, first published in 1988, is an unabridged republication of the work originally published by E. L. Roberts & Co., Chicago, in 1903, under the title *Number 500 General Catalogue of E. L. Roberts & Co.* A note on the page numbering has been added (on this page). The illustrations originally in color (pages 81–87, 146, 148, 149, 151, 153, 155, 157, 159, 329–340, 358, 359, 362, 363, 365, 367, 370, 372, 374, 376, 377 and 379) are reproduced in black and white in the present edition.

Manufactured in the United States of America
Dover Publications, Inc., 31 East 2nd Street, Mineola, N.Y. 11501

Library of Congress Cataloging in Publication Data

Number 500 general catalogue of E.L. Roberts & Co.
Roberts' illustrated millwork catalog : a sourcebook of turn-of-the-century architectural woodwork/E.L. Roberts & Co.
p.   cm.
Reprint. Originally published : Chicago : E.L. Roberts & Co., 1903 under title : Number 500 general catalogue of E.L. Roberts & Co.
Includes index.
ISBN 0-486-25697-9 (pbk.)
1. Woodwork—United States—Catalogs. 2. Woodwork—Canada—Catalogs. 3. Architecture, Modern—19th century—United States. 4. Architecture, Modern—19th century—Canada. I. E.L. Roberts & Co. II. Title. III. Title : Illustrated millwork catalog.
TH1155.N86 1988
729'.6—dc 19   88-16205
                                                              CIP

NUMBER

500

GENERAL CATALOGUE

OF

E. L. ROBERTS & CO.

WHOLESALE MANUFACTURERS OF

DOORS, GLAZED SASH, BLINDS

MOULDINGS, FINE STAIRWORK,
ART AND WINDOW GLASS, MANTELS, GRILLES,
PARQUETRY FLOORS

AND

EVERYTHING IN THE LINE OF MILLWORK IN ANY WOOD

NOTE

THIS CATALOGUE IS NOT COMPLETE UNLESS ACCOMPANIED
BY OUR PRICE SUPPLEMENT

ORDER BY NUMBER ONLY

CAUTION.

Owing to the duplication of numbers and names by various parties referring to entirely different subjects, care must be used to specify where the numbers or names are obtained.

We assume that numbers or names of designs (if they appear herein) refer to this catalogue unless otherwise specified. In referring to other catalogues simply give firm name and year of publication.

Copyrighted 1903 by E. L. Roberts & Co.

DO NOT CUT THIS BOOK

INTRODUCTORY

WE take pleasure in presenting to you our general catalogue number 500. More novel and useful features are to be found within its covers than in any sash and door catalogue yet published. We have replaced the stereotyped matter now in general use by absolutely new and original designs. This important change will enable the progressive dealer to secure orders from the critical buyers who demand stylish and tasteful goods. We have issued separately in supplement form the official sash, door and blind list, as it is much used in figuring bills and estimates, and much easier to handle than the heavier catalogue. We will be pleased to make quotations on anything in our line shown in other books or from architects' details. We trust that these catalogues will prove of mutual advantage and hope to receive your orders and inquiries.

E. L. ROBERTS & CO.

TWENTY-SECOND STREET AND UNION PLACE, CHICAGO, U. S. A.

INDEX.

BIRDSEYE VIEW OF OUR IMMENSE PLANT—THE LARGEST IN CHICAGO.

DIRECTIONS FOR ORDERING
CIRCLE AND SEGMENT TOP WINDOWS.

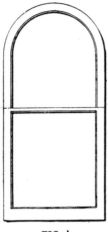

FIG. 1

For window frames, circle inside and outside.

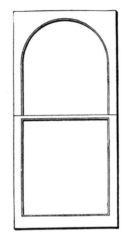

FIG. 2

For window frames, circle outside, square inside.

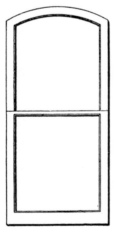

FIG. 3

For window frames, segment inside and outside.

Always use these figures, viz. 1, 2, 3 or 4 in ordering segment or circle top windows or frames.

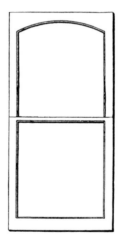

FIG. 4

For window frames, segment outside, square inside.

Windows made in the above styles can be filled with any number of lights required.

Always give the radius on segment, circle or gothic openings.

The regular radius of a circle top is ½ the width and on segment and gothic top the full width of opening.

For elliptic or irregular openings always furnish pattern.

A window indicates two pieces. A sash indicates one piece. A pair of blinds indicates two pieces. A blind indicates one piece. A set of sash or blinds indicates more than two pieces, and order should be accompanied with sketch.

DIRECTIONS FOR ORDERING.

Save valuable time by closely following the directions below.

Doors, blinds and sash are often ordered 1¼, 1½ and 2 inches thick. Do not use these terms, as it only delays orders. The regular thicknesses are 1⅛, 1⅜ and 1¾ inches, and all other thicknesses must be made to order at extra price.

Unless otherwise specified, or covered by standing instructions to the contrary, we will understand all orders as calling for REGULAR WESTERN STYLES OF GOODS, as described in this Catalogue.

The universal rule in ordering mill-work is to give the width first and then the height.

WINDOWS AND SASH.

A—The term Sash indicates a single piece.

B—The term Window means two pieces, an upper and a lower Sash, made with either plain or check rail.

C—In ordering regular sizes of Sash or Windows, give size of glass and number of lights and thickness; if a Window, whether check or plain rail; state whether open or glazed, and if glazed, whether with single or double strength glass.

D—In ordering odd sizes, give size of opening to be filled and describe as above.

E—When measurements are given in inches, it usually indicates the glass size, and we will so understand it; when given in feet and inches the outside measure or opening is understood.

F—In ordering segment, circle, gothic or elliptic top openings, see opposite page.

BLINDS.

In Ordering, Specify Whether Outside (O. S.) or Inside (I. S.) Blinds are Wanted.

G—OUTSIDE BLINDS. In ordering Outside Blinds, if regular, give size of glass and number of lights in window for which they are intended and size of opening to be filled. If odd, give thickness and state if rolling slats (R. S.), stationary slats (S. S.), or half rolling and half stationary slats (½ R. S., ½ S. S.) are required. If other than these styles are required, order must so state.

H—The regular opening for Outside Blinds is one (1) inch longer than Check Rail Windows of corresponding glass size. Where Blinds of extra length for brick buildings are desired, order must so state and Blinds will then be made two (2) inches longer than sash opening.

I—Our Standard Blinds are 1⅛ inch thick, full rolling slats made for regular openings, as above described. When not otherwise specified we assume this to be the style desired, and fill orders accordingly.

J—INSIDE BLINDS. In ordering it is best to give exact outside measure of opening to be filled. Give thickness, number of folds and state if all panels, all slats or half panel and half slats, referring to style desired as shown in cuts on page 77, giving sketch of any unusual arrangement of panels.

K—If Blinds are to be cut, state how many times and give distance from top of window to center of meeting rail.

L—If Blinds are to fold into pockets, give size of pockets.

M—State quality, whether No. 1, for paint or oil finish.

N—When description of Window only is given, as in ordering O. S. Blinds, we furnish our standard measurement of Inside Blinds, which is the same as the check rail window opening, 1⅛ inch thick, four fold where practicable, style made to cut once at check rail.

DOORS.

O—In ordering always give width, height, thickness, number of panels and quality. If full instructions are not given, to save time in shipment, we assume that our Standard Door 1⅜ inch, Four Panel O. G. "A" quality is desired, and will fill order accordingly.

P—If other than Four Panel O. G. Doors are required, for Panel Doors give number and ar-

rangement of panels and style of Sticking; for Sash Doors give number of style desired; indicate whether open or glazed, and if glazed, style of glazing.

Q—Where Moulded Doors are required state whether flush or raised mould is desired, and if to be moulded on one or two sides.

FRAMES.

R—In ordering, state whether for Outside or Inside Frames.

S—For Window Frames give size, thickness and full description of window, stating whether for frame, brick or brick veneer building, referring to styles shown on pages 71, 72, 73 and 74. If for frame or brick veneer building, give width of studding. If for brick building, give thickness of wall. State if frames are desired with or without pulleys.

T—For Outside Door Frames give size and thickness of door and state whether frames are required with stops or with rabbeted jambs, and if sill is to be pine or oak, referring to styles on pages 71, 72, 73 and 74. If for frame building, give width of studding; if for brick building, give thickness of wall.

U—For Inside Door Frames give size and thickness of door and width and thickness of jambs; state whether stops or rabbeted jambs are required.

MOULDINGS.

V—In ordering, give numbers as shown in this catalogue and name kind of wood. If other styles than are shown herein are required, furnish detail or sketch with correct measurements.

V7—Unless otherwise instructed, we will fill orders with our Standard White Pine Mouldings, Paint Quality, in miscellaneous long lengths, 10, 12, 14 and 16 feet long.

OFFICIAL GRADES SASH, DOORS AND BLINDS.

Adopted by the Wholesale Sash, Door and Blind Manufacturers'
Association of the Northwest.

DOORS.

AAA. Oil Finish Doors.—Material for AAA. Oil Finish Doors must be clear, no white sap admitted. Workmanship must be good.

AA. Oil Finish Doors.—Material For AA. Oil Finish Doors must be clear, with the exception that white sap will be admitted, not to exceed twenty-five (25) per cent of the face of any one piece. Workmanship must be good.

A. Doors.—Material in A. Doors must be clear, with the exception that water stains and small pin knots not exceeding one-fourth ($\frac{1}{4}$) inch in diameter may be admitted. No piece to contain more than two (2) such defects, and no door more than five (5) such defects on each side; white sap not considered a defect. Workmanship must be good.

B. Doors.—Material in B. Doors may contain knots not to exceed one (1) inch in diameter, and blue sap showing on both sides not to exceed fifty (50) per cent in any one piece of the door, and gum spots showing on one side (1) of a piece only and other slight defects, shall not exceed ten (10) in number on each side and each white pine stile, bottom and lock rail must contain at least one (1) and not to exceed three (3) such defects; plugs admitted and not regarded as a defect. Slight defects in workmanship admitted.

C. Doors.—Material in C. Doors may contain all stained sap and small worm holes and fine shake; also knots not exceeding one and three-fourths ($1\frac{3}{4}$) inches in diameter. Twenty (20) defects may be allowed on each side, also slight defects in workmanship. Each piece of white pine in a No. C Door must contain a defect. Not more than six (6) defects allowed in any one piece.

D. Doors.—D Doors are regarded as a cull door and must contain large coarse knots and may contain rot, worm holes, shake and other serious defects.

A Standard Door may be through tennon, blind tennon or dowelled.

WINDOWS.

Check Rail Windows may contain two (2) knots three-eighths ($\frac{3}{8}$) inch in diameter or one red knot five-eighths ($\frac{5}{8}$) inch in diameter in each piece of a window. White sap and not over thirty-three and one-third ($33\frac{1}{3}$) per cent blue sap may be admitted in any one window. Workmanship must be good.

Plain Rail Windows and Sash may contain blue sap and small knots.

BLINDS.

No. 1. Outside Blinds must be made of clear lumber, except that small, sound pin knots, water stain and white sap may be admitted. Workmanship must be good.

WOODS ADMISSIBLE.

Woods other than Michigan, Wisconsin and Minnesota white pine admitted in Doors, Blinds and Windows, except Oil Finish Goods.

WINDOWS, SASH AND TRANSOMS.

PLAIN RAIL WINDOWS.

8-light plain rail windows, see page 2 of price supplement accompanying this catalogue.

12-light plain rail windows, see page 3 of price supplement accompanying this catalogue.

CHECK RAIL WINDOWS.

8-light check rail windows, see page 4 of price supplement accompanying this catalogue.

12-light check rail windows, see page 5 of price supplement accompanying this catalogue.

4-light check rail windows, see pages 6 and 7 of price supplement accompanying this catalogue.

2-light check rail windows, see pages 8, 9, 10 and 11 of price supplement accompanying this catalogue.

2-light pantry check rail windows, see page 12 of price supplement accompanying this catalogue.

4-light pantry check rail windows, see page 12 of price supplement accompanying this catalogue.

Factory check rail windows, see page 13 of price supplement accompanying this catalogue.

SINGLE SASH.

1-light stall sash, see page 13 of price supplement accompanying this catalogue.

4-light barn sash, see page 13 of price supplement accompanying this catalogue.

Hot bed sash, see page 13 of price supplement accompanying this catalogue.

2 and 3-light cellar sash, see page 16 of price supplement accompanying this catalogue.

1-light front sash, see page 17 of price supplement accompanying this catalogue.

TRANSOMS.

1 and 2-light transoms, see pages 14 and 15 of price supplement accompanying this catalogue.

FRONT WINDOWS.
CHECK RAIL.

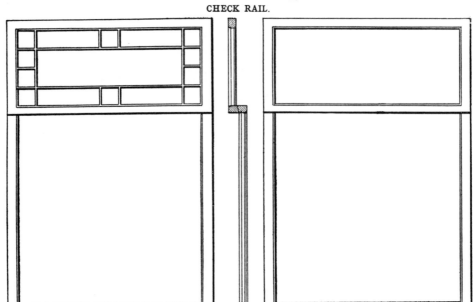

67   68

For prices of above windows in standard sizes, see page 18 of our price supplement accompanying this catalogue.

FRONT SASH.
STATIONARY.

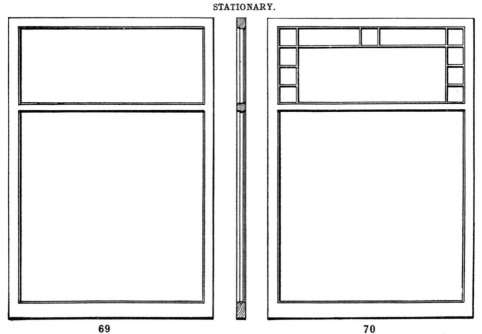

69   70

For prices of above sash in standard sizes, see page 18 of our price supplement accompanying this catalogue.

FRONT SASH AND TRANSOMS
STATIONARY.

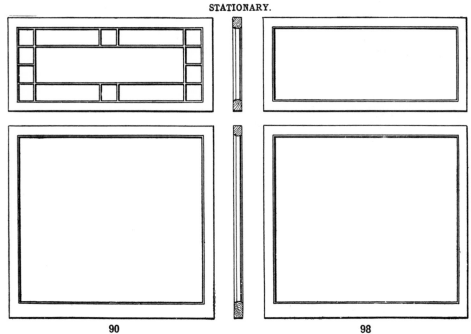

90   98

For prices of above designs in standard sizes, see page 19 of our price supplement accompanying this catalogue.

FRONT WINDOWS.
CHECK RAIL.

132   133

For prices of above windows in standard sizes, see page 19 of our price supplement accompanying this catalogue.

FRONT SASH.
STATIONARY.

R 133½   R 133½ A

Above sash glazed D. S. glass in bottom and leaded clear glass in top.
For prices in standard sizes, see page 20 of our price supplement accompanying this catalogue.

FRONT WINDOWS.
CHECK RAIL.

R 133½ B   R 133½ C

Above windows glazed D. S. glass in bottom and leaded clear glass in top.
For prices in standard sizes, see page 20 of our price supplement accompanying this catalogue.

FRONT SASH.
STATIONARY.

R 133½ D   **R 133½ E**

Bottom sash of above glazed D. S. glass. Top leaded art glass.
For prices in standard sizes, see page 21 of our price supplement accompanying this catalogue.
For colors of above, see designs R3110 and R3117, page 358.

FRONT WINDOWS.
CHECK RAIL.

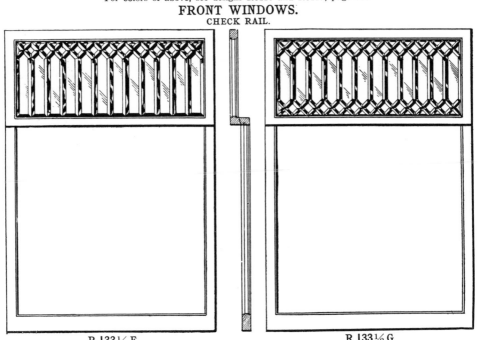

R 133½ F   **R 133½ G**

Above windows glazed D. S. glass in bottom and leaded bevel plate glass in top.
For prices in standard sizes, see page 21 of our price supplement accompanying this catalogue.

QUEEN ANNE WINDOWS.

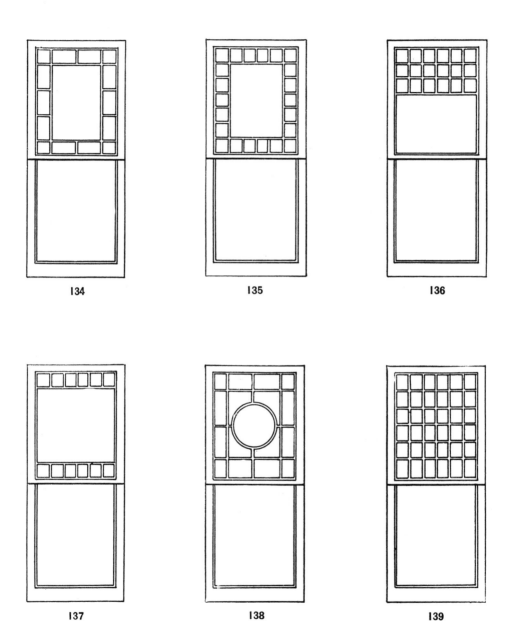

For prices of above windows in standard sizes, see page 22 of our price supplement
accompanying this catalogue.

QUEEN ANNE WINDOWS.

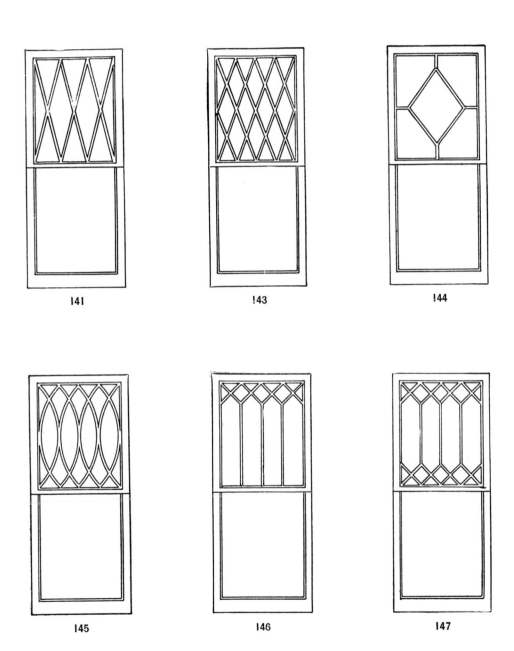

For prices of above windows in standard sizes, see page 22 of our price supplement accompanying this catalogue.

QUEEN ANNE SASH, WINDOWS AND TRANSOMS.

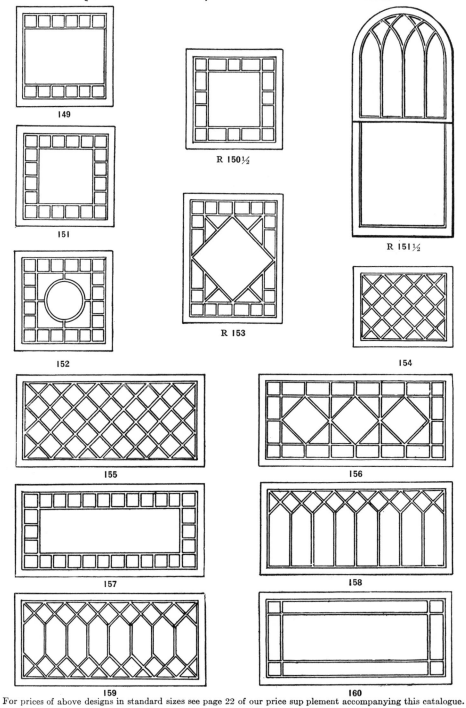

149

R 150½

151

R 153

152

R 151½

154

155

156

157

158

159

160

For prices of above designs in standard sizes see page 22 of our price sup plement accompanying this catalogue.

TRANSOMS.

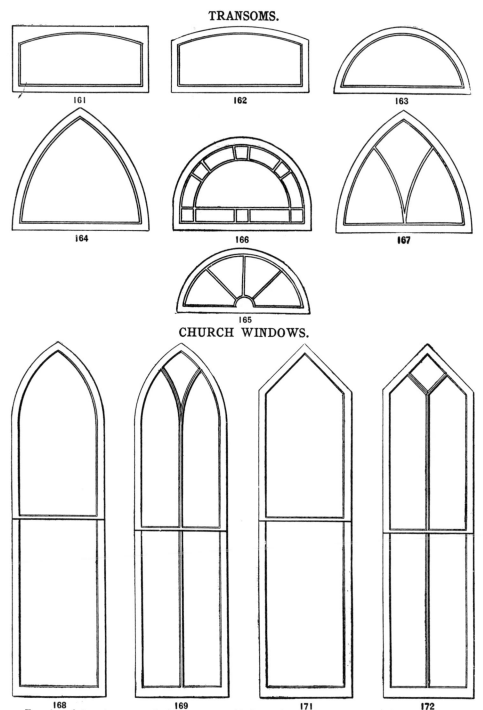

161

162

163

164

166

167

165

CHURCH WINDOWS.

168   169   171   172

For prices of above transoms and windows see page 23 of our price supplement accompanying this catalogue.
For other designs in lead and colors see pages 329 to 340 of this catalogue

GABLE SASH AND FRAMES.

SASH, R 173
FRAME, R 173½

SASH, R 174
FRAME, R 174½

SASH, R 175
FRAME, R 175½

SASH, R 176
FRAME, R 176½

SASH, R 177
FRAME, R 177½

SASH, R 178
FRAME, R 178½

SASH, R 179
FRAME, R 179½

SASH, R 180
FRAME, R 180½

SASH, R 181
FRAME, R 181½

SASH, R 182
FRAME, R 182½

SASH, R 183
FRAME, R 183½

SASH, R 184
FRAME, R 184½

For complete list of prices and standard sizes of above designs see page 23 of our price
supplement accompanying this catalogue.
For leaded and colored designs see pages 329 to 340 of this catalogue.

STORM SASH.

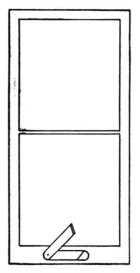

Two-Light
Ventilator Closed.

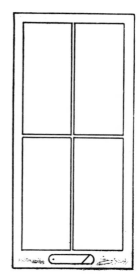

Four-Light
Ventilator Open.

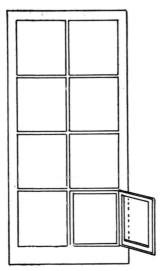

Eight-Light
Swing Light Ventilator.

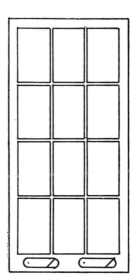

Twelve-Light
Double Ventilator.

Size of openings, same as blinds.
We can make one or more ventilators in bottom rail of sash, as shown in cuts.
If ventilators are wanted order must so state.
For prices of storm sash see rules 54 to 57, page 25 of our price supplement accompanying this catalogue.

BENT OR BOW WINDOWS.

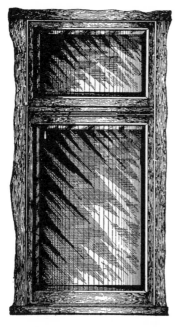

R 185   R 185½

We manufacture bent windows (glazed with window, plate or art glass), at moderate prices.
In ordering give radius to outside of top sash and exact width straight across between jambs.
If jambs are not parallel, a full-sized plan of sill is necessary.

For church windows and transoms see page 65.

FRONT WINDOWS.

WINDOW DESIGN, R 186
GLASS DESIGN, R 186½

In ordering follow instructions on pages 54 and 55.

WINDOW DESIGN R 187

CENTER GLASS DESIGN, R 187½   SIDE LIGHT GLASS DESIGN, R 188

Give sizes in writing for prices.

For other designs in lead and colors see pages 329 to 340.

WINDOW AND DOOR FRAMES.

There are many styles of frames used in various sections and cities of this country, and to avoid confusion in the operation of this department of our business, we show on following pages the standard frames of this market. Unless furnished with a detail showing different construction we always furnish frames for brick or stone buildings as shown on page 71, and for frame buildings as shown on page 72. We usually make inside door frames or jambs as follows:

For 2-in. studding and plastering 2 sides ⅞x3¾ and O G stop No. 8095 K.D.
" 4 "   "   "   "   2 "   ⅞x5⅝ "   "   "   " 8095 "
" 6 "   "   "   "   2 "   ⅞x7½ "   "   "   " 8095 "

In ordering or asking for estimate on frames read instruction at bottom of page 55 and study the details on pages 71, 72, 73 and 74 for style desired.

Always state whether they are to be put together or knock down and with or without pulleys. The quantity and kind of wood required regulates the price of frames. For this reason we prefer to make quotations on each requirement and can thus give you the benefit of best prices the specifications will warrant.

STANDARD BOX FRAMES FOR BRICK OR STONE BUILDING.

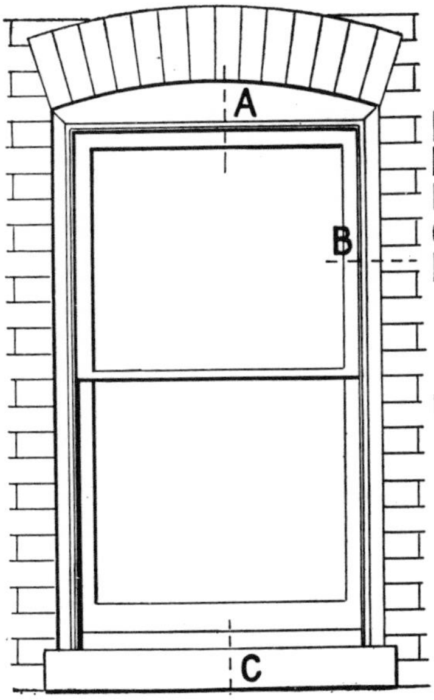

- D. HEAD CASING... 1⅛x4½
- E. HANGING STILE.. 1⅛x2 *8441
- F. BLIND STOP ⅞x2¼
- G. HEAD JAMB 1¾x4⅞
- H. PARTING STOP ½x13/16 *8432
- I. INSIDE STOP ⅜x1⅜ *8084
- K. BACK LINING 13/16x4⅛
- L. INSIDE CASING 13/16x4⅛
- M. PULLEY STILE 13/16x4⅛
- N. OUTSIDE CASING 13/16x4⅝
- O. SILL 1¾x5¾
- P. HEAD JAMB LINING
- R. JAMB LINING
- S. STOOL

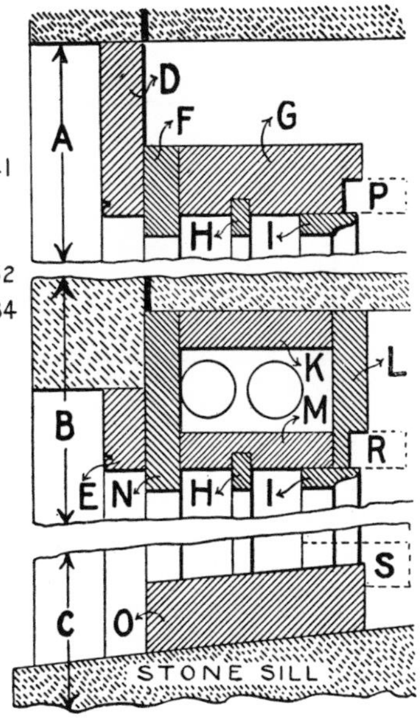

R 188A

STANDARD DOOR FRAME FOR BRICK OR STONE BUILDING.

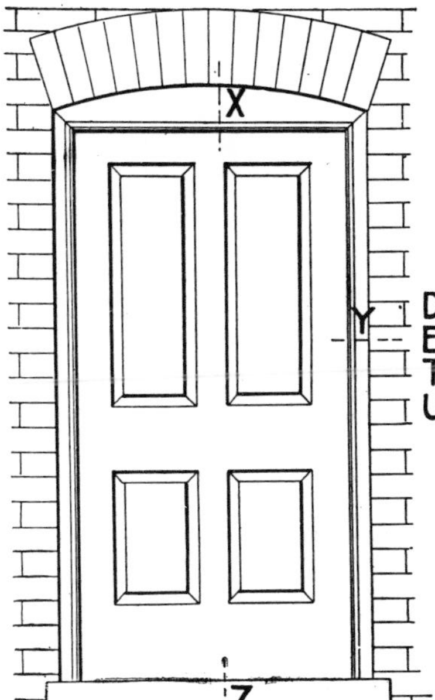

- D. HEAD CASING 1⅛x4½
- E. HANGING STILE. 1⅛x2 *8441
- T. HEAD JAMB 1¾x5¾
- U. SIDE JAMB 1¾x5¾

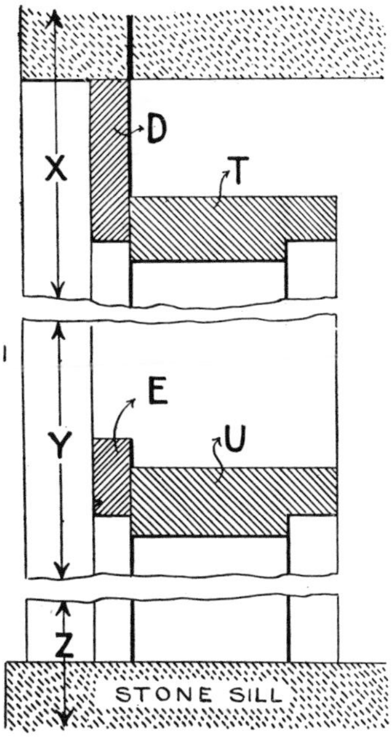

R 188B

Always read opposite page in ordering or asking for estimate on frames.

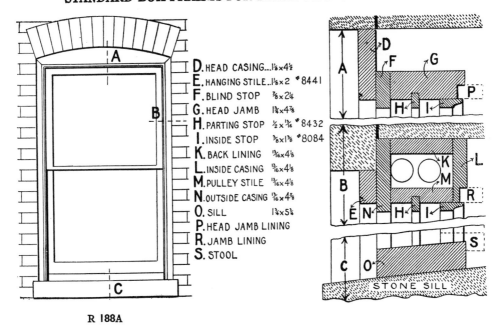

STANDARD DRIP CAP WINDOW FRAME FOR FRAME BUILDING.

For 4 inch studding, ⅞ inch sheathing and plastering.

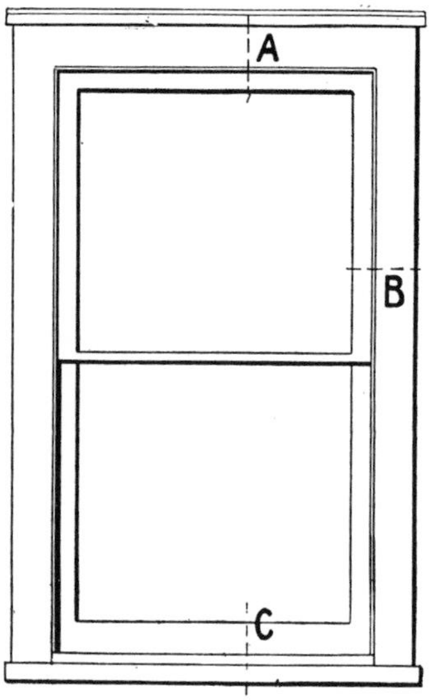

D. DRIP CAP........1⅛ x 1⅝ ..*8283
E. HEAD CASING...1⅛x4½
F. BLIND STOP.....13/16 x 1⅜ ..*8430
G. HEAD JAMB....13/16 x 4¾ *8431
H. PARTING STOP.. ½ x 13/16 *8432
I. INSIDE STOP.... ⅜ x 1⅜ *8084
K. SHEATHING......⅞ THICK
L. PLASTERING
M. OUTSIDE CASING. 1⅛x4½
N. PULLEY STILE.. 13/16 x 4¾ ..*8431
O. SUB SILL .... 13/16 x 5¾ ..*8440
P. MAIN SILL ......1¾ x 3¾ ..*8439

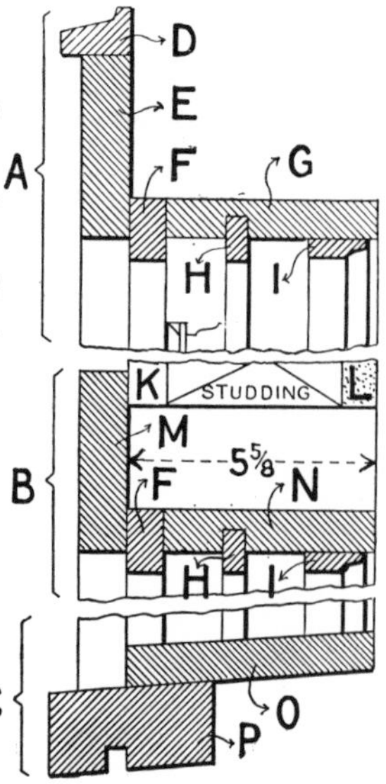

R 188½

STANDARD DRIP CAP DOOR FRAME FOR FRAME BUILDING.

For 4 inch studding, ⅞ inch sheathing and plastering.

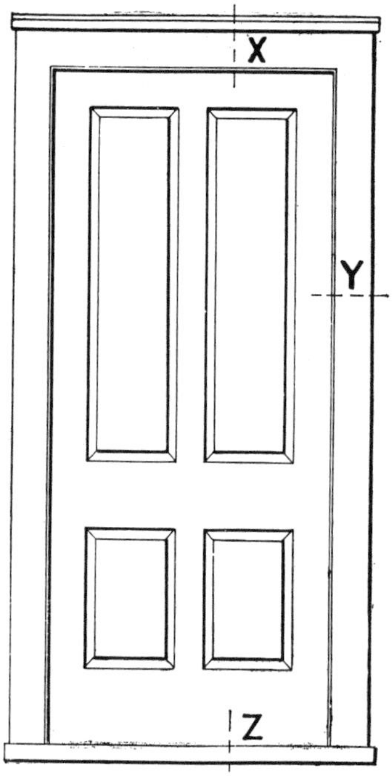

D. DRIP CAP........1⅛x 1⅝ *8283
E. HEAD CASING 1⅛x4½
K. SHEATHING
L. PLASTERING
M. OUTSIDE CASING...1⅛x4½
R. HEAD JAMB........1⅜x 5⅝
S. SIDE JAMB........1⅜x 5⅝
T. SILL..............1¾x 7½

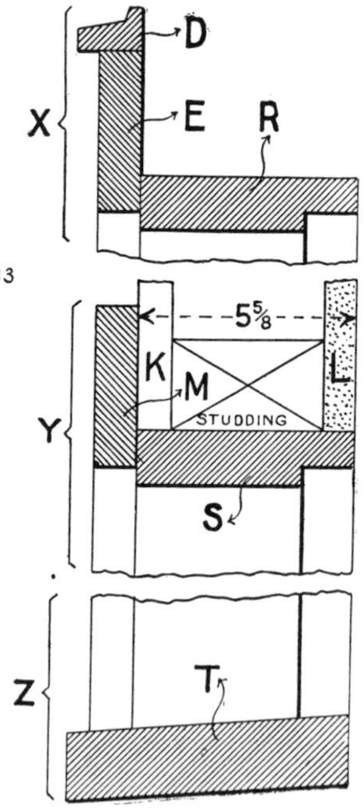

R 188½ A

Always read page 70 in ordering or asking for estimate on frames.

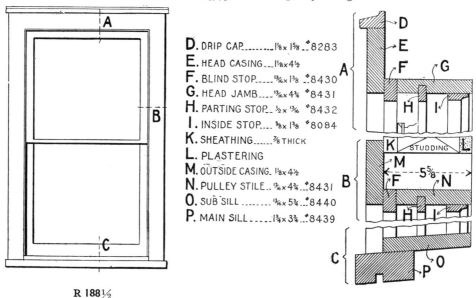

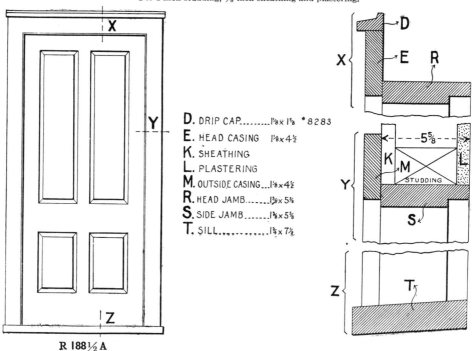

SPECIAL WINDOW FRAMES FOR FRAME BUILDING.

The construction is same as the design on opposite page.   Door frames are made to match.

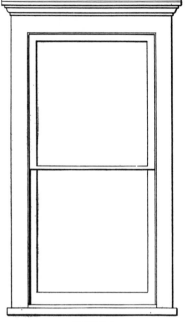

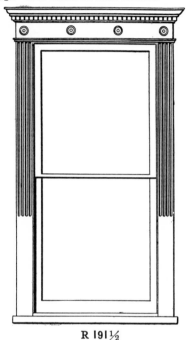

R 189½   R 191½

The door frames are same construction as the designs on opposite page.

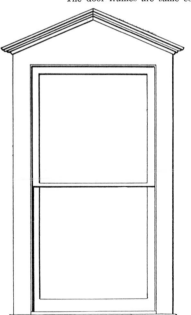

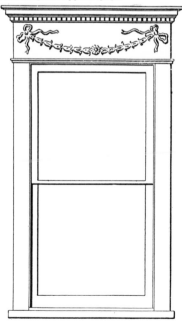

R 191½ A   R 191½ B

Always read page 70 in ordering or asking for estimate on frames.

SPECIAL "JIB" OR "POCKET HEAD" WINDOW FRAME FOR FRAME BUILDING.

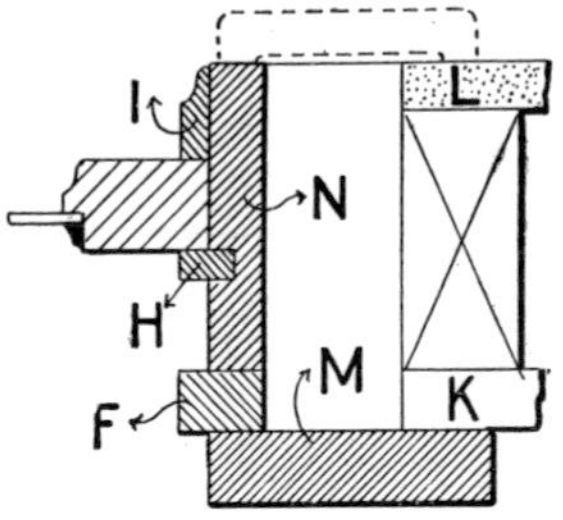

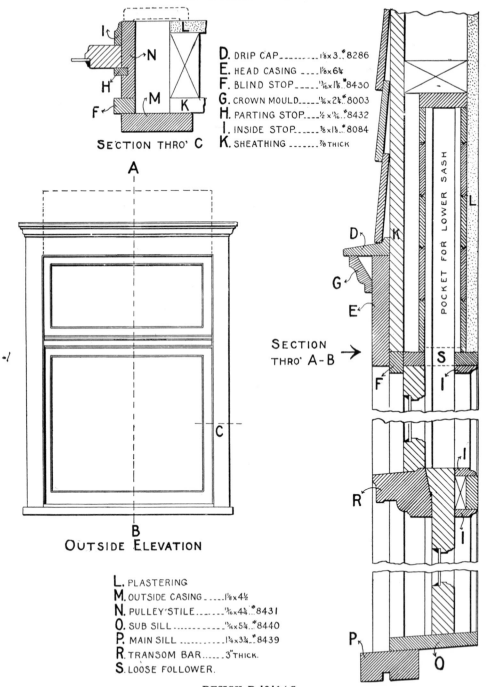

SECTION THRO' C

D. DRIP CAP .... 1 1/8 x 3 .. *8286
E. HEAD CASING .... 1 1/8 x 6 3/4
F. BLIND STOP ..... 13/16 x 1 3/8 .. *8430
G. CROWN MOULD ..... 13/16 x 2 1/4 .. *8003
H. PARTING STOP .... 1/2 x 13/16 .. *8432
I. INSIDE STOP ...... 3/8 x 1 3/8 .. *8084
K. SHEATHING .... 7/8 THICK

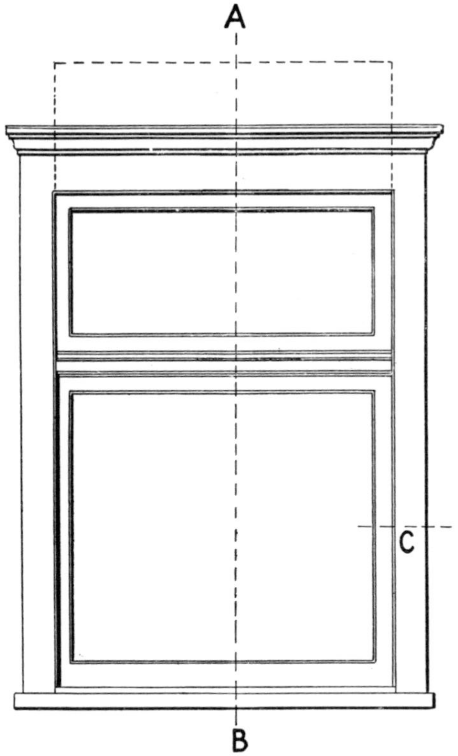

OUTSIDE ELEVATION

L. PLASTERING
M. OUTSIDE CASING ..... 1 1/8 x 4 1/2
N. PULLEY STILE .... 13/16 x 4 3/4 ... *8431
O. SUB SILL .... 13/16 x 5 3/4 ... *8440
P. MAIN SILL .... 1 3/4 x 3 3/4 ... *8439
R. TRANSOM BAR ...... 3" THICK.
S. LOOSE FOLLOWER.

SECTION THRO' A-B →

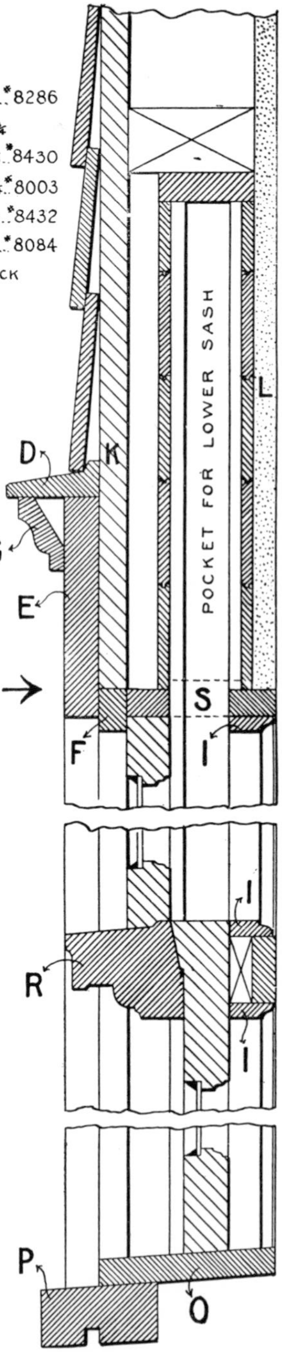

DESIGN R 191½ C

Always read page 70 in ordering or asking for estimate on frames.

VENETIAN BLINDS.

Best Venetian Blind Made.

They do not interfere with draperies. See cut above.

Ordinary Venetian blinds originated in Europe several centuries ago, and are still universally used, which ought to be sufficient testimonial of their durability.

Our blind has many improvements, making it all the more desirable, and is the peer of anything made for a similar purpose.

They have constantly grown in public favor since their introduction several years ago, and there are now thousands of them in use in all parts of the United States, in all kinds of good buildings and residences.

They are made of thin wood slats 2 and 2⅜ inches wide, hung on best woven ladder tapes; hang within window frames, between stop beads or jambs; are never swinging out in the room, "sticking fast" or "coming off the roller," and are perfectly noiseless in use and operation. Have a light, airy appearance, slats being but one-eighth inch thick, and an individuality in style and general make up, and are suitable for the finest mansions, country residences, club houses, hotels, hospitals, office and apartment buildings, court houses, schools and colleges, and verandas, as well as public and private buildings of less pretensions,—in fact, any place where a handsome, durable and handy device is wanted to control the light.

SEE NEXT PAGE.

VENETIAN BLINDS.

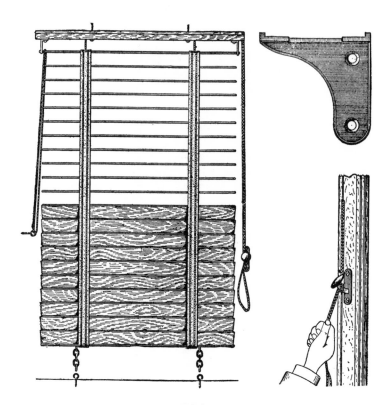

Above cut shows details and method of application.

They require no special frame, can be hung at the top, as this cut suggests, or hung at the side on brackets, as shown above. All hardware, fittings, cord, cord-holder, chain and staples for sill fasteners, everything complete goes with our blinds.

2-INCH SLATS

Are intended for residences, etc.

2⅜-INCH SLATS

Cost less, make a lighter blind, and are for larger windows, public buildings, etc., although either width is well adapted for any purpose.

For prices of Venetian blinds see page 32 of our price supplement accompanying this catalogue.

VENETIAN BLINDS.

DIRECTIONS FOR ORDERING.
By carefully following the sketches and using the form below delay and error will be avoided.

Reference can be made to the above cut to describe where dimensions are taken by saying if taken at "a," "b" or "c," and if taken at "c" how much lap was allowed on face of casing.

a—Between stop beads.
b—Between jambs.
c—Face of casing and tell how much if any lap has been allowed on each side.

CAUTION—Be careful to give exact dimensions.

Number of Blinds.	* Width between window jambs.	Height of frame from window sill.	Height of sill from floor.	Width of stop beads.	Width of jamb from stop bead to face of casing	Are slats to be 2 in. or 2⅜ in. wide?	Kind of Wood and Finish.
	Feet Inches	Feet Inches	Feet Inches	Inches	Inches		

* It is generally better to hang blinds between window jambs, but sometimes preferable to hang them between the stop beads; in the latter case the distance between the "stop beads" must be given, and at the head of the column the word "jambs" changed to "stop beads."

INSIDE FOLDING BLINDS.

Our inside blinds are unexcelled in every respect.   Write us for discounts and we will be pleased to make the best quotations consistent with good workmanship and materials.   We make them in any wood, and call special attention to our hardwood work.

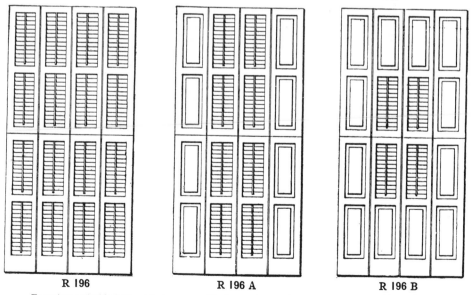

R 196   R 196 A   R 196 B

For prices on inside folding blinds see page 30 of our price supplement accompanying this catalogue.

HILL'S PATENT SLIDING BLINDS.

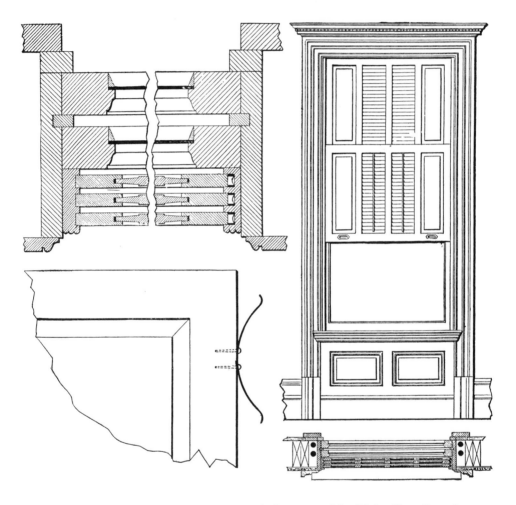

Above section shows that no special frame is required to use our sliding blinds.   The guideway is
fastened on pulley stile, acting as a stop for the sash.
Read carefully opposite page in ordering or asking for estimate.

For prices on Hill's Patent Sliding Blinds see page 33 of our price supplement
accompanying this catalogue.

HILL'S PATENT SLIDING BLINDS.

These sliding blinds are made ½-inch in thickness, and though constructed of light material possess great strength and lasting qualities.

Can be closed with the window raised and cannot blow open or rattle, thus giving the best medium of ventilation.

They do not interfere with curtains or window ornaments, and admit light and air from any part of the window.

These blinds are specially made to order in the white or finished complete; either varnished in the natural colors of the different woods or stained and varnished, or wood filled and cabinet or rubbed finish. All trimmings and hardware we furnish, which is included in the price of the blinds given on page 33 of our price supplement.

DIVISIONS IN WIDTH.

This has reference to the number of parts or panels in which each section is divided. To look well the divisions should not be excessively wide or narrow. The maximum widths given under each number of divisions in the price list will show panels about 7 inches wide, the minimum widths about 4 inches wide. This classification will always be used unless otherwise ordered.

PLEASE NOTE — That list prices include all necessary hardware or trimming, and in comparing costs with folding blinds or other makes of sliding blinds, this should be taken into consideration.

Will make net estimates on weighted blinds or on special designs from architect's details.

DIRECTIONS FOR ORDERING.

Give the exact measurement of the opening which the blinds are to fill. Where guideways take the place of stops, state distance from face of casing to inner face of lower sash. If windows are circle head or segment inside, send exact pattern or give radius. Full information for adjusting these blinds accompany each order.

For prices of these blinds see page 33 of our price supplement accompanying this catalogue.

INTERIOR OF FACTORY.

View in our door department, where the cores for our excellent veneered doors are
prepared for the gluing room.

PAINTED PANEL DOORS.

200
4 Panels, O G Sticking.

201
5 Panels, O G Sticking.

We carry these doors in stock ready for immediate shipment in following sizes only:

2- 6x6- 6   1⅛ and 1⅜ inches thick.
2- 8x6- 8   1⅛ and 1⅜ inches thick.
2-10x6-10   1⅛ and 1⅜ inches thick.
3- 0x7- 0   1⅛ and 1⅜ inches thick.

These doors are made of thoroughly kiln-dried materials, will stand as well as any door made. They are well covered by two coats of specially prepared French drab paint applied by hand with a brush by skilled painters. All of our painted doors have an elegant gloss finish.

FOR NET PRICES SEE OUR CURRENT DISCOUNT AND PRICE LIST.

PAINTED SASH DOORS.

210
2-Panel 4-Light Sash Door.

211
2-Panel 2-Light Sash Doors.

We carry these doors in stock ready for immediate shipment in following sizes only:

2- 6x6- 6   1⅜ inches thick.
2- 8x6- 8   1⅜ inches thick.
2-10x6-10   1⅜ inches thick.
3- 0x7- 0   1⅜ inches thick.

These doors are made of thoroughly kiln-dried materials and will stand as well as any door made.
Our painted doors have always been the standard of excellence.   Many manufacturers
dip their doors in a paint vat and then drain them off.   These doors
can always be distinguished by their appearance around
the mouldings and panels.   Our doors are
always painted by hand.

FOR NET PRICES, BOTH OPEN AND GLAZED, SEE OUR CURRENT DISCOUNT AND PRICE LIST.

PAINTED SASH DOORS.

212
2-Panel and 1-Light Sash Door.

213
2-Panel and 2-Light Circle Top Sash Door.

We carry these doors in stock ready for immediate shipment in following sizes only:

2- 6x6- 6   1⅜ inches thick.
2- 8x6- 8   1⅜ inches thick.
2-10x6-10   1⅜ inches thick.
3- 0x7- 0   1⅜ inches thick.

These doors are made of thoroughly kiln-dried materials and will stand as well as any door made.
They are painted with specially prepared French drab paint applied by hand
with a brush by skilled painters.   All our painted doors
have an elegant gloss finish.

FOR NET PRICES, BOTH OPEN AND GLAZED, SEE OUR CURRENT DISCOUNT AND PRICE LIST.

GRAINED PANEL DOORS.

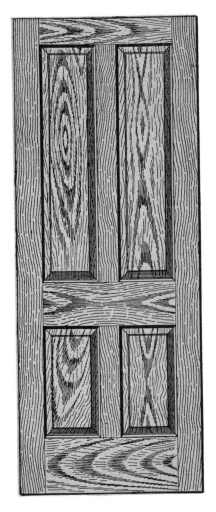

200
4 Panels, O G Sticking.

201
5 Panels, O G Sticking.

We carry these doors in stock ready for immediate shipment in following sizes only :

2- 6x6- 6　1⅛ and 1⅜ inches thick.
2- 8x6- 8　1⅛ and 1⅜ inches thick.
2-10x6-10　1⅛ and 1⅜ inches thick.
3- 0x7- 0　1⅛ and 1⅜ inches thick.

These doors are made of thoroughly kiln-dried materials and will stand as well as any door made.
They are painted and grained in oak effect by hand. We do no machine
graining and employ only skilled grainers, thus insuring a
natural variety in style.

FOR NET PRICES, BOTH OPEN AND GLAZED, SEE OUR CURRENT DISCOUNT AND PRICE LIST.

GRAINED SASH DOORS.

210
2-Panel and 4-Light Sash Door.

211
2-Panel and 2-Light Sash Door.

We carry these doors in stock ready for immediate shipment in following sizes only:

2- 6x6- 6 1⅜ inches thick.
2- 8x6- 8 1⅜ inches thick.
2-10x6-10 1⅜ inches thick.
3- 0x7- 0 1⅜ inches thick.

These doors are made of thoroughly kiln-dried materials and will stand as well as any door made.
They are painted and grained in oak effect by hand and are ready to hang in place.
We employ only skilled grainers to do this work, insuring uniform
and satisfactory work.

FOR NET PRICES, BOTH OPEN AND GLAZED, SEE OUR CURRENT DISCOUNT AND PRICE LIST.

GRAINED SASH DOORS.

212	**213**
2-Panel 1-Light Sash Door.	2-Panel 2-Light Circle Top Sash Door.

We carry these doors in stock ready for immediate shipment in following sizes only:

2- 6x6- 6   1⅜ inches thick.
2- 8x6- 8   1⅜ inches thick.
2-10x6-10   1⅜ inches thick.
3- 0x7- 0   1⅜ inches thick.

These doors are made of thoroughly kiln-dried materials and will stand as well as any door made. They are painted and grained in oak effect by hand, ready to hang in place. We employ only skilled grainers, thus insuring uniformly reliable results.

FOR NET PRICES, BOTH OPEN AND GLAZED, SEE OUR CURRENT DISCOUNT AND PRICE LIST.

PAINTED AND GRAINED FRONT DOORS.

OOM BULL	JOHN PAUL
Painted and Glazed Cut Glass.	Grained Oak and Glazed Cut Glass

We carry these doors in stock ready for immediate shipment in following sizes only:

2- 6x6- 6   1⅜ inches thick only.
2- 8x6- 8   1⅜ inches thick only.
2-10x6-10   1⅜ inches thick only.
3- 0x7- 0   1⅜ inches thick only.

These doors are painted and grained to match in style and color the doors on pages 81 to 86.
The glass is the same quality as used in our more expensive doors.

FOR NET PRICES, GLAZED, SEE OUR CURRENT DISCOUNT AND PRICE LIST.

SWING WATER CLOSET DOORS.

R 196½

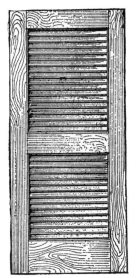

R 197

R 197½

R 198

We make these doors to order in soft or hard woods.

FOR LIST PRICE, IN ORDINARY SIZES, SEE PAGE 34 OF PRICE SUPPLEMENT ACCOMPANYING THIS CATALOGUE.

SIDE LIGHTS FOR DOORS.

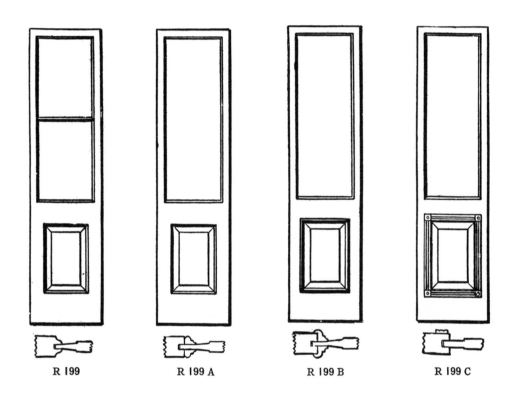

R 199   R 199 A   R 199 B   R 199 C

For prices of above side lights, both open and glazed in standard sizes, see page 34 of our price
supplement accompanying this catalogue. We also make to order side lights to
match any door shown herein or from architect's details
at reasonable prices.

CUPBOARD DOORS.

For prices of panel or glass doors for china closets and cupboards see page 34 of
price supplement accompanying this catalogue.

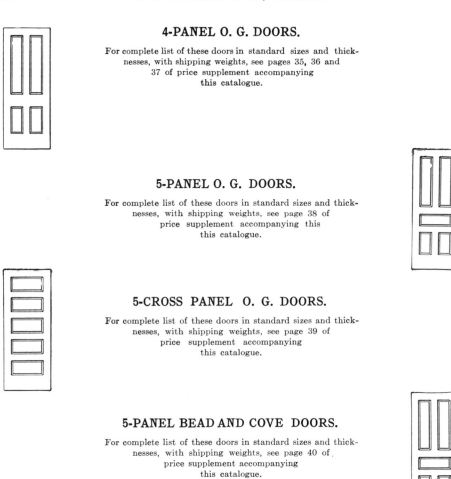

4-PANEL O. G. DOORS.

For complete list of these doors in standard sizes and thicknesses, with shipping weights, see pages 35, 36 and
37 of price supplement accompanying
this catalogue.

5-PANEL O. G. DOORS.

For complete list of these doors in standard sizes and thicknesses, with shipping weights, see page 38 of
price supplement accompanying this
this catalogue.

5-CROSS PANEL O. G. DOORS.

For complete list of these doors in standard sizes and thicknesses, with shipping weights, see page 39 of
price supplement accompanying
this catalogue.

5-PANEL BEAD AND COVE DOORS.

For complete list of these doors in standard sizes and thicknesses, with shipping weights, see page 40 of
price supplement accompanying
this catalogue.

5-CROSS PANEL BEAD AND COVE DOORS.

For complete list of these doors in standard sizes and thicknesses, with shipping weights, see page 41 of
price supplement accompanying
this catalogue.

4-PANEL FLUSH AND RAISED MOULDED DOORS.

For complete list of these doors in standard sizes and thicknesses, with shipping weights, see page 42 of
price supplement accompanying
this catalogue.

O. G. SASH DOORS.

For complete list of these doors, both open and glazed, in standard sizes and
thicknesses, with shipping weights, see page 43 of our
price supplement accompanying this catalogue.

O. G. SASH DOORS.

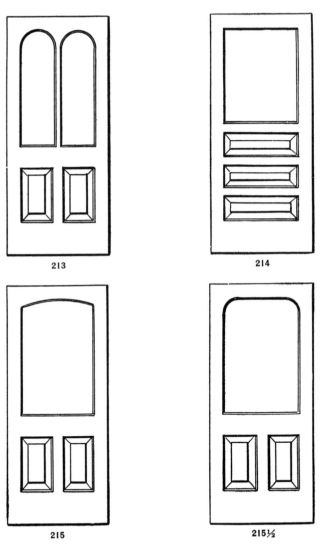

For complete list of these doors, both open and glazed, in standard sizes and
thicknesses, with shipping weights, see page 43 of our price
supplement accompanying this catalogue.

FRONT DOORS.

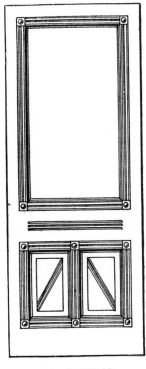

231 GARFIELD   233 JENNY LIND

For complete list of these doors, both open and glazed, in standard sizes and thicknesses, with shipping weights, see page 43 of price supple-
ment accompanying this catalogue.

MODERN FRONT DOORS.
"BATTENBERG" SERIES

BATTENBERG No. 1   BATTENBERG No. 2

Strictly "A" quality.   The glass designs in these doors are faithful reproductions of the famous Battenberg Lace.

These designs carried in stock in following sizes only:

2-6 x 6-6, 1⅜-in. thick.   2-10 x 6-10, 1⅜-in. thick.
2-8 x 6-8, 1⅜-in. thick.   2- 8 x 7- 0, 1⅜-in. thick
3-0 x 7-0, 1⅜-in. thick.

These doors are carefully manufactured from thoroughly kiln-dried stock, and the handsome glass designs make them popular with the trade.

For net prices of these doors see our current discount and net-price list.

MODERN FRONT DOORS.
BATTENBERG AND "BOXER" SERIES.

BATTENBERG No. 3

Fine "B" quality. The glass design in this door is a faithful reproduction of a beautiful pattern of the famous Battenberg Lace.

BOXER "A"

5½ inch Stiles. Wide Lock Rail, Strictly "A" quality; Glazed Clear D. S. Glass.

These designs carried in stock in following sizes only:

2-6 x 6-6, 1⅜-in. thick.   2-10 x 6-10, 1⅜-in. thick.
2-8 x 6-8, 1⅜-in. thick.   2- 8 x 7- 0, 1⅜-in. thick.
          3-0 x 7-0, 1⅜-in. thick.

Careful builders require wide stiles on their front doors. Our "Boxer" series was designed to meet this demand.

For net prices on these doors see our current discount and net-price list.

MODERN FRONT DOORS.

BOXER SERIES."

BOXER "B"   **BOXER "C"**

Strictly "A" quality; glazed Florentine glass.   Strictly "A" quality; glazed cut glass.

5½ inch Stiles.   Wide Lock Rail.

These designs carried in stock in following sizes only:

2-6 x 6-6, 1⅜-in. thick.   2-10 x 6-10, 1⅜-in. thick.
2-8 x 6-8, 1⅜-in. thick.   2- 8 x 7- 0, 1⅜-in. thick.
3-0 x 7-0, 1⅜-in. thick.

A stock of these doors with their good wide stiles, lock rails, and excellent glass
designs will help you sell other goods.
For net prices of these doors see our current discount and net-price list.

MODERN FRONT DOORS.
"BOXER SERIES."

BOXER "D"

Strictly "A" quality; glazed heavy beveled
Florentine glass, with wheel-cut miters
in center.

BOXER "E"

Strictly "A" quality; glazed bevel plate.

5½ inch Stiles.   Wide Lock Rail.

These designs carried in stock in following sizes only:

2-6 x 6-6, 1⅜-in. thick.   2-10 x 6-10, 1⅜-in. thick.
2-8 x 6-8, 1⅜-in. thick.   2- 8 x 7- 0, 1⅜-in. thick.
3-0 x 7-0, 1⅜-in. thick.

The wide stiles and lock rails of this series make them very popular with builders
as they have plenty of room for hardware.
For net prices of these doors see our current discount and net-price list.

MODERN FRONT DOORS.

"GEMS OF THE TRADE" SERIES.

EMERALD	TOPAZ
Strictly "A" q ality; glazed cut glass.	Strictly "A" quality; glazed combination cut and chipped design; bevel effect.

These designs carried in stock in following sizes only:

2-6 x 6-6, 1⅜-in. thick.   2-10 x 6-10, 1⅜-in. thick.
2-8 x 6-8, 1⅜-in. thick.   2- 8 x 7- 0, 1⅜-in. thick.
3-0 x 7-0, 1⅜-in. thick.

These doors are solid moulded inside and flush moulded outside with egg and dart moulding.
The garland is genuine wood carving.
For net prices of these doors see our current discount and net-price list.

MODERN FRONT DOORS.
"GEMS OF THE TRADE" SERIES.

OPAL	GARNET
Strictly "A" quality; glazed colored art and beveled plate in lead; subdued effect.	Strictly ' A" quality; glazed colored art and beveled plate in lead; bright colors.

These designs carried in stock in following sizes only:

2–6 x 6–6, 1⅜-in. thick.　　2–10 x 6–10, 1⅜-in. thick.
2–8 x 6–8, 1⅜-in. thick.　　2– 8 x 7– 0, 1⅜-in. thick.
3–0 x 7–0, 1⅜-in. thick.

The leaded glass in these doors is well made of nicely selected colors.
The garland is genuine wood carving and the panels are flush moulded outside with egg and dart moulding.
For net prices of these doors see our current discount and net-price list.

MODERN FRONT DOORS.

"GEMS OF THE TRADE" SERIES.

MOONSTONE

Strictly "A" quality; glazed clear beveled plate.

TEXAS

Strictly "A" quality; glazed cut glass.

These designs carried in stock in following sizes only:

2-6 x 6-6, 1⅜-in. thick.   2-10 x 6-10, 1⅜-in. thick.
2-8 x 6-8, 1⅜-in. thick.   2- 8 x 7- 0, 1⅜-in. thick.
3-0 x 7-0, 1⅜-in. thick.

These doors have always been a help to the trade in selling other goods.
If business is dull, a few of these doors prominently displayed will be of service.
For net prices see our current discount and net-price list.

MODERN FRONT DOORS.

"GEMS OF THE TRADE" SERIES.

BOKAY

Strictly "A" quality; glazed combination cut and chipped design; bevel effect.

PALMA

Strictly "A" quality; glazed cut glass.

These designs carried in stock in following sizes only:

2-6 x 6-6, 1⅜-in. thick.   2-10 x 6-10, 1⅜-in. thick.
2-8 x 6-8, 1⅜-in. thick.   2- 8 x 7- 0, 1⅜-in. thick.
3-0 x 7-0, 1⅜-in. thick.

The whole "Gems of the Trade" series has always been popular.
If you have none of these in stock you have undoubtedly lost many sales you could have otherwise secured.
For net prices see our current discount and net-price list.

MODERN FRONT DOORS.
"ROUGH RIDER" SERIES.

MUSTANG

Choice "B" quality; glazed cut glass.

These designs carried in stock in following sizes only:

2-6 x 6-6, 1⅜-in. thick.   2-10 x 6-10, 1⅜-in. thick.
2-8 x 6-8, 1⅜-in. thick.   2- 8 x 7- 0, 1⅜-in. thick.
3-0 x 7-0, 1⅜-in. thick.

Where medium priced front doors of good design and manufacture are required this series fills the bill.
For net prices see our current discount and net-price list.

MODERN FRONT DOORS.
"ROUGH RIDER" SERIES.

BRONCO	CAYUSE
Choice "B" quality; glazed cut glass.	Choice "B" quality; glazed cut glass.

These designs carried in stock in following sizes only:

2-6 x 6-6, 1⅜-in. thick.   2-10 x 6-10, 1⅜-in. thick.
2-8 x 6-8, 1⅜-in. thick.   2- 8 x 7- 0, 1⅜-in. thick.
3-0 x 7-0, 1⅜-in. thick.

While these doors are graded "B" quality they are almost as good as "A" quality.
For net prices see our current discount and net-price list.

MODERN FRONT DOORS.

VENEERED "UNSELECTED" WISCONSIN BIRCH.

L 375

Glazed beveled plate glass
stiles, 4⅞in. Bottom rail, 9½ in.

L 379

Glazed beveled plate glass
stiles, 5½ in. Bottom rail, 9½ in.

We carry these doors in stock ready for prompt shipment in following sizes only:

2- 8 x 6- 8	—1⅜	in.	thick.		
2- 8 x 7- 0	"	"	"		
2- 8 x 6- 8	—1¾	"	"		
2-10 x 6-10	"	"	"		
2- 8 x 7- 0	"	"	"		
2-10 x 7- 0	"	"	"		
3- 0 x 7- 0	"	"	"		
3- 4 x 7- 0	"	"	"		

It is worth your while to read pages 144 to 165 regarding birch.
For prices of these doors see special birch price list.

MODERN FRONT AND VESTIBULE DOORS.

VENEERED "UNSELECTED" WISCONSIN BIRCH.

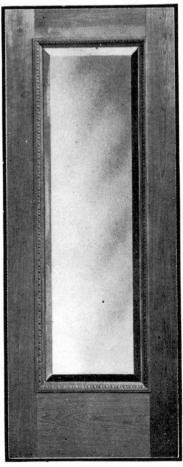

L 379½

Glazed leaded D. S. glass
stiles, 5½ in. Bottom rail, 9½ in.

We carry door L 379½ in stock in following
sizes only:

    2- 8 x 6- 8—1⅜ in. thick.
    2- 8 x 7- 0   "   "   "
    2- 8 x 6- 8—1¾ "   "
    2-10 x 6-10   "   "   "
    2- 8 x 7- 0   "   "   "
    2-10 x 7- 0   "   "   "
    3- 0 x 7- 0   "   "   "
    3- 4 x 7- 0   "   "   "

L 380

Glazed beveled plate glass
stiles, 5½ in. Bottom rail, 12 in.

Vestibule door design.

L 380

has machine-pressed egg
and dart moulding outside and
plain moulding inside.

This door made to order
on special order only.

For price of these doors see our special birch price list.
Read pages 144 to 165 regarding birch.

VIEWS IN OUR MANUFACTURING PLANT.

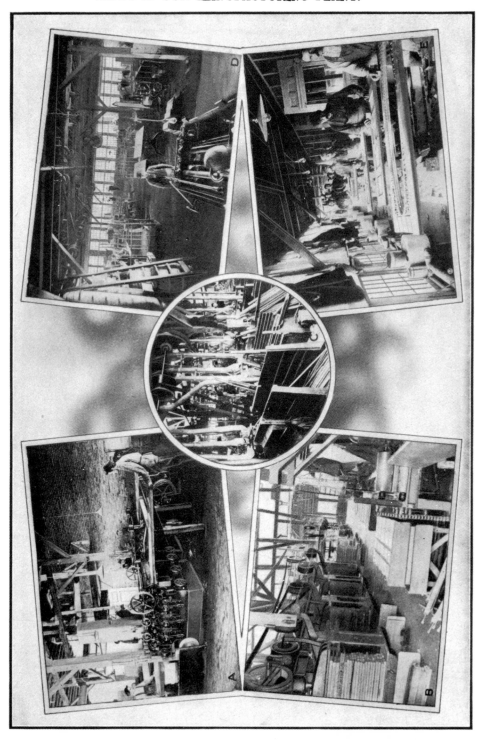

"A"—Triple sanders and polishers.   "B"—Group of steam-power presses—total capacity 1,200 doors per day,
pressure, 1,000 lbs. to the square inch.   "C"—View in moulding department.
"D"—A section of main machine room.   "E—"Group of bench workers.

MODERN HARDWOOD DOORS.

VENEERED "UNSELECTED" WISCONSIN BIRCH.

We carry these doors in stock in following sizes only:
See the power presses used in our veneered door department, on opposite page.

L 377 STOCK SIZES 1⅜ IN. THICK.	
2- 0 x 6- 0	6+Panel.
2- 0 x 6- 6	"
2- 4 x 6- 6	"
2- 6 x 6- 6	"
2- 0 x 6- 8	"
2- 2 x 6- 8	"
2- 4 x 6- 8	"
2- 6 x 6- 8	"
2- 8 x 6- 8	"
2-10 x 6-10	"
2- 0 x 7- 0	"
2- 2 x 7- 0	"
2- 4 x 7- 0	"
2- 6 x 7- 0	"
2- 8 x 7- 0	"
2-10 x 7- 0	"
3- 0 x 7- 0	"
2- 6 x 7- 6	"
2- 8 x 7- 6	"
2- 6 x 8- 0	7+Panel.
2- 8 x 8- 0	"
3- 0 x 8- 0	"

L 377 STOCK SIZES 1¾ IN. THICK.	
2- 6 x 6- 8	6+Panel.
2- 8 x 6- 8	"
2-10 x 6-10	"
2- 6 x 7- 0	"
2- 8 x 7- 0	"
2-10 x 7- 0	"
3- 0 x 7- 0	"
2- 6 x 7- 6	"
2- 8 x 7- 6	"
2-10 x 7- 6	"
3- 0 x 7- 6	"
2- 6 x 8- 0	7+Panel.
2- 8 x 8- 0	"
3- 0 x 8- 0	"

L 377

These doors have flat panels and are cove and bead solid moulded.
All stiles and rails are veneered on soft wood built up cores, which prevents warping out of shape
as is the case in solid hardwood doors.
For prices see page 44 of our price supplement accompanying this catalogue.

SPECIAL PANEL DOORS.

 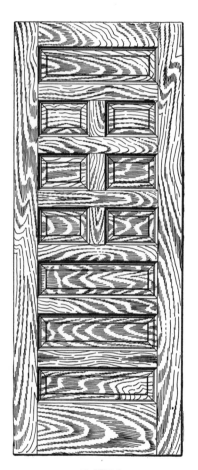

R 806   R 806½

We make these doors to order of soft or hard woods.
For prices in soft woods see page 45 of our price supplement accompanying this catalogue.
See pages 144 to 165 regarding birch as an interior finish.

SPECIAL PANEL DOORS.

R 808   R 808½

We make these doors to order of soft or hard woods.
For prices in soft woods see page 45 of our price supplement accompanying this catalogue.
See pages 144 to 165 regarding birch as an interior finish.

SPECIAL PANEL DOORS.

R 809½   R 809½A

We make these doors to order of soft or hard woods.
For prices in soft woods see page 45 of our price supplement accompanying this catalogue.
See pages 144 to 165 regarding birch as an interior finish.

SPECIAL PANEL DOORS.

R 809½B   R 809½C

We make these doors to order of soft or hard woods.
For prices in soft woods see page 45 of our price supplement accompanying this catalogue.
See pages 144 to 165 regarding birch as an interior finish.

SPECIAL VESTIBULE DOORS.

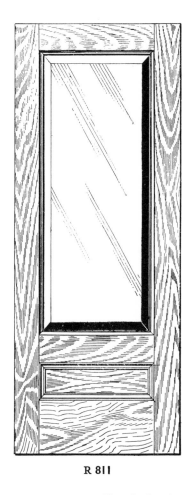

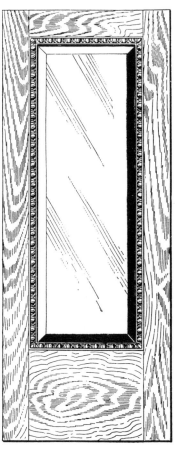

R 811   R 813

We make these doors to order of soft or hard woods.
For prices in soft woods see page 45 of our price supplement accompanying this catalogue.
See pages 144 to 165 regarding birch as an interior finish.
For designs of front doors carried in stock see pages 94 to 105.

SPECIAL VESTIBULE DOORS.

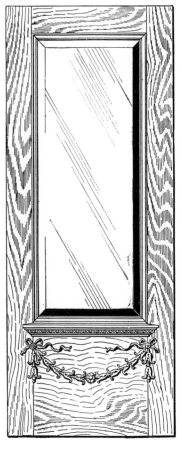
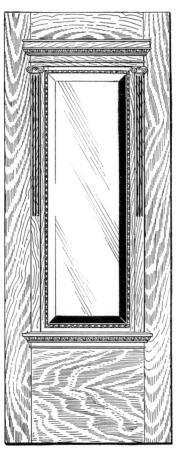

R 813½   R 814

We make these doors to order of soft or hard woods
For prices in soft woods see page 45 of our price supplement accompanying this catalogue.
See pages 144 to 165 regarding birch as an interior finish.
For designs of front doors carried in stock see pages 94 to 105.

SPECIAL VESTIBULE DOORS.

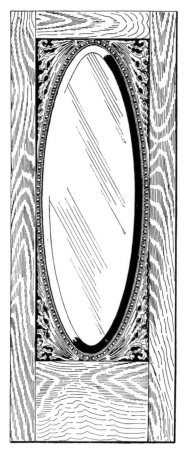

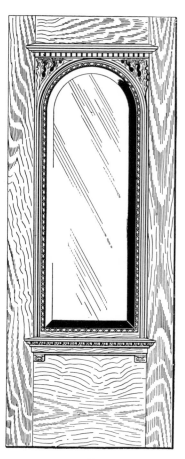

R 815   R 816

We make these doors to order of soft or hard woods.
For prices in soft woods see page 45 of our price supplement accompanying this catalogue.
See pages 144 to 165 regarding birch as an interior finish.
For designs of front doors carried in stock see pages 94 to 105.

SPECIAL VESTIBULE DOORS.

R 817

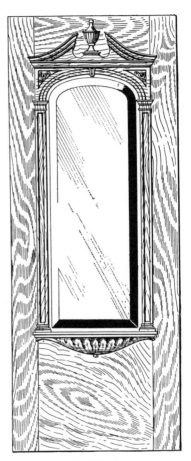

R 817½

We make these doors to order of soft or hard woods.
For price in soft woods see page 45 of our price supplement accompanying this catalogue.
See pages 144 to 165 regarding birch as an interior finish.
For designs of front doors carried in stock see pages 94 to 105.

SPECIAL FRONT DOORS.

R 818   R 819½

We make these doors to order of soft or hard woods.
For prices in soft woods see page 46 of our price supplement accompanying this catalogue.
See pages 144 to 165 regarding birch as an interior finish.
For designs of front doors carried in stock see pages 94 to 105.

SPECIAL FRONT DOORS.

R 820   R 821 ½

We make these doors to order of soft or hard woods.
For prices in soft woods see page 46 of our price supplement accompanying this catalogue.
See pages 144 to 165 regarding birch as an interior finish.
For designs of front doors carried in stock see pages 94 to 105.

SPECIAL FRONT DOORS.

R 822½   R 823½

We make these doors to order of soft or hard woods.
For prices in soft woods see page 46 of our price supplement accompanying this catalogue.
See pages 144 to 165 regarding birch as an interior finish.
For designs of front doors carried in stock see pages 94 to 105.

SPECIAL FRONT DOORS.

R 824½   R 825

We make these doors to order of soft or hard woods.
For prices in soft woods see page 46 of our price supplement accompanying this catalogue.
See pages 144 to 165 regarding birch as an interior finish.
For designs of front doors carried in stock see pages 94 to 105.

SPECIAL FRONT DOORS.

R 826½   R 827½

We make these doors to order of soft or hard woods.
For prices in soft woods see page 46 of our price supplement accompanying this catalogue.
See pages 144 to 165 regarding birch as an interior finish.
For designs of front doors carried in stock see pages 94 to 105.

SPECIAL FRONT DOORS.

R 828½   R 829½

We make these doors to order of soft or hard woods.
For prices in soft woods see page 46 of our price supplement accompanying this catalogue.
See pages 144 to 165 regarding birch as an interior finish.
For designs of front doors carried in stock see pages 94 to 105.

SPECIAL DUTCH DOOR.

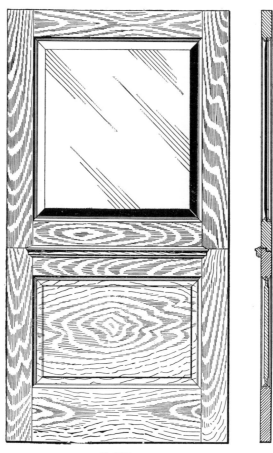

R 830

This door is made in two parts as shown by section.
The top section is hinged so as to swing into the hall while the lower section remains locked.
When required the entire door can be opened the same as a single door.
Most of the designs on pages 116 to 121 can be made in this manner.
We make these doors to order of soft or hard woods.
For prices in soft woods see page 46 of our price supplement accompanying this catalogue.
See pages 144 to 165 regarding birch as an interior finish.
For designs of front doors carried in stock see pages 94 to 105.

SPECIAL DOUBLE FRONT DOORS.

<table>
<tr><td>R 831</td><td>R 832</td></tr>
</table>

These designs are drawn for double door openings. In ordering double doors always state if
they are to be rabbeted in center or left plain for astragal joint. If rabbeted,
state which door opens in as you face them on the outside. If
astragal is wanted state which style—see page 439.

Other designs, pages 112 to 121, can be made in pairs when desired.

We make these doors to order of soft or hard woods.

For prices in soft woods see page 46 of our price supplement accompanying this catalogue.

See pages 144 to 165 regarding birch as an interior finish.

For designs of front doors carried in stock see pages 94 to 105.

STORE DOORS.

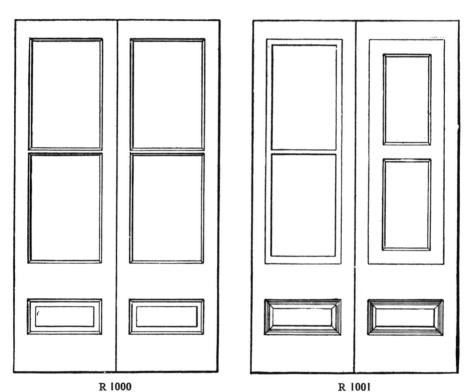

R 1000
Not made for shutters.

R 1001
Made for shutters.
Right side of cut shows shutters in place.

These doors made any size or thickness to order in all woods.
For list prices in ordinary sizes see page 47 in price supplement accompanying this catalogue.
In ordering state if they are to be rabbeted together in center or left plain for astragal joint.
If rabbeted, state which door opens in as you face them on the outside.
If astragal is wanted state which style—see page 439.
We never furnish astragals or rabbet doors unless ordered.

SPECIAL STORE DOORS.

R 1002½   R 1003½

These doors made any size or thickness to order in all woods.
For list prices in ordinary sizes see page 47 in price supplement accompanying this catalogue.
In ordering state if they are to be rabbeted together in center or left plain for astragal joint.
If rabbeted, state which door opens in as you face them on the outside.
If astragal is wanted state which style—see page 439.
We never furnish astragals or rabbet doors unless ordered.

STORE FRONTS.

For the convenience of our customers we have prepared the entirely new and practical designs shown on pages 127 to 130, drawn to a scale with large scale details. These drawings show ordinary proportions and the construction of the fronts in all their parts. They will be found of great convenience in ordering, and erecting the work at the building. In ordering or asking for estimate always furnish the following information:

First—With or without glass.

Second—If glass is wanted state whether plate or double strength.

Third—With or without recess for doors and side lights.

Fourth—For frame or brick building.

Fifth—State if sash, doors, transoms and panels only are wanted or the front complete except bulkheading. The bulkheading is made of flooring, which every dealer carries in stock, and we never include same unless so instructed.

MEASUREMENTS REQUIRED.

Give all measurements indicated by the following letters, shown on small scale plan and elevation. A. B. C. D. E. F. G. H. K. M.

Some of these letters are also used in the larger details, to indicate the same parts more clearly. By closely following above suggestions much time and trouble will be saved all parties concerned.

STORE FRONTS
FOR FRAME BUILDING.

R 1005½   R 1006½

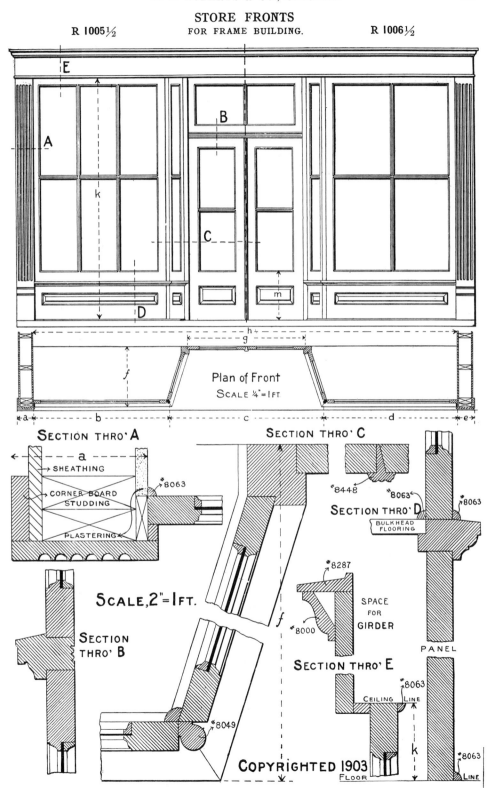

E

A

B

C

D

k

m

h
g

Plan of Front
SCALE ¼"=1FT.

f

a   b   c   d   e

SECTION THRO' A

a

SHEATHING

CORNER BOARD
STUDDING

PLASTERING

#8063

SECTION THRO' C

#8448   #8063   #8063

SECTION THRO' D

BULKHEAD
FLOORING

#8287

SPACE
FOR
GIRDER

#8000

PANEL

SCALE, 2"=1FT.

SECTION THRO' B

f

#8049

SECTION THRO' E

CEILING LINE

#8063

k

#8063

FLOOR   LINE

COPYRIGHTED 1903

Read instructions on page 126 carefully in ordering or asking for estimate.

STORE FRONTS
FOR FRAME BUILDING.

R 1007½　　　　　　　　　　　　　　　　　　R 1008½

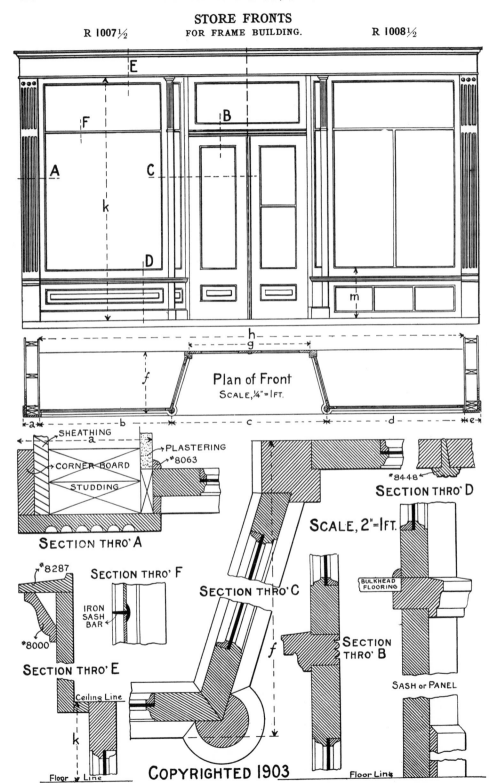

Plan of Front
SCALE, ¼" = 1 FT.

SHEATHING
PLASTERING
*8063
CORNER BOARD
STUDDING

SECTION THRO' A

*8448
SECTION THRO' D

SCALE, 2" = 1 FT.

BULKHEAD FLOORING

*8287

SECTION THRO' F

IRON SASH BAR

*8000

SECTION THRO' E

SECTION THRO' C

SECTION THRO' B

SASH or PANEL

Ceiling Line

Floor Line

Floor Line

COPYRIGHTED 1903

Read instructions on page 126 carefully in ordering or asking for estimate.

STORE FRONTS

R1009½   FOR BRICK BUILDING.   R 1010½

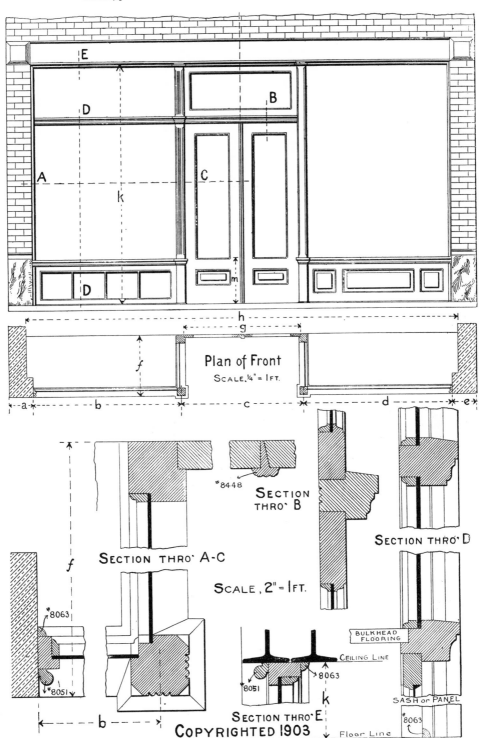

Plan of Front

SCALE. ¼" = 1 FT.

*8448

SECTION THRO' B

SECTION THRO' A-C

SCALE, 2" = 1 FT.

SECTION THRO' D

*8063

*8051

BULKHEAD FLOORING

CEILING LINE

*8063

*8051

SASH or PANEL

SECTION THRO' E

*8063

Floor Line

COPYRIGHTED 1903

Read instructions on page 126 carefully in ordering or asking for estimate.

STORE FRONTS

R 1011½   FOR FRAME BUILDING.   R 1012½

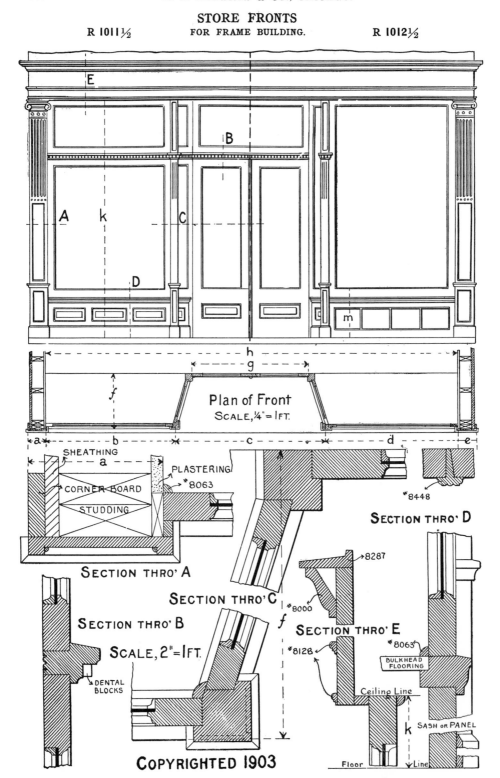

Plan of Front
SCALE, ¼" = 1 FT.

SHEATHING
PLASTERING
*8063
CORNER BOARD
STUDDING

*8448

SECTION THRO' D

*8287

*8000

SECTION THRO' A

SECTION THRO' C

SECTION THRO' B

SCALE, 2" = 1 FT.

DENTAL BLOCKS

*8128

SECTION THRO' E

*8063

BULKHEAD FLOORING

Ceiling Line

SASH OR PANEL

Floor   Line

COPYRIGHTED 1903

INTERIOR FINISH.

We make a specialty of fine interior finish in soft or hard woods. Where architect's details are furnished (unless instructed to the contrary), we follow them closely, observing the lines and spirit of the drawings throughout. Four things are required to produce good mouldings—dry lumber, sharp knives, high speed of the cutting heads and slow feed. This is what we give our customers and that is why architects and owners favor our work.

For designs of interiors finished in "unselected" birch see pages 146 to 159.

CAP TRIM.

For Windows and Doors.   Made of any Wood.

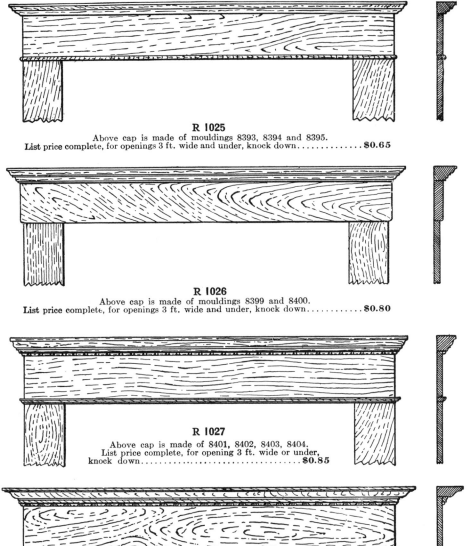

R 1025

Above cap is made of mouldings 8393, 8394 and 8395.
List price complete, for openings 3 ft. wide and under, knock down.............$0.65

R 1026

Above cap is made of mouldings 8399 and 8400.
List price complete, for openings 3 ft. wide and under, knock down...........$0.80

R 1027

Above cap is made of 8401, 8402, 8403, 8404.
List price complete, for opening 3 ft. wide or under,
knock down..................................$0.85

R 1028

Above cap is made of 8405, 8406, 8407, 8408, 8409.
List price complete, for opening 3 ft. wide and under, knock down.............$0.95
For openings wider than 3 feet, add to above prices for each additional
foot or fraction thereof, 25 per cent.
Always state whether you want them put together or K. D.
We make extra charge for putting caps together.
ABOVE PRICES SUBJECT TO MOULDING DISCOUNT.

CAP TRIM.

For Windows and Doors.   Made of Any Wood.

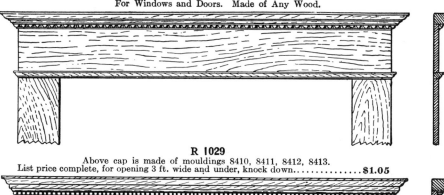

R 1029
Above cap is made of mouldings 8410, 8411, 8412, 8413.
List price complete, for opening 3 ft. wide and under, knock down..............$1.05

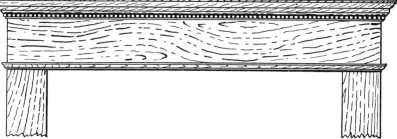

R 1030
Above cap is made of mouldings 8410, 8411, 8412, and small dentil mould ⅝ x ¾ inches.
List price complete, for opening 3 ft. wide and under, knock down..............$1.15

R 1031
Above cap is made of mouldings 8393, 8394, 8395, and thin carved blocks as shown.
List price complete, for opening 3 ft. wide and under, knock down..............$1.60

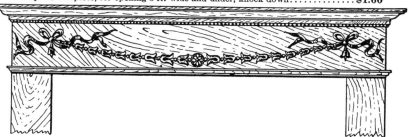

R 1032
Above cap is made of mouldings 8405, 8406, 8407, 8408, turned bead and carving planted on as shown.
List price, (without carvings) for opening 3 ft. wide and under, knock down.......$1.05
For price of carvings see page 142.
Always state whether you want them put together or K. D.
For openings wider than 3 feet, add to above prices for each additional
foot or fraction thereof, 25 per cent.
ABOVE PRICES SUBJECT TO MOULDING DISCOUNT.

COMPOSITION ORNAMENTS.

The composition ornaments shown on opposite page are made to closely resemble the wood in grain and color on which they are to be mounted. It is impossible to produce in wood the beautiful detailed effects obtained in these goods and the material used is much more durable than wood carving. The prices given below are for the **ornaments only** mounted on the caps the size noted. This will enable you to use any detail of cap trim or wood desired, without affecting price of ornaments.

For openings 3 feet in width and under, 6 to 7 inches high between neck and cap moulding.

R1040................$3.60
R1041............... 3.00
R1042............... 3.00
R1043............... 3.00

Larger sizes in proportion.

For prices of these ornaments unmounted, carefully packed in box for shipment, deduct 15 per cent. from prices quoted above.

For genuine wood carvings and rosettes see pages 142 and 143.

ABOVE PRICES SUBJECT TO DISCOUNT.

COMPOSITION MOUNTINGS FOR INTERIOR WOODWORK.

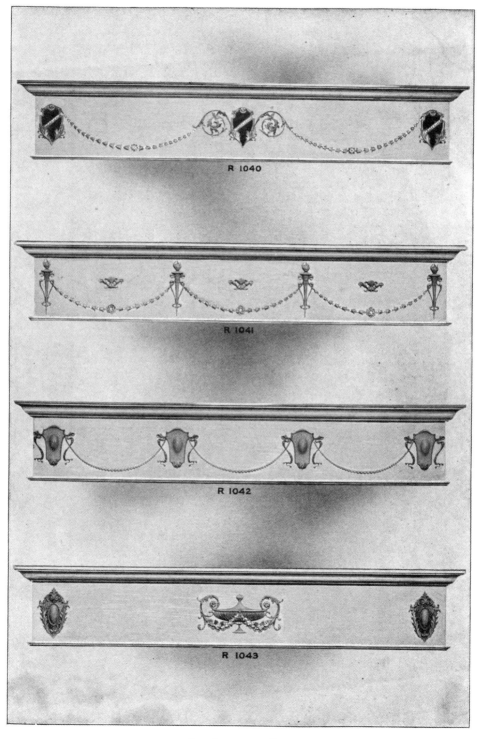

For prices see opposite page.

COMPOSITION ORNAMENTS.

The elegant designs shown on opposite page are made for both interior and exterior work. Prices given below are for exterior work in sizes noted. Other sizes in proportion.

R 1050		R 1053	
10 inches diam., each..**$1.30**		10 inches diam., each..**$1.10**	
14 " " " .. **1.90**		14 " " " .. **1.50**	
16 " " " .. **2.60**		16 " " " .. **2.10**	

R 1051		R 1054	
15 inches long, each..**$1.30**		10 inches diam., each..**$1.30**	
20 " " " .. **1.90**		14 " " " .. **1.90**	
24 " " " .. **2.60**		16 " " " .. **2.60**	

R 1052		R 1055	
10 inches diam., each..**$1.30**		10 inches diam., cach..**$1.30**	
14 " " " .. **2.10**		14 " " " .. **1.90**	
16 " " " .. **2.60**		16 " " " .. **2.60**	

R 1056—R 1057—R 1058

For space 12 inches or less in height.

24 inches long, each....**$2.30**
30 " " " **3.00**
36 " " " **3.80**

If these designs are made for interior work, deduct 15 per cent. from above.
Above prices subject to discount.
For genuine wood carvings see pages 142 and 143.

COMPOSITION ORNAMENTS.

CORNER BLOCKS.

Prices are for blocks 1⅛ inches thick and 5⅝ inches square or under.   Order must state sizes wanted.

R 1101
$7.80 per 100.

R 1101½
$7.00 per 100.

R 1102
$24.00 per 100.

R1104
$6.60 per 100.

R 1105
$7.80 per 100.

R 1106
$5.50 per 100.

R 1108
$22.00 per 100.

R 1110
$5.00 per 100.

R 1113
$9.00 per 100.

R 1115
$10.20 per 100.

R 1117
$7.00 per 100.

R 1119
$8.40 per 100.

R 1121
$6.60 per 100.

R 1122
$7.20 per 100.

R 1129
$30.00 per 100.

Blocks thicker or larger than listed sizes, extra price.

ABOVE PRICES SUBJECT TO DISCOUNT.

HEAD BLOCKS.

Prices are for blocks size and thickness shown under each design or smaller.   Order must state sizes wanted.

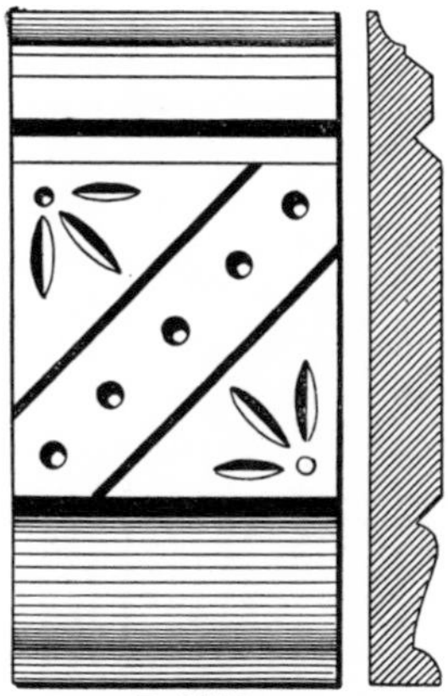

R 1131
1⅛x5⅝x11. $13.20 per 100.

R 1132
1⅛x5⅝x11. $13.20 per 100.

R 1134½
1⅛x5⅝x11. $36.00 per 100.

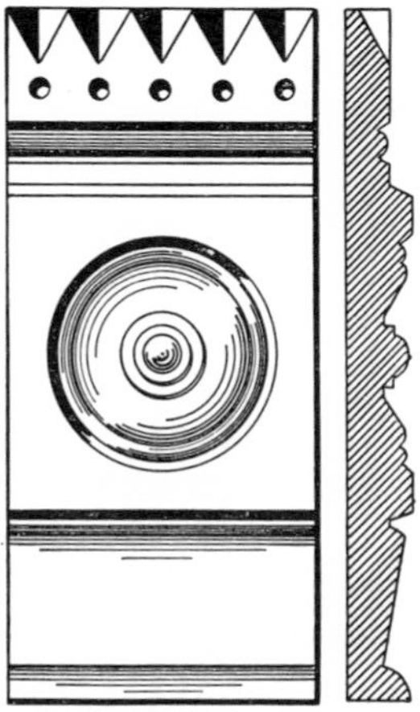

R 1135½
1⅛x5⅝x12. $15.00 per 100.

R 1135
1⅛x5⅝x11. $10.00 per 100.

R 1137
1⅛x5⅝x12. $24.00 per 100.

R 1139
1⅛x5⅝x11. $19.20 per 100.

R 1140
1⅛x5⅝x11. $20.40 per 100.

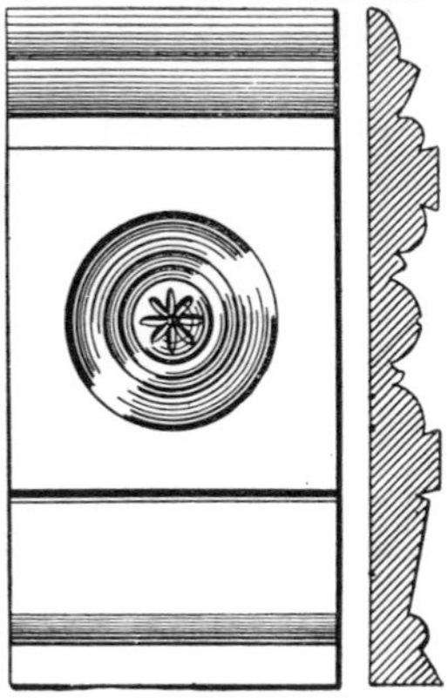

R 1141
1⅛x5⅝x11. $14.40 per 100.

Blocks thicker or larger than listed sizes extra price.
ABOVE PRICES SUBJECT TO DISCOUNT.

HEAD BLOCKS.

Prices are for blocks, sizes and thickness shown under each design or smaller.   Order must state sizes wanted.

R 1142
1⅛x5⅝x11. $13.20 per 100.

R 1143
1⅛x5⅝x11. $14.40 per 100.

R 1147½
1⅜x5⅝x11. $40.00 per 100.

R 1150
1⅛x5⅝x11. $15.00 per 100.

R 1151
1⅛x5⅝x11. $15.00 per 100.

R 1152½
1⅛x5⅝x11. $14.40 per 100.

R 1154
1⅛x5⅝x11. $14.40 per 100.

R 1155
1⅛x5⅝x11. $15.60 per 100.

R 1156
1⅛x5⅝x11. $16.80 per 100.

Blocks thicker or larger than listed sizes extra price.
ABOVE PRICES SUBJECT TO DISCOUNT,

BASE OR PLINTH BLOCKS.

Prices are for blocks, sizes and thickness shown under each design or smaller.   Order must state sizes wanted.

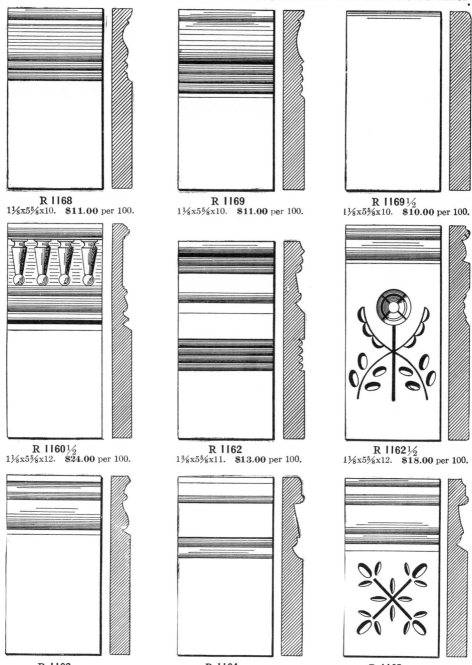

R 1168
1⅛x5⅝x10. **$11.00** per 100.

R 1169
1⅛x5⅝x10. **$11.00** per 100.

R 1169½
1⅛x5⅝x10. **$10.00** per 100.

R 1160½
1⅛x5⅝x12. **$24.00** per 100.

R 1162
1⅜x5⅝x11. **$13.00** per 100.

R 1162½
1⅛x5⅝x12. **$18.00** per 100.

R 1163
1⅛x5⅝x10. **$10.00** per 100.

R 1164
1⅛x5⅝x10. **$10.00** per 100.

R 1165
1⅛x5⅝x10. **$16.80** per 100.

Blocks thicker or larger than listed sizes extra price.
ABOVE PRICES SUBJECT TO DISCOUNT.

GENUINE WOOD CARVINGS.

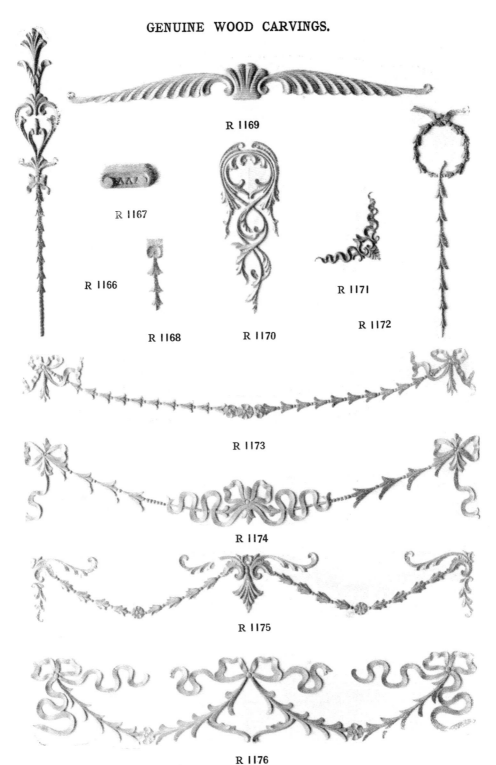

R 1169

R 1167

R 1166

R 1168

R 1170

R 1171

R 1172

R 1173

R 1174

R 1175

R 1176

For prices of above ornaments see page 232.

GENUINE WOOD CARVINGS AND ROSETTES.

R 1177

R 1179

R 1178

R 1180

R 1181

R 1182

R 1183

R 1184

R 1185

R 1186

R 1187

R 1188

For prices of above ornaments see page 232.

UNSELECTED BIRCH.

A SPLENDID HARDWOOD.   EXCEEDINGLY LOW IN PRICE.

The interior of your buildings can be fitted out with hardwood trim and veneered doors in the following effects at very low prices:

**NATURAL BIRCH, BLACK WALNUT
MAHOGANY, CHERRY, BUTTERNUT**

and many other imitations equally effective.

For doors see pages 104 to 107.   For mouldings and interior designs see pages 146 to 165.

"UNSELECTED BIRCH."

The term, "unselected birch," refers only to the color of the wood (NOT THE QUALITY). Our unselected birch goods are free from defects, such as knots, shake and check. The doors are as durably constructed as any hardwood veneered doors on the market, and the trim carefully and smoothly manufactured. The heart of a birch log is reddish brown, and the outside portion, or sap, is white. When selected for color the heart is known as "selected red birch," and the sap "selected white birch. The selected birch is, therefore, much more expensive than the unselected. Our unselected birch stock veneered doors and trim run more strongly to red than to white in color. The variegated color effect of unselected birch, when finished natural, is rich and pleasing, but where an even color is wanted it is cheaply obtained by staining. Where customers desire, we will do the staining for them at a reasonable extra price.

AUDITORIUM HOTEL BUILDINGS, CHICAGO.
FINISHED IN "UNSELECTED" WISCONSIN BIRCH.

The new building to the left of picture is the new 'Annex" finished throughout above first floor by us in "Unselected" Wisconsin birch, stained mahogany, see sample on page 149. This finish is supposed by many guests to be genuine mahogany, so perfect is the imitation.

COLOR SAMPLES OF "UNSELECTED" WISCONSIN BIRCH.

STAINED "GOLDEN BIRCH."

The upper part of this sample is white and the lower red.   Notice that the stain fully equalizes the color.

STAINED "MEDIUM MAHOGANY."

The upper part of this sample is red and the lower white.   Notice that the stain fully equalizes the color.
See instructions for finishing, page 147.

INSTRUCTIONS FOR FINISHING
"UNSELECTED" WISCONSIN BIRCH.

The methods that apply to the finish of hardwoods in general are applicable to birch. The first requisite is perfectly dry material. Many architects, contractors and owners do not realize that any and all woodwork after being once thoroughly kiln-dried and then exposed (in the white) rapidly absorbs moisture in the degree that may exist in the atmosphere to which it is exposed. Thus, **perfectly kiln-dried goods** after being exposed (in the white) in warehouses, freight cars, or newly constructed buildings are **liable** to be unfit for a satisfactory finish, either paint or varnish. After the woodwork is in place, the building should be heated to a temperature from 10° to 30° warmer than normal, and maintained night and day for a period of not less than two weeks, this precautionary measure will absolutely prevent the unsightly appearance of open joints and unfinished lines of exposed wood caused by shrinkage after finish is applied. The results illustrated by color reproductions on preceding and following pages are obtained by applying one coat of stain and one coat of shellac. To this foundation should be added two coats of standard varnish. The smooth, mirror-like finish so desirable is produced by rubbing the varnished surface, the height of the polish being regulated by the amount of rubbing and polishing done. Any painter familiar with use of stain and varnish can produce the color effects and finish of our samples. The staining or filling of both face and back of hardwood work before shipping closes the pores of the wood and prevents much of the trouble caused by swelling from exposure during or after shipment. It sometimes happens in the smaller towns that there is a scarcity or painters or finishers familiar with staining hardwood work. For these reasons we will, when requested, stain the work before shipping at reasonable extra price for labor, materials and extra packing. We invite correspondence and will quote prices promptly.

COLOR SAMPLES OF "UNSELECTED" WISCONSIN BIRCH.

STAINED WALNUT.

The upper part of this sample is white and the lower red.   Notice that the color is equalized by the stain.

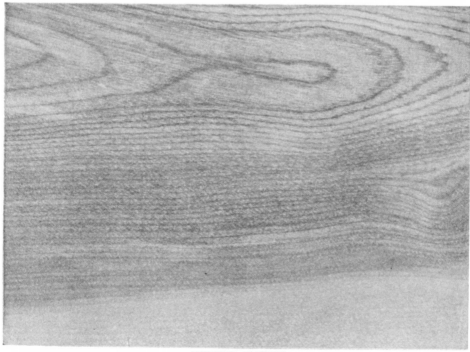

FINISHED NATURAL.

The upper part of this sample is red and the lower white.   The variegated color effect is preferred by many
critics to any other finish.
See instructions for finishing on page 147.

COLOR SAMPLES OF "UNSELECTED" WISCONSIN BIRCH.

STAINED CHERRY.

The upper part of this sample is white and the lower red.   Notice that the color is equalized by the stain.

STAINED LIGHT MAHOGANY.

The upper part of this sample is red and the lower white.   The stain so fully equalizes the color that the difference cannot be seen.

See instructions for finishing on page 147.

DETAILS OF RECEPTION HALL TRIM IN "UNSELECTED" BIRCH.

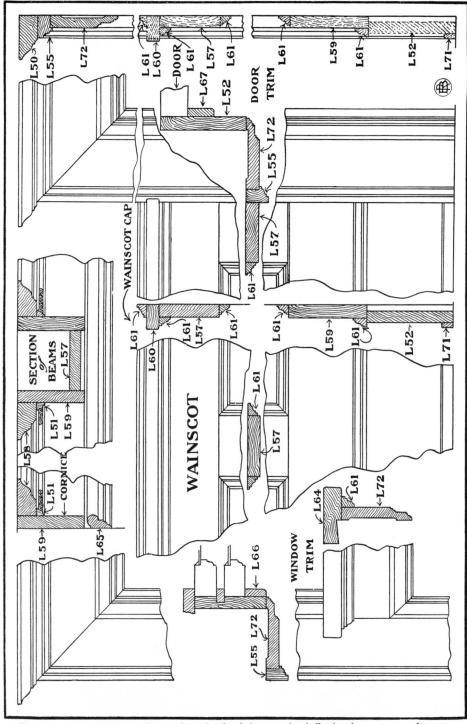

The above sections form complete working details of the reception hall trim shown on opposite page.
For full-sized sections and list prices see pages 160 to 164.

RECEPTION HALL, FINISHED EXCLUSIVELY IN "UNSELECTED" BIRCH.

In above sketch the trim is "Unselected" birch, stained mahogany. The panels in wainscot can be either cement or burlaps, tinted as shown. See complete working details on opposite page.

DETAILS OF PARLOR TRIM IN "UNSELECTED" BIRCH.

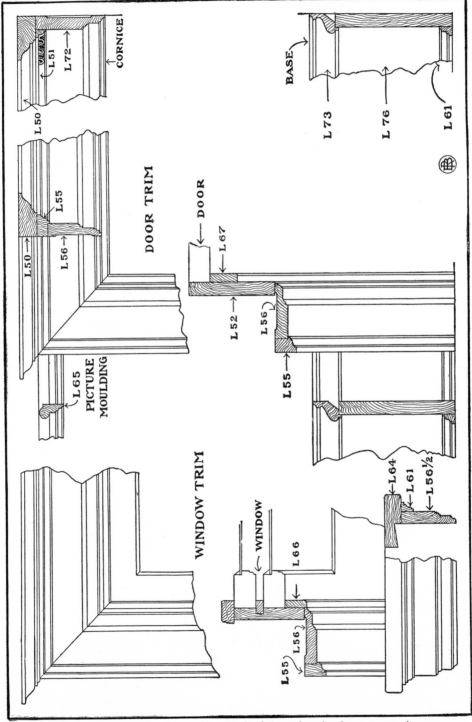

The above sections form complete working details of the parlor trim shown on opposite page.
For full-sized sections and list prices see pages 160 to 164.

PARLOR DESIGN, FINISHED EXCLUSIVELY IN "UNSELECTED" BIRCH.

In above sketch the trim is "Unselected" birch, finished with white enamel, and the doors and consol in mahogany stain. The cornice is tinted to harmonize with the decorations.
See complete working details on opposite page.

DETAILS OF LIBRARY TRIM IN "UNSELECTED" BIRCH.

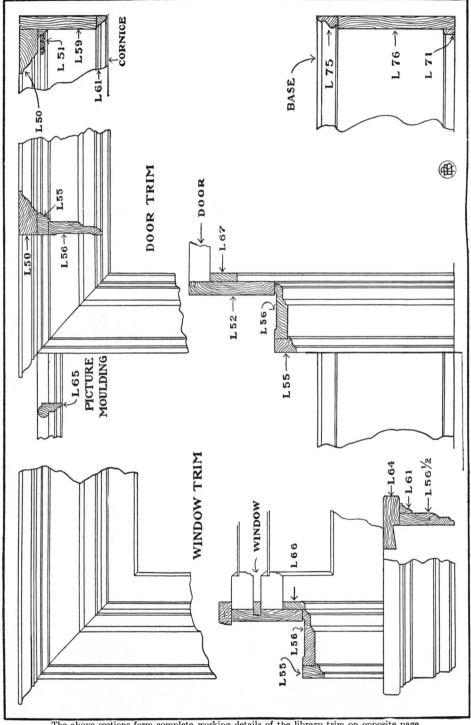

The above sections form complete working details of the library trim on opposite page.
For full-sized sections and list prices see pages 160 to 164.

LIBRARY DESIGN, FINISHED EXCLUSIVELY IN "UNSELECTED" BIRCH.

In above sketch the trim is "Unselected" birch, stained medium mahogany. See complete working details on opposite page.

DETAILS OF DINING-ROOM TRIM IN "UNSELECTED" BIRCH.

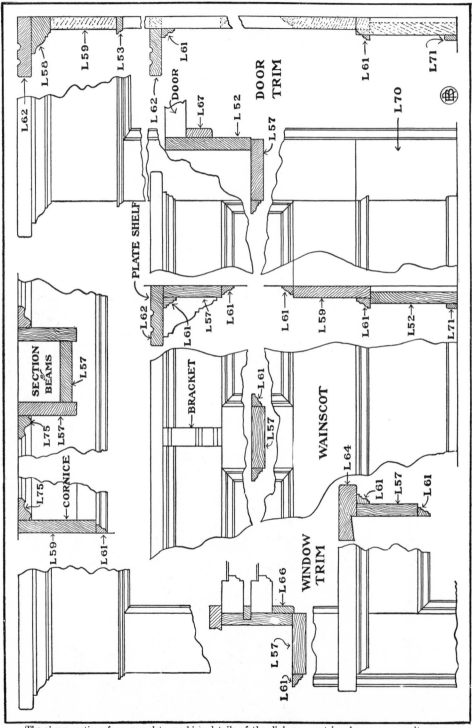

The above sections form complete working details of the dining-room trim shown on opposite page.
For full-sized sections and list prices, see pages 160 to 164.

DINING-ROOM DESIGN, FINISHED EXCLUSIVELY IN "UNSELECTED" BIRCH.

In above sketch the trim is "Unselected" birch stained walnut. The panels in wainscot can be either cement or burlaps, tinted as shown. See complete working details on opposite page.

DETAILS OF CHAMBER TRIM IN "UNSELECTED" BIRCH.

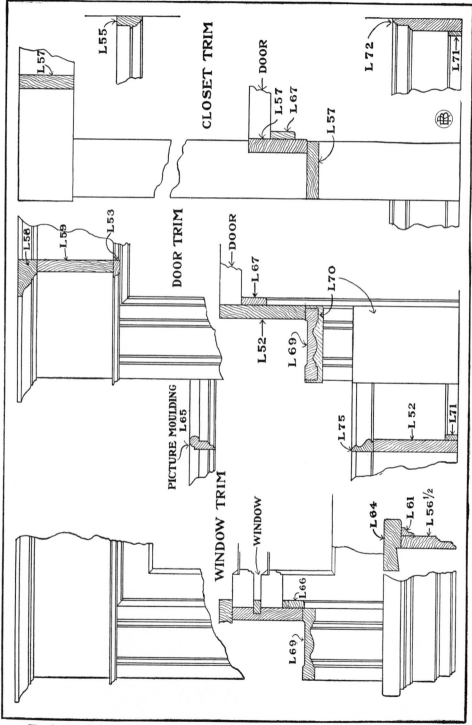

The above sections form complete working details of the chamber trim shown on opposite page.
For full-sized sections and list prices see pages 160 to 164.

CHAMBER DESIGN, FINISHED EXCLUSIVELY IN "UNSELECTED" BIRCH.

In above sketch the trim is finished natural and the doors in mahogany stain.   Where economy demands, yellow pine trim can be substituted for the birch.   See complete working details on opposite page.

FULL SIZED DETAILS OF OUR "UNSELECTED" BIRCH MOULDINGS.

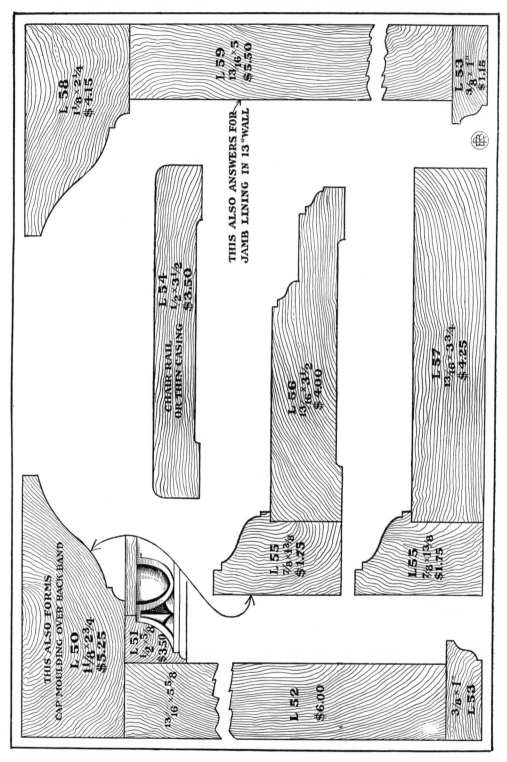

For practical applications of these designs see pages 150 to 159.   Prices listed are per 100 lineal feet
State quantities required in writing for discounts.

FULL SIZE DETAILS OF OUR "UNSELECTED" BIRCH MOULDINGS.

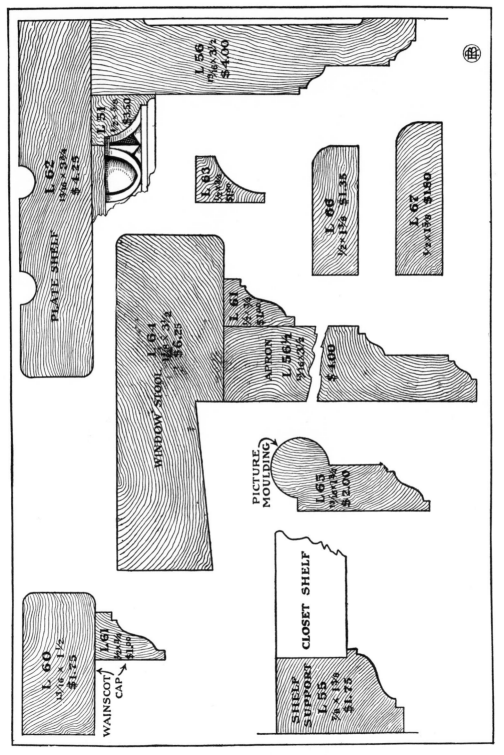

For practical applications of these designs see pages 150 to 159. Prices listed are per 100 lineal feet. State quantities required in writing for discounts.

FULL SIZED DETAILS OF OUR "UNSELECTED" BIRCH MOULDINGS.

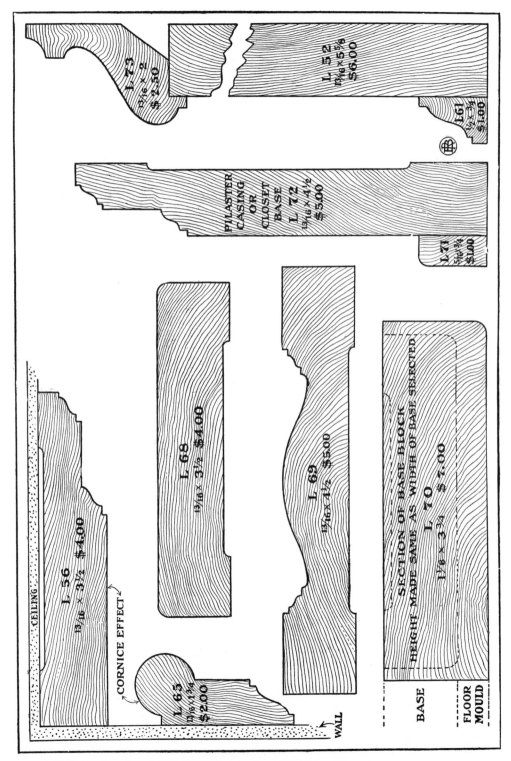

For practical applications of these designs see pages 150 to 159.   Prices listed are per 100 lineal feet.
State quantities required in writing for discounts.

FULL SIZED DETAILS OF OUR "UNSELECTED" BIRCH MOULDINGS.

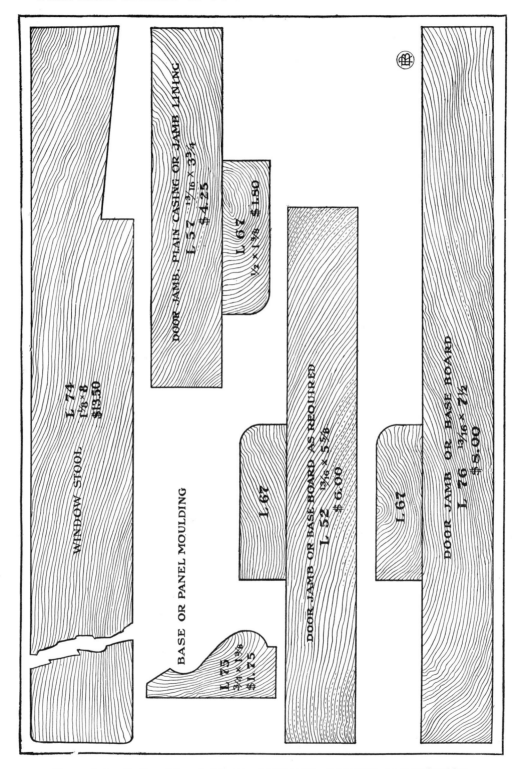

WINDOW STOOL
L 74
1⅛ × 8
$13.50

DOOR JAMB PLAIN CASING OR JAMB LINING
L 57   ¹³⁄₁₆ × 3¾
$4.25

L 67
½ × 1⅜ $1.80

BASE OR PANEL MOULDING

L 75
¾ × 1⅜
$1.75

L 67

DOOR JAMB OR BASE BOARD AS REQUIRED
L 52   ¹³⁄₁₆ × 5⅝
$6.00

L 67

DOOR JAMB OR BASE BOARD
L 76   ¹³⁄₁₆ × 7½
$8.00

For practical applications of these designs see pages 150 to 159.   Prices listed are per 100 lineal feet.
State quantities required in writing for discounts.

COMPLETE PRICE LIST OF "UNSELECTED" BIRCH MOULDINGS.

Shown on Pages 160 to 163.

Design.	List Price.	Design.	List Price.	Design.	List Price.	Design.	List Price.
L50	$5.25	L57	$4.25	L64	$6.25	L71	$1.00
L51	3.50	L58	4.15	L65	2.00	L72	5.00
L52	6.00	L59	5.50	L66	1.35	L73	2.50
L53	1.15	L60	1.75	L67	1.80	L74	13.50
L54	3.50	L61	1.00	L68	4.00	L75	1.75
L55	1.75	L62	4.25	L69	5.00	L76	8.00
L56	4.00	L63	1.00	L70	7.00		

These mouldings are smoothly run from thoroughly kiln dried stock and therefore require but little sandpapering to prepare them for the finishers.

For practical applications of these designs, see pages 150 to 159. Prices listed are per 100 lineal feet. State quantities required in writing for discounts.

INTERIOR OF RESIDENCE FINISHED IN UNSELECTED BIRCH.

The trim is finished in white enamel and the doors stained mahogany to match the
genuine mahogany mantel and furniture.

CORNER BEADS AND BASE ANGLES.

In White or Yellow Pine.

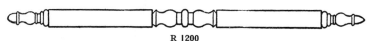

R 1200

Round turned, 1⅜ inch x 4 feet, each, 18c.   1¾ inch x 4 feet, each, 22c.

R 1201

Square turned, 1⅜ inch x 4 feet, each, 22c.   1¾ inch x 4 feet, each, 26c.

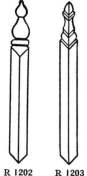

R 1202   R 1203

1⅜ x 12 to 14 inches.
R 1202 each, 5c.
R 1203 each, 6c.

SINK AND TABLE LEGS.

Prices named below are for poplar, pine or cypress.

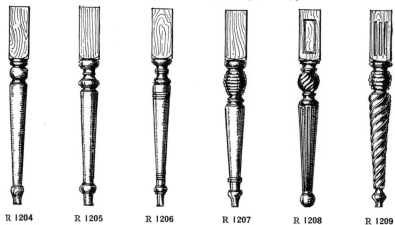

R 1204   R 1205   R 1206   R 1207   R 1208   R 1209

Size.	R 1204	R 1205	R 1206	R 1207	R 1208	R 1209
1¾ x 2 - 6	$0.20	$0.20	$0.22	$0.22	$....	$....
2¼ x 2 - 6	.28	.28	.30	.30	....	....
3¾ x 2 - 6	.56	.56	.60	.60	2.20	2.10

For prices in plain oak, add 25 per cent. to above.   Special prices in large quantities.

TURNED ROSETTES ON OPPOSITE PAGE.

Price per 100, white pine or poplar.
For patterns R 1210, R 1211 and R 1213.

½ in. diam.	¾ in. diam.	1 in. diam.	1½ in. diam.	2 in. diam.	2½ in. diam.	3 in. diam.	3½ in. diam.	4 in. diam.	4½ in. diam.	5 in. diam.	5½ in. diam.	6 in. diam.
$2.50	$3.50	$4.00	$4.50	$5.00	$5.50	$6.00	$6.50	$7.00	$8.00	$9.00	$11.00	$13.50

For patterns R 1214, R 1215 and R 1216.

½ in. diam.	¾ in. diam.	1 in. diam.	1½ in. diam.	2 in. diam.	2½ in. diam.	3 in. diam.	3½ in. diam.	4 in. diam.	4½ in. diam.	5 in. diam.	5½ in. diam.	6 in. diam.
$3.00	$4.00	$4.50	$5.00	$5.50	$6.00	$6.50	$7.00	$8.00	$9.00	$10.00	$12.00	$15.00

For rosettes of common hardwoods add 40 per cent. to above prices.
Special prices in large quantities.

ABOVE PRICES SUBJECT TO DISCOUNT.

TURNED ROSETTES.
White Pine or Poplar.

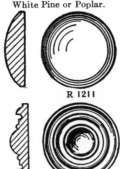

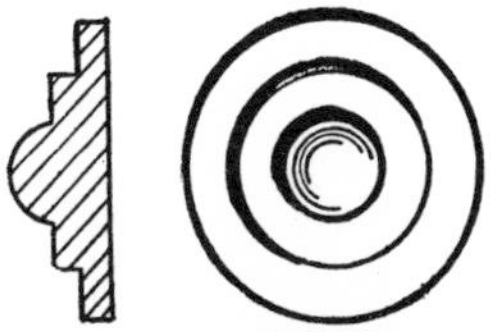

R 1210 R 1211 R 1213

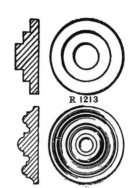

R 1214 R 1215 R 1216

For prices see bottom of opposite page.

TURNED DOWELS.
Pine, Poplar, Cypress and Common Hardwoods.

⅜ to ½-inch, 3-foot lengths..............per 100 feet, **$1.50**
⅝ to ¾-inch, 3-foot lengths..............per 100 feet, **2.00**
Can furnish Dowels up to 1⅜-inch diameter.
For orders of less than 250 feet of a size and kind, add 15 per cent. to above prices.

TURNED BALLS AND DROPS.

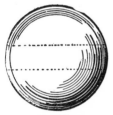 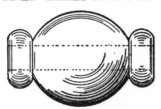 

R 1220 R 1221 R 1222

Oak or Birch—Bored ¼ or 5-16-in. hole.
⅝ and ¾ inch ....per 100, **$0.80**
⅞ inch............................" 100, **1.00**
1 " ...." 100, **1.40**
1¼ " ...." 100, **1.60**
Double or cross boring, **60c** per 100 extra.

1⅜ inch Whitewood, ⅜ hole......per 100, **$1.60**
1⅜ " Oak or Birch, ⅜ " ...." 100, **2.70**
1¾ " " " ½ " ...." 100, **4.20**
1¾ " Whitewood, ½ " ...." 100, **2.00**
2 " " ⅝ " ...." 100, **2.50**
Double or cross boring, **60c** per 100 extra.

Above prices cover only the woods as specified in the sizes given. If of other woods or of other sizes than given, in orders of less than 250 of a kind, we add **$1.00** extra for setting up machine.

TRIMMINGS FOR GRILLE WORK.
Turned for ¼ or 5-16 inch holes.

R 1223 R 1224 R 1225

Designs R1223, R1224 and R1225...............per 100, **$5.00**

Above prices are for oak or birch only, in the sizes specified. If of other woods, on orders of less than 250 of a kind, we add **$1.00** extra for setting up machine.

ABOVE PRICES SUBJECT TO DISCOUNT.

STAIRWORK.

We have a large and most complete stair department in charge of a competent stair builder of long experience. Where desired we send a working plan drawn to a scale upon receipt of order with complete measurements. This enables our customers to check up and correct any misunderstandings that might possibly occur, before the work is too far advanced. All designs on pages 170 to 205 are absolutely new and original and develop many pleasing features. All newels and balusters are drawn to a scale and are therefore seen in proper proportions. We have priced the rails, newels and balusters on each page for ready reference. No prices on complete stairways have been made, as no two stairways are built exactly alike in width, height and plan, and prices are therefore misleading. We will be pleased to make close estimates on any of the designs shown on receipt of design selection, kind of wood and the measurements indicated on opposite page.

STAIR GROUND PLANS.

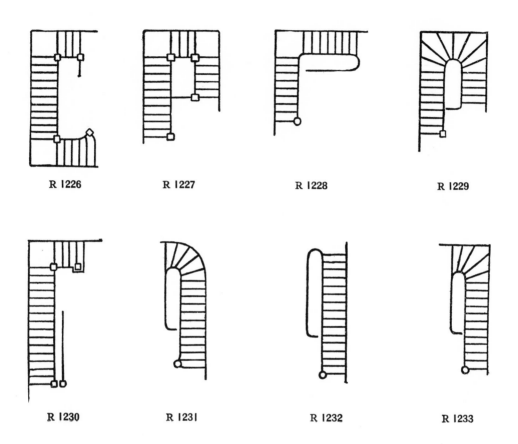

| R 1226 | R 1227 | R 1228 | R 1229 |

| R 1230 | R 1231 | R 1232 | R 1233 |

DIRECTIONS NECESSARY FOR ORDERING OR SECURING ESTIMATES
ON STAIRWAYS.

FIRST. Give rough or scale plan of main floor and floor above, with careful measurements of space to be occupied by the stairs on the main floor and rough well hole opening on floor above.

SECOND. Give height from top of main finished floor to top of finished floor above.

THIRD. On open stairs give width of stairs from finished plaster wall to outside face of rough carriages. If box stairs give width between finished plastered walls.

FOURTH. Give width of joist on floor above main floor and state whether single or double floor on floor above main floor.

FIFTH. Where carriages are already in place give number of treads and risers and the width of tread and height of riser as cut out on the carriages.

NOTE. All treads are made $1\frac{1}{8}$ inch thick and risers $\frac{7}{8}$ inch thick, and no rough carriages are furnished unless we are instructed to the contrary.

STARTING NEWELS.

R 1260	R 1261	R 1262
Price, Each, $5.00.	Price, Each, $7.00.	Price, Each, $10.00.

Above prices are for newels of plain oak, with shaft 6 x 6 inches.
For yellow pine, deduct 5 per cent.   For quartered oak, add 25 per cent.
Unless otherwise instructed we will make base to receive one riser only.
A proportionate extra charge is made for newels with bases to receive more than two risers.
These newels will be found in the stair designs on following pages.

Special prices in large quantities.

ABOVE PRICES SUBJECT TO DISCOUNT.

STARTING NEWELS.

R 1263
ice, Each, $6.00.

R 1264
Price, Each, $8.00.

R 1265
Price, Each, $9.50.

Above prices are for newels of plain oak, with shaft 6 x 6 inches.
For yellow pine, deduct 5 per cent.   For quartered oak, add 25 per cent.
Unless otherwise instructed we will make base to receive one riser only.
A proportionate extra charge is made for newels with bases to receive more than two risers.
These newels will be found in the stair designs on following pages.

Special prices in large quantities.

ABOVE PRICES SUBJECT TO DISCOUNT.

STARTING NEWELS.

R 1266	R 1267	R 1268
Price, Each, **$7.50.**	Price, Each, **$11.00.**	Price, Each, **$15.00.**

Above prices are for newels of plain oak, with shaft 6 x 6 inches.
For yellow pine, deduct 5 per cent.   For quartered oak, add 25 per cent.
Unless otherwise instructed we will make base to receive one riser only.
A proportionate extra charge is made for newels with bases to receive more than two risers.
These newels will be found in the stair designs on following pages.

Special prices in large quantities.

ABOVE PRICES SUBJECT TO DISCOUNT.

STARTING NEWELS.

R 1269	R 1270	R 1271
Price, Each, **$11.00**.	Price, Each, **$5.00**.	Price, Each, **$15.00**.

Above prices are for newels of plain oak, with shaft 6 x 6 inches.
For yellow pine, deduct 5 per cent.   For quartered oak, add 25 per cent.
Unless otherwise instructed we will make base to receive one riser only.
A proportionate extra charge is made for newels with bases to receive more than two risers.
These newels will be found in the stair designs on following pages.

Special prices in large quantities.

ABOVE PRICES SUBJECT TO DISCOUNT.

STARTING NEWELS.

R 1272
Price, Each, **$20.00.**

R 1273
Price, Each, **$16.50.**

R 1274
Price, Each, **$18.00.**

Above prices are for newels of plain oak, with shaft 6 x 6 inches.
For yellow pine, deduct 5 per cent. For quartered oak, add 25 per cent.
Unless otherwise instructed we will make base to receive one riser only.
A proportionate extra charge is made for newels with bases to receive more than two risers.
These newels will be found in the stair designs on following pages.

Special prices in large quantities.

ABOVE PRICES SUBJECT TO DISCOUNT.

STARTING NEWELS.

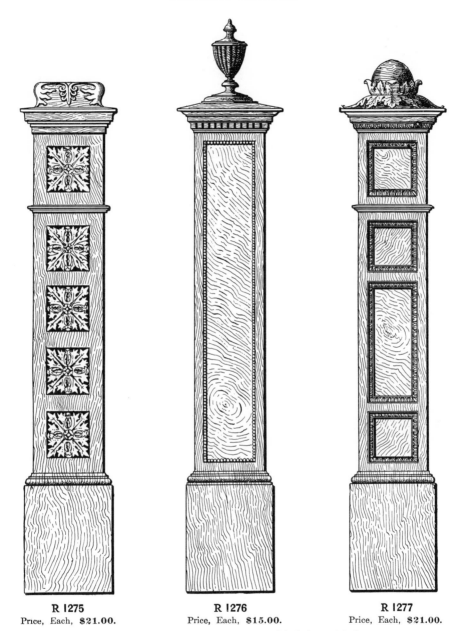

R 1275
Price, Each, **$21.00.**

R 1276
Price, Each, **$15.00.**

R 1277
Price, Each, **$21.00.**

Above prices are for newels of plain oak, with shaft 6 x 6 inches.
For yellow pine, deduct 5 per cent.   For quartered oak, add 25 per cent.
Unless otherwise instructed we will make base to receive one riser only.
A proportionate extra charge is made for newels with bases to receive more than two risers.
These newels will be found in the stair designs on following pages.

Special prices in large quantities.

ABOVE PRICES SUBJECT TO DISCOUNT.

ANGLE NEWELS.

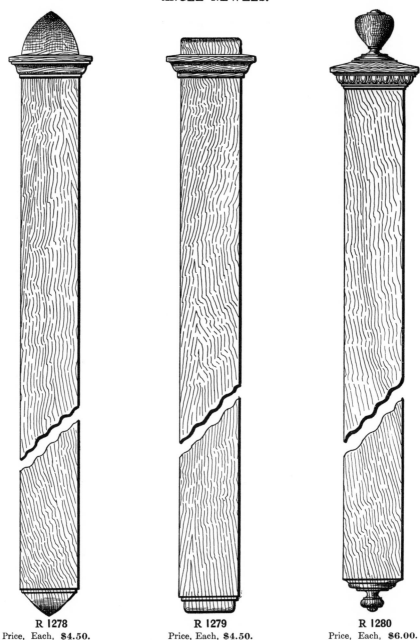

R 1278
Price, Each, **$4.50.**

R 1279
Price, Each, **$4.50.**

R 1280
Price, Each, **$6.00.**

Above prices are for newels of plain oak, with shaft 5 x 5 inches.
For yellow pine, deduct 5 per cent. For quartered oak, add 25 per cent.
Unless otherwise instructed we will make them to receive two risers only.
A proportionate extra charge is made for newels to receive more than two risers.
These newels will be found in the stair designs on following pages.
Special prices in large quantities.

ABOVE PRICES SUBJECT TO DISCOUNT.

ANGLE NEWELS.

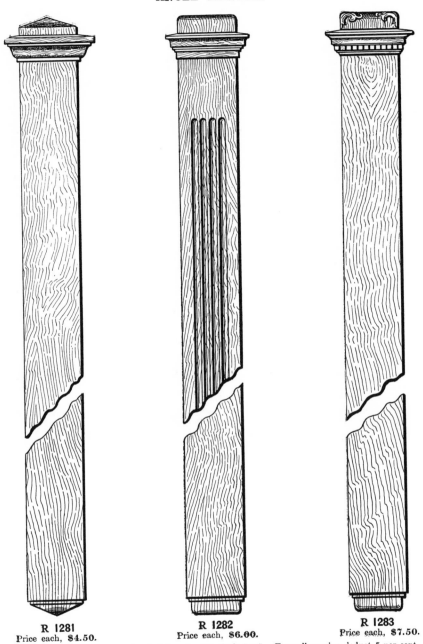

R 1281
Price each, **$4.50.**

R 1282
Price each, **$6.00.**

R 1283
Price each, **$7.50.**

Above prices are for newels of plain oak with shaft 5 x 5. For yellow pine deduct 5 per cent.
For quartered oak add 25 per cent. Unless otherwise instructed we will make them
to receive two risers only. A proportionate extra charge is made for
newels to receive more than two risers. These newels will
be found in the stair designs on following pages.
Special prices in large quantities.

ABOVE PRICES SUBJECT TO DISCOUNT.

E. L. ROBERTS & CO., CHICAGO.

ANGLE NEWELS.

R 1284	R 1285	R 1286
Price each, **$10.50.**	Price each, **$5.50.**	Price each, **$10.50.**

Above prices are for newels of plain oak with shaft 5 x 5. For yellow pine deduct 5 per cent. For quartered oak add 25 per cent. Unless otherwise instructed we will make them to receive two risers only. A proportionate extra charge is made for newels to receive more than two risers. These newels will be found in the stair designs on following pages. Special prices in large quantities.

ABOVE PRICES SUBJECT TO DISCOUNT.

ANGLE NEWELS.

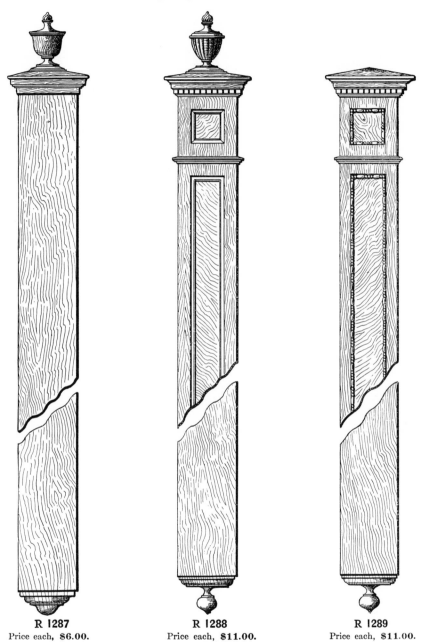

R 1287
Price each, **$6.00.**

R 1288
Price each, **$11.00.**

R 1289
Price each, **$11.00.**

Above prices are for newels of plain oak with shaft 5 x 5. For yellow pine deduct 5 per cent.
For quartered oak add 25 per cent. Unless otherwise instructed we will make them
to receive two risers only. A proportionate extra charge is made for
newels to receive more than two risers. These newels will
be found in the stair designs on following pages.
Special prices in large quantities.

ABOVE PRICES SUBJECT TO DISCOUNT.

ANGLE NEWELS.

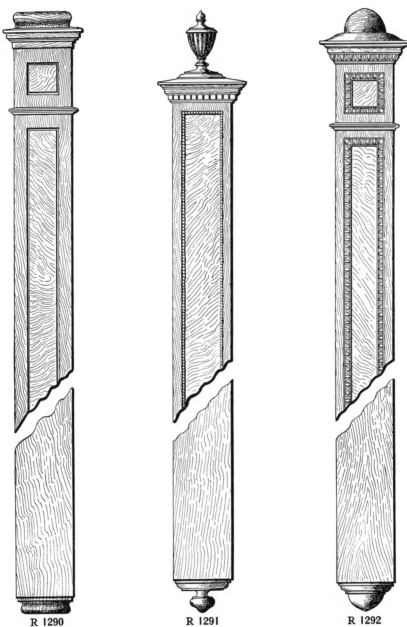

R 1290   R 1291   R 1292
Price each, $10.50.   Price each, $13.50.   Price each, $14.00.
Above prices are for newels of plain oak with shaft 5 x 5.   For yellow pine deduct 5 per cent.
For quartered oak add 25 per cent.   Unless otherwise instructed we will make them
to receive two risers only.   A proportionate extra charge is made for
newels to receive more than two risers.   These newels will
be found in the stair designs on following pages.
Special prices in large quantities.

ABOVE PRICES SUBJECT TO DISCOUNT.

STAIR RAILS.

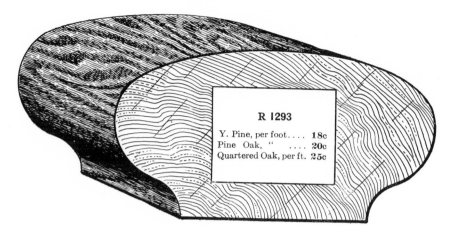

R 1293

Y. Pine, per foot	....	18c
Pine Oak, "	....	20c
Quartered Oak, per ft.		25c

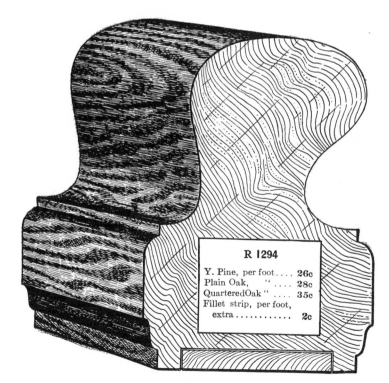

R 1294

Y. Pine, per foot	....	26c
Plain Oak, "	....	28c
Quartered Oak "	....	35c
Fillet strip, per foot, extra	....	2c

Above cuts are actual size for 1¾ inch balusters.
Special prices in large quantity.

ABOVE PRICES SUBJECT TO DISCOUNT.

STAIR RAILS.

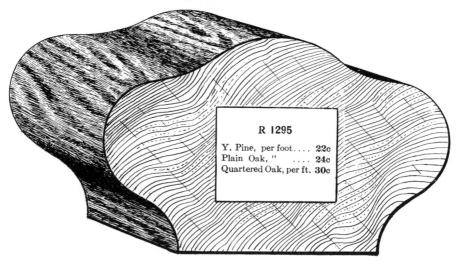

R 1295

Y. Pine, per foot.... **22c**
Plain Oak, " **24c**
Quartered Oak, per ft. **30c**

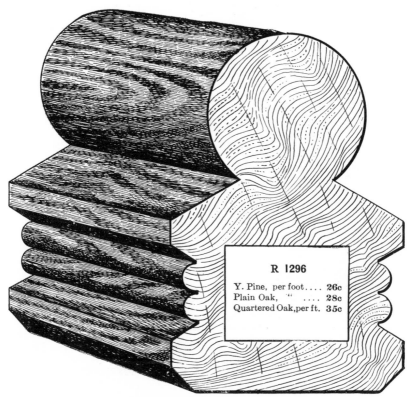

R 1296

Y. Pine, per foot.... **26c**
Plain Oak, " **28c**
Quartered Oak, per ft. **35c**

Above cuts are actual size for 1¾-inch balusters.
Can be plowed for fillet strip same as R1294 at 2c. per lineal foot **extra.**
Special price in large quantity.
ABOVE PRICES SUBJECT TO DISCOUNT.

STAIR RAILS.

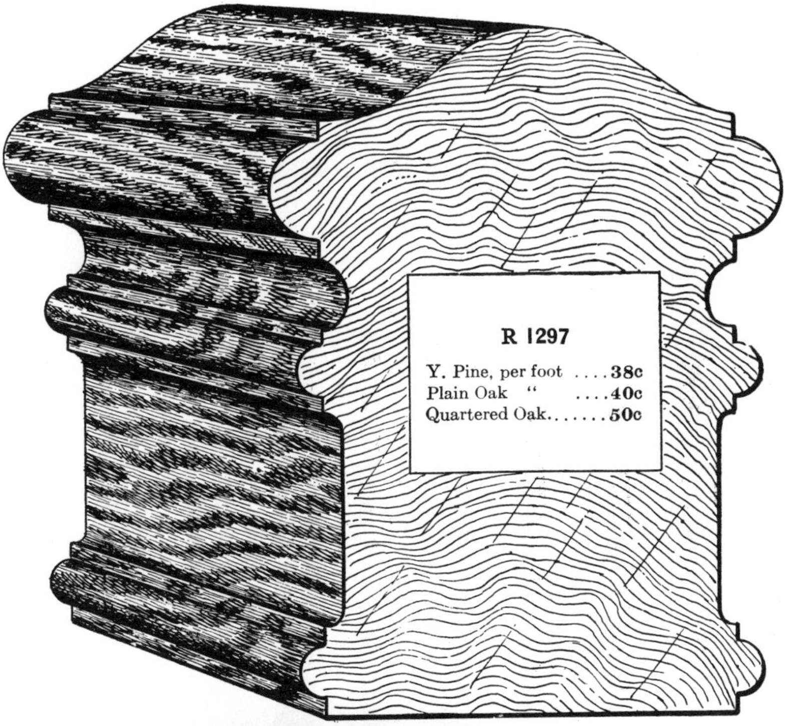

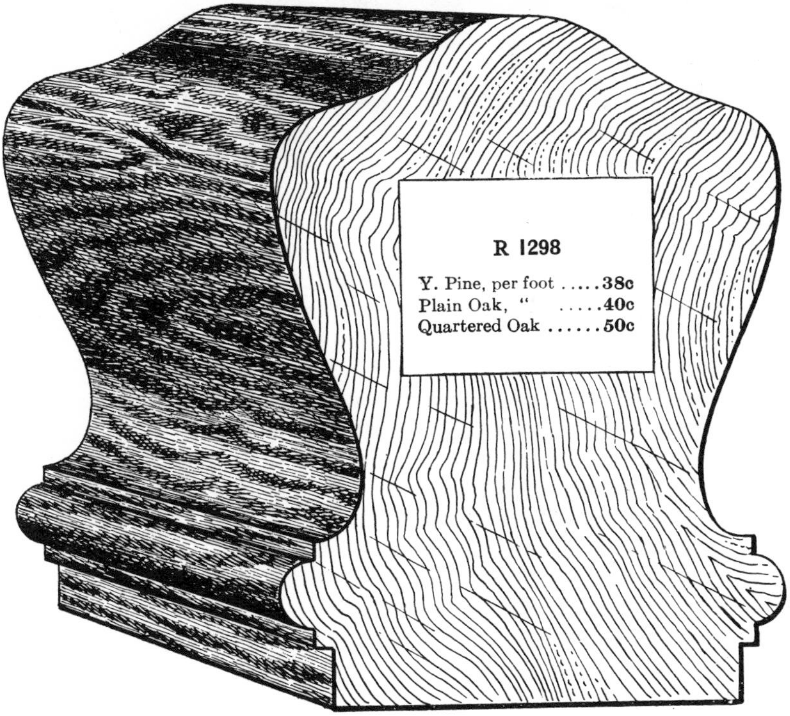

R 1297

Y. Pine, per foot **38c**
Plain Oak   " **40c**
Quartered Oak.......**50c**

R 1298

Y. Pine, per foot **38c**
Plain Oak, " **40c**
Quartered Oak **50c**

Above cuts are actual size for 1¾-inch balusters.
Can be plowed for fillet strip same as R1294 at 2c. per foot **extra.**
Special prices in large quantity.
ABOVE PRICES SUBJECT TO DISCOUNT.

STAIR BALUSTERS.

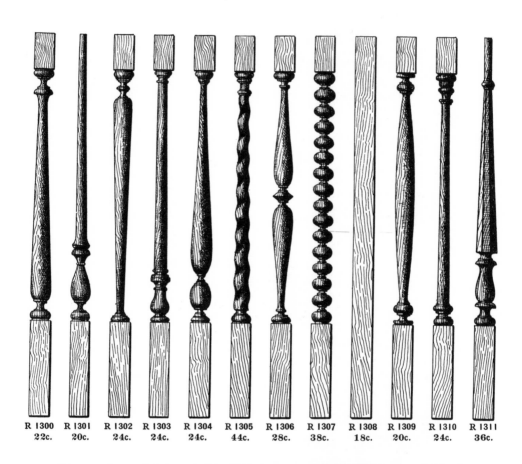

R 1300	R 1301	R 1302	R 1303	R 1304	R 1305	R 1306	R 1307	R 1308	R 1309	R 1310	R 1311
22c.	20c.	24c.	24c.	24c.	44c.	28c.	38c.	18c.	20c.	24c.	36c.

Prices named are per baluster made 1⅜ or 1¾ inches square and 28 to 32 inches long of plain oak.
For prices of yellow pine balusters deduct 2 cents.
Special prices in large quantities.

ABOVE PRICES SUBJECT TO DISCOUNT.

STAIR BALUSTERS.

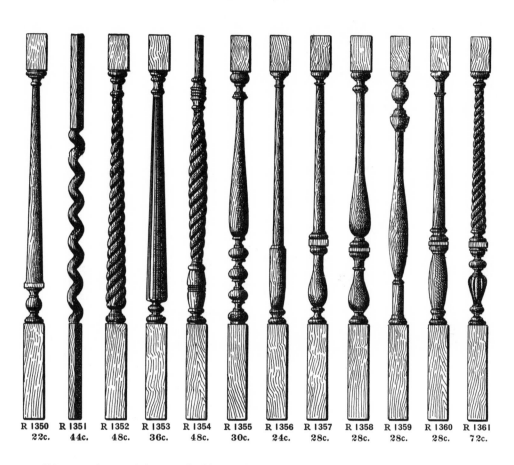

R 1350	R 1351	R 1352	R 1353	R 1354	R 1355	R 1356	R 1357	R 1358	R 1359	R 1360	R 1361
22c.	44c.	48c.	36c.	48c.	30c.	24c.	28c.	28c.	28c.	28c.	72c.

Prices named are per baluster made 1⅜ or 1¾ inches square and 28 to 32 inches long, of plain oak.
For prices of yellow pine balusters deduct 2 cents.
Special prices in large quantities.

ABOVE PRICES SUBJECT TO DISCOUNT.

STAIR DESIGN.

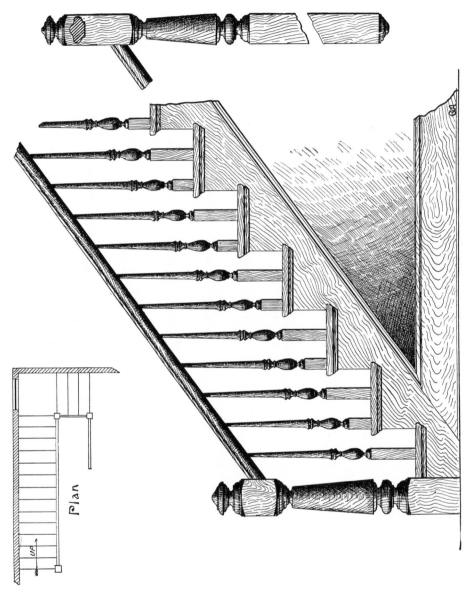

R 1400

In this stairway the following designs are used:
Starting newel, R1270; Angle newel, R1285; Rail, R1295; Baluster, R1301.
In ordering or asking for estimate see pages 168 and 169.

For parquetry and hardwood floor designs see pages 325 to 340.

STAIR DESIGN.

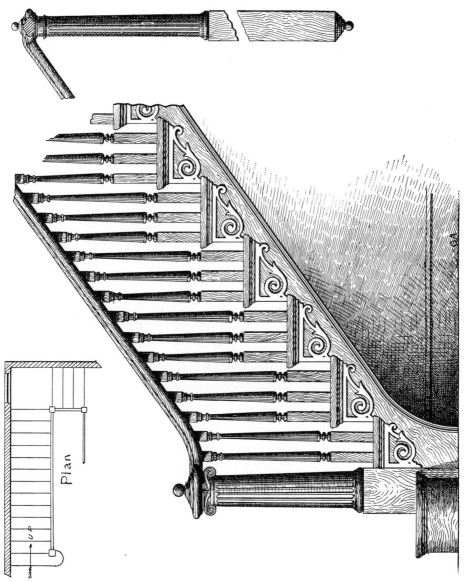

R 1401

In this stairway the following designs are used:
Starting newel, R1274; Angle newel, R1286; Rail, R1295; Baluster, R1353.
In ordering or asking for estimate see pages 168 and 169.

For parquetry and hardwood floor designs see pages 325 to 340.

STAIR DESIGN.

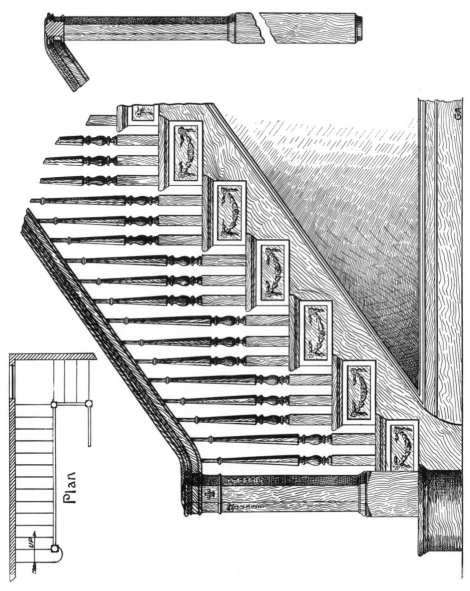

R 1402

In this stairway the following designs are used:
Starting newel, R1271; Angle newel, Special; Rail, R1297; Baluster, R1311.
In ordering or asking for estimates see pages 168 and 169.

For parquetry and hardwood floor designs see pages 325 to 340.

STAIR DESIGN.

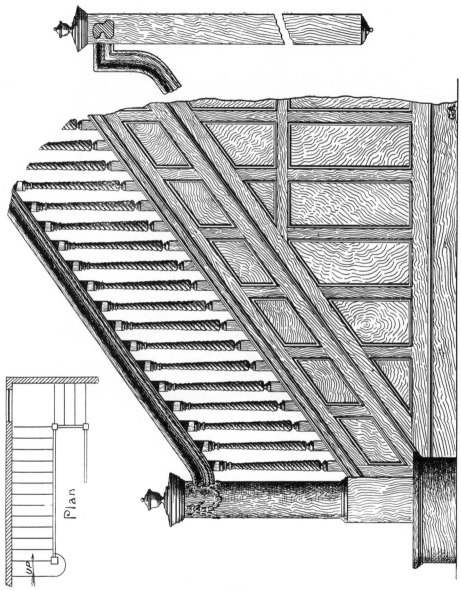

R 1403

In this stairway the following designs are used:
Starting newel, R1273; Angle newel, R1287; Rail, R1294; Baluster, R1352.
In ordering or asking for estimate see pages 168 and 169.

For parquetry and hardwood floor designs see pages 325 to 340.

STAIR DESIGN.

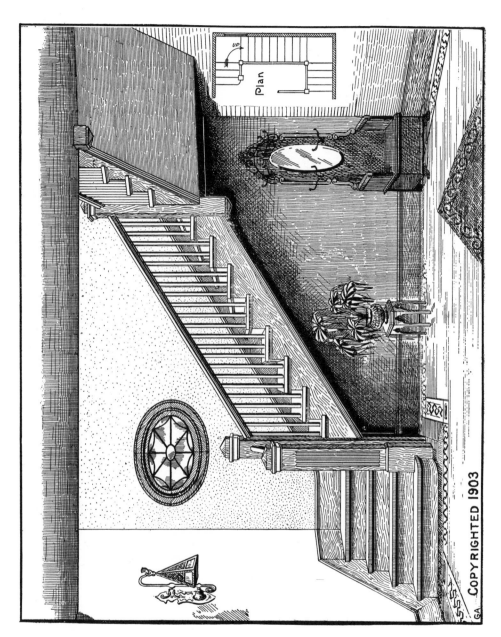

R 1404

In this stairway the following designs are used:
Starting newel, R1263; Angle newel, R1281; Rail, R1296; Baluster, R1308.
In ordering or asking for estimates see pages 168 and 169.

For parquetry and hardwood floor designs see pages 325 to 340.

STAIR DESIGN.

R 1405

In this stairway the following designs are used:
Starting newel, R1260; Angle newel, R1278; Rail, R1293; Baluster, R1301.
In ordering or asking for estimate see pages 168 and 169.

For parquetry and hardwood floor designs see pages 325 to 340.

STAIR DESIGN.

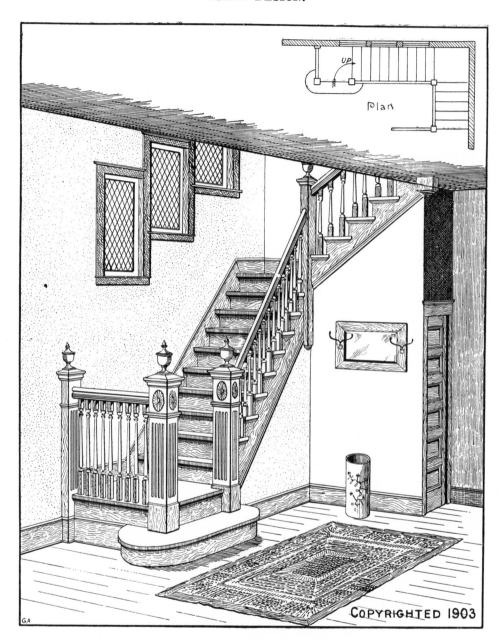

R 1406

In this stairway the following designs are used:
Starting newel, R1266; Angle newel, R1287; Rail, R1296; Baluster, R1300.
In ordering or asking for estimate see pages 168 and 169.

For parquetry and hardwood floor designs see pages 325 to 340.

STAIR DESIGN.

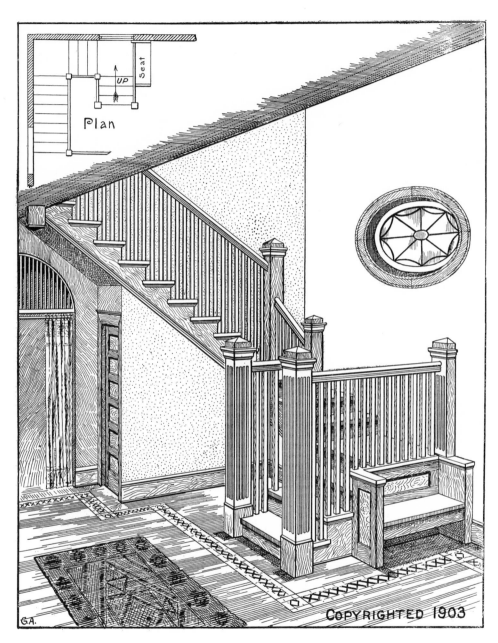

Plan   UP   Seat

COPYRIGHTED 1903

R 1407

In this stairway the following designs are used:
Starting newel, R1263; Angle newel, R1281; Rail, R1296; Baluster, R1308.
In ordering or asking for estimate see pages 168 and 169.

For parquetry and hardwood floor designs see pages 325 to 340.

STAIR DESIGN.

R 1408

In this stairway the following designs are used:
Starting newel, R1265; Angle newel, R 1283; Rail, R1296; Baluster, R1300.
In ordering or asking for estimate see pages 168 and 169.

For parquetry and hardwood floor designs see pages 325 to 340.

STAIR DESIGN.

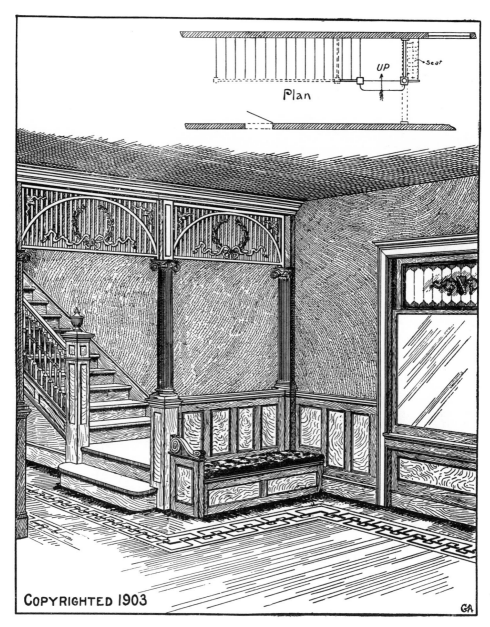

R 1409

In this stairway the following designs are used:
Starting newel, R1267; Angle newel, R1288; Rail, R1294; Baluster, R1306.
In ordering or asking for estimate see pages 168 and 169.

For parquetry and hardwood floor designs see pages 325 to 340.

STAIR DESIGN.

R 1410

In this stairway the following designs are used:
Starting newel, Special; Angle newel, Special; Rail, R1293; Baluster, R1304.
In ordering or asking for estimate see pages 168 and 169.

For parquetry and hardwood floor designs see pages 325 to 340.

STAIR DESIGN.

R 1411

In this stairway the following designs are used:
Starting newel, R1261; Angle newel, R1279; Rail, R1294; Baluster, R1302.
In ordering or asking for estimate see pages 168 and 169.

For parquetry and hardwood floor designs see pages 325 to 340.

STAIR DESIGN.

R 1412

In this stairway the following designs are used:
Starting newel, R1272; Angle newel, R1284; Rail, R1297; Baluster, R1304.
In ordering or asking for estimate see pages 168 and 169.

For parquetry and hardwood floor designs see pages 325 to 340.

STAIR DESIGN.

Plan

COPYRIGHTED 1903

R 1413

An excellent colonial design of moderate cost.

In this stairway the following designs are used:

Starting newel, Special; Angle newel, Special; Rail, R1295; Baluster, R1303.

In ordering or asking for estimate see pages 168 and 169.

For parquetry and hardwood floor designs see pages 325 to 340.

STAIR DESIGN.

R 1414

In this stairway the following designs are used:
Starting newel, R1268; Angle newel, R1289; Rail, R1294; Baluster, R1305.
In ordering or asking for estimate see pages 168 and 169.

For parquetry and hardwood floor designs see pages 325 to 340.

STAIR DESIGN.

Plan

COPYRIGHTED 1903

G.A.

R 1415

In this stairway the following designs are used:
Starting newel, R1262; Angle newel, R1280; Rail, R1294; Baluster, R1300.
In ordering or asking for estimate see pages 168 and 169.

For parquetry and hardwood floor designs see pages 325 to 340.

STAIR DESIGN.

Plan

COPYRIGHTED 1903

R 1416

In this stairway the following designs are used:
Starting newel, R1264; Angle newel, R1279; Rail, R1294; Baluster, R1300.
In ordering or asking for estimate see pages 168 and 169.

For parquetry and hardwood floor designs see pages 325 to 340.

STAIR DESIGN.

R 1417

In this stairway the following designs are used:
Starting newel, R1267; Angle newel, R1288; Rail, R1294; Baluster, R1304.
In ordering or asking for estimate see pages 168 and 169.

For parquetry and hardwood floor designs see pages 325 to 340.

STAIR DESIGN.

R 1418

In this stairway the following designs are used:
Starting newel, Special; Angle newel, R1289; Rail, R1295; Baluster, R1307.
In ordering or asking for estimate see pages 168 and 169.
In ordering or asking for estimate state whether with or without bookcase.

For parquetry and hardwood floor designs see pages 325 to 340.

STAIR DESIGN.

R 1419

This elegant Moorish design can be used in any reception hall of moderate size.
The trim and doors should be made to match as shown in design.
In ordering or asking for estimate see pages 168 and 169.

For parquetry and hardwood floor designs see pages 325 to 340.

STAIR DESIGN.

R 1430
Made in any wood.
In ordering or asking for estimate see pages 168 and 169.
For parquetry and hardwood floor designs see pages 325 to 340.

STAIR DESIGN.

R 1431
Made in any wood.
In ordering or asking for estimate see pages 168 and 169.
For parquetry and hardwood floor designs see pages 325 to 340.

STAIR DESIGN.

R 1432
Made in any wood.
In ordering or asking for estimate see pages 168 and 169.
For parquetry and hardwood floor designs see pages 325 to 340.

STAIR DESIGN.

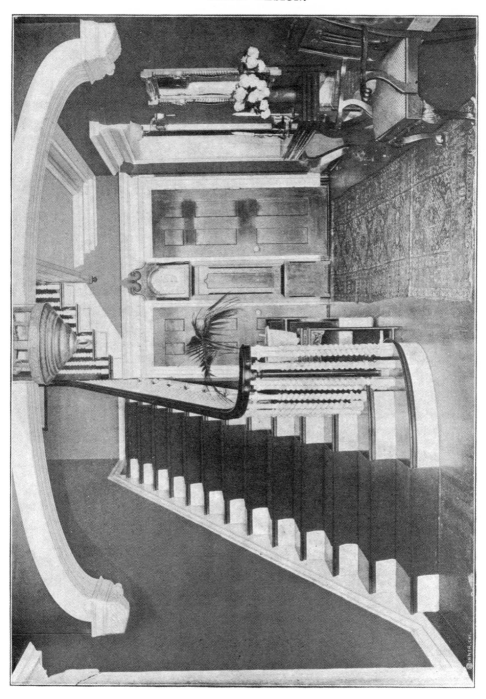

R 1433
Made in any wood.
In ordering or asking for estimates see pages 168 and 169.
For parquetry and hardwood floor designs see pages 325 to 340.

PANELED WAINSCOTING.
MADE IN PINE OR HARDWOODS.

R 1650

Above cut shows effect in oak.

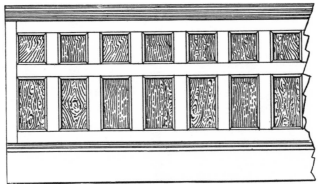

R 1651

Above shows effect in white pine stiles and rails and yellow pine panels.

R 1652

Above shows effect in oak or hardwoods of similar grain.

Always give quantity, height and kind of wood in asking for estimate.

PRESSED MOULDINGS.

Prices are for pine, poplar, cypress and common hardwoods.

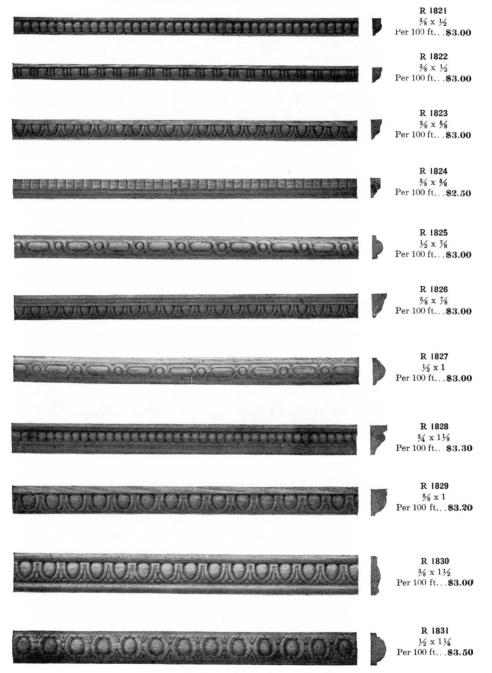

R 1821
⅜ x ½
Per 100 ft...**$3.00**

R 1822
⅜ x ½
Per 100 ft...**$3.00**

R 1823
⅜ x ⅝
Per 100 ft...**$3.00**

R 1824
⅜ x ⅝
Per 100 ft...**$2.50**

R 1825
½ x ⅞
Per 100 ft...**$3.00**

R 1826
⅝ x ⅞
Per 100 ft...**$3.00**

R 1827
½ x 1
Per 100 ft...**$3.00**

R 1828
¾ x 1⅛
Per 100 ft...**$3.30**

R 1829
⅝ x 1
Per 100 ft...**$3.20**

R 1830
⅜ x 1½
Per 100 ft...**$3.00**

R 1831
½ x 1¼
Per 100 ft...**$3.50**

ABOVE PRICES SUBJECT TO DISCOUNT.

PRESSED MOULDINGS.

Prices are for pine, poplar, cypress and common hardwoods.

R 1832
½ x 1¾
Per 100 ft...$3.50

R 1833
⅞ x 1¾
Per 100 ft...$4 50

R 1834
⅞ x 2
Per 100 ft...$4.50

R 1835
⅞ x 2⅛
Per 100 ft...$5.30

R 1836
⅞ x 2¼
Per 100 ft...$5.30

R 1837
⅞ x 2⅜
Per 100 ft...$5.50

R 1838
⅞ x 2½
Per 100 ft...$5.50

ABOVE PRICES SUBJECT TO DISCOUNT.

PRESSED MOULDINGS.

Prices are for pine poplar, cypress and common hardwoods.

R 1839
$\frac{7}{8}$x2$\frac{1}{8}$
Per 100 ft.
$5.30

R 1840
$\frac{7}{8}$x2$\frac{3}{4}$
Per 100 ft.
$6 50

R 1841
$\frac{7}{8}$x3$\frac{1}{2}$
Per 100 ft.
$8.00

R 1842
$\frac{1}{2}$x4
Per 100 ft
$8.00

R 1843
$\frac{7}{8}$x4
Per 100 ft.
$8.00

ABOVE PRICES SUBJECT TO DISCOUNT.

TURNED AND ROPED MOULDINGS.

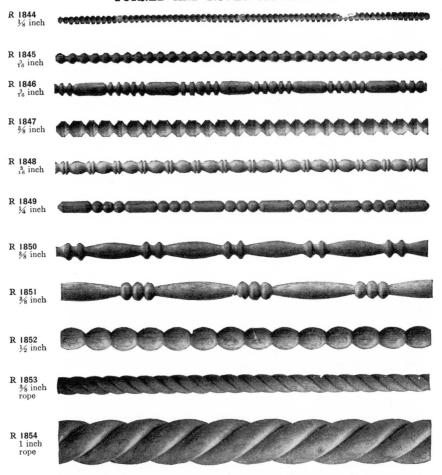

R 1844
1/8 inch

R 1845
3/16 inch

R 1846
3/16 inch

R 1847
3/8 inch

R 1848
3/16 inch

R 1849
1/4 inch

R 1850
3/8 inch

R 1851
3/8 inch

R 1852
1/2 inch

R 1853
3/8 inch
rope

R 1854
1 inch
rope

Price list of turned mouldings, R1844 to R1852 inclusive, in lengths of from 2 to 3 feet, in white pine, yellow pine, cypress, poplar and common hardwoods.

Full round, 1/8 to 7/8 inch diameter	per 100	feet	$3.60
" over 7/8 to 1 1/8 inch diameter	100	"	5.40
" " 1 1/8 to 1 3/8 "	" 100	"	13.20
Half round, 1/4 to 3/4 inch diameter	" 100	"	2.20
" over 7/8 to 1 1-16 inches diameter	" 100	"	3.40
Quarter round, 3-16 x 3-16 to 3/8 x 3/8 inch	" 100	"	1.50
7-16 x 7-16 to 1/2 x 1/2 "	" 100	"	1.80
" 5/8 x 5/8 inch	" 100	"	4.00
" 3/4 x 3/4 "	" 100	"	5.40
7/8 x 7/8 "	" 100	"	7.20
" 1 x 1 "	" 100	"	10.80

ROPE MOULDINGS.

R1853 or R1854

In white pine yellow pine, cypress, poplar and common hardwoods.

1/4 to 1/2 inch diameter	per 100	feet	$ 5.50
5/8 to 7/8 "	" 100	"	7.00
1 to 1 1/8 "	" 100	"	11.00
1 1/4 to 1 3/8 "	" 100	"	14.00
1 5/8 to 1 7/8 "	" 100	"	21.00
2 "	" 100	"	28.00

Walnut and cherry, 10 per cent. higher than above list On mahogany special prices will be quoted on application
Above prices cover orders of 100 feet of a kind and over. If less than 100 feet, we add **$2.00** extra for setting up machine.

ABOVE PRICES SUBJECT TO DISCOUNT

PORCH MATERIALS.

The large and massive porch of classic design is now recognized as a necessary feature of the modern residence. But few manufacturers or persons aside from the leading architects are posted as to their proper proportions, and the appearance of many otherwise handsome buildings is therefore ruined. Even the careless observer of these improperly built porches will know there is something wrong with the building but would be unable to say just how to remedy the evil. We have made a careful study of this subject and are prepared to furnish our customers with porch materials of excellent design and manufacture at competitive prices. On page 218 will be found the details of a standard design with all parts in proportion and properly named. The use of the terms shown on this design in correspondence will save delays and misunderstandings. Always send a floor plan design and complete measurements in ordering or asking for estimate on porches. We invite your careful inspection of the following pages, as they will greatly assist you in handling your customers.

PORCH COLUMNS.

The prices named below are for designs on opposite page in the diameters most commonly used. The height of each column as given is in correct proportion to the diameter of the design selected.

Design Number.	Name.	Diam. of Shaft at Base.	Diam. of Shaft at Neck.	Total Height Including Cap and Base.	Price Each Inc. Cap & Base.
R1855½	Tuscan	8 inches	6⅜ inches	4 ft. 8 inches	$4.50
"	"	9 "	7⅛ "	5 " 3 "	5.50
"	"	10 "	8 "	5 " 10 "	7.00
"	"	12 "	9½ "	7 " 0 "	11.00
R1856½	Doric	8 "	6¾ "	5 " 4 "	8.40
"	"	9 "	7½ "	6 " 0 "	9.70
"	"	10 "	8⅜ "	6 " 8 "	10.70
"	"	12 "	10 "	8 " 0 "	14.00
R1857½	Colonial	8 "	6½ "	6 " 0 "	5.00
"	"	9 "	7½ "	6 " 9 "	6.00
"	"	10 "	8½ "	7 " 6 "	7.00
"	"	12 "	10 "	9 " 0 "	11.00
R1858½	Ionic	8 "	6½ "	6 " 0 "	10.30
"	"	9 "	7½ "	6 " 9 "	12.40
"	"	10 "	8½ "	7 " 6 "	15.00
"	"	12 "	10 "	9 " 0 "	21.00
R1859½	Corinthian	8 "	6½ "	6 " 8 "	12.50
"	"	9 "	7½ "	7 " 6 "	15.00
"	"	10 "	8½ "	8 " 4 "	17.00
"	"	12 "	10 "	10 " 0 "	23.00

ABOVE PRICES SUBJECT TO DISCOUNT.

Where a slender column is desired, place a pedestal under the column, this gives the additional height without increasing the diameter of the column. It is the invariable rule that the diameter of the column must increase proportionately with the height of the shaft. For cut illustrating this point, see designs R1861½ and R1861½A page 220. In these two designs the height from floor to entablature is the same but the column in design R1861½ is much less in diameter than that in R1861½A owing to the length of shaft in R1861½ being decreased by the pedestal.

PORCH COLUMNS.

Architecturally correct in name and detail.
Scale ¾ inch to the foot.

R 1855½	R 1856½	R 1857½	R 1858½	1859½
Tuscan.	Doric.	Colonial.	Ionic.	Corinthian.

NOTE: These columns are all the same diameter, but the proportionate height varies in the different orders of architecture. We make these columns from 6 to 36 inches in diameter and height in proportion. The shaft is built up of staves locked together in the most careful manner and will not open up at the joints. The ornamental capitals are made of composition for exterior use. We have classic models and tables giving proper proportions of the various parts and unless instructed to the contrary make our columns correct in every detail. If given the height and style of column will gladly advise our customers the proper diameter and general proportions so they can order correctly.

For prices of columns as shown above, see opposite page.

CLASSIC PORCH DETAILS.

See complete elevation on opposite page.

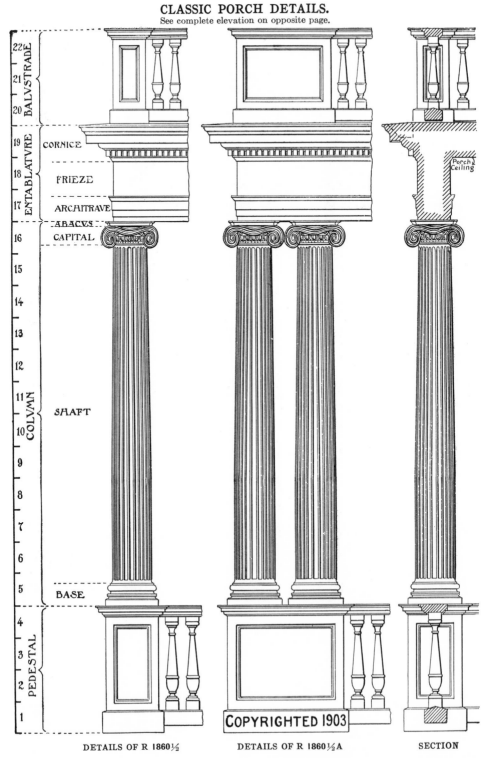

DETAILS OF R 1860½   DETAILS OF R 1860½A   SECTION

In above details the following designs are employed: Column, R1858½ with pedestal; Top rail, R1941½;
Bottom rail, R1942½; Baluster R1900½.
Read pages 215 and 217 regarding porch work.

CLASSIC PORCH DESIGN.
See details on opposite page.

COMPLETE ELEVATION OF DESIGN R 1860½ A
The details on opposite page are carefully drawn to a scale and the total height from porch floor to top of balcony newel is divided into 22 equal divisions. These divisions show the proportionate relation of column, pedestal, entablature and balcony balustrade, to each other.

E. L. ROBERTS & CO.. CHICAGO.

CLASSIC PORCH DETAILS.

See complete elevation on opposite page.

COPYRIGHTED 1903

DETAILS OF R 1861½   R 1861½ A   SECTION

In above details the following designs are employed: Column R1858½. Balcony newel, R1939½;
Top rail, R1941½; Bottom rail, R1942½; Baluster, R1900½.
Read pages 215, 216 and 217, regarding porch work.

CLASSIC PORCH DESIGN.

See details on opposite page.

COMPLETE ELEVATION OF DESIGN R 1861½.

The details on opposite page are carefully drawn to a scale, and the total height from porch floor to top of balcony newel of design R1861½ is divided into 31 equal divisions, and design R1861½A into 18 equal divisions. These divisions show the proportionate relations of columns, entablature and balcony balustrade to each other.

CLASSIC PORCH DETAILS.

See complete elevation on opposite page.

*8012

*8003

*8131

COPYRIGHTED 1903

ELEVATION DETAILS OF R 1862½.

In above details the following designs are employed: Section column, R1855½; Balcony newel, R1937½;
Top rail, R1944½; Bottom rail, R1946½. Balcony baluster, R1870½.
Read pages 215 and 217 regarding porch work.

CLASSIC PORCH DESIGN.
See details on opposite page

COMPLETE ELEVATION OF DESIGN R 1862½.

The details on opposite page are carefully drawn to a scale, and the total height from porch floor to top of balcony newel is divided into 23 equal divisions. These divisions show the proportionate relations of columns, entablature and balcony balustrade to each other.

CLASSIC PORCH DESIGN.

DESIGN R 1862½ A

Always furnish complete floor plan, and read pages 215 and 217 in ordering or asking for estimate.

MODERN PORCH DESIGN.

DESIGN R 1862½ B

Always furnish complete floor plan and read pages 215 and 217 in ordering or asking for estimate.

MODERN PORCH DESIGN.

DESIGN R 1862½ C
Always furnish complete floor plan and read pages 215 and 217 in ordering or asking for estimate.

PORCH BALUSTERS

OF PINE OR POPLAR.

For prices see bottom of page.

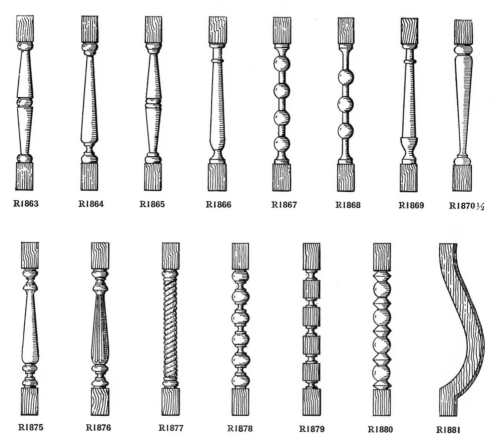

R1863   R1864   R1865   R1866   R1867   R1868   R1869   R1870½

R1875   R1876   R1877   R1878   R1879   R1880   R1881

PRICE PER BALUSTER.

SIZE.	1¾ x 1¾ inches square.							
	R1863	R1864	R1865	R1866	R1867	R1868	R1869	R1870½
	$ cts.	$ cts.	$ cts.	$ cts.	$ cts.	$ cts.	$ cts.	$ cts.
16 or 18 Inches Long......	.10	.11	.10	.10	.11	.11	.11	.11
20 or 24 Inches Long......	.11	.12	.11	.11	.12	.12	.12	.12
26 or 28 Inches Long......	.12	.13	.12	.12	.13	.13	.13	.13

SIZE.	1¾ x 1¾ inches square.						
	R1875	R1876	R1877	R1878	R1879	R1880	R1881
	$ cts.	$ cts.	$ cts.	$ cts.	$ cts.	$ cts.	$ cts.
16 or 18 Inches Long......	.12	.16	.30	.16	.16	.16	.20
20 or 24 Inches Long......	.14	.18	.32	.18	.18	.18	.22
26 or 28 Inches Long......	.16	.20	.34	.20	.20	.20	.24

Special prices in large quantities.

ABOVE PRICES SUBJECT TO DISCOUNT.

TURNED PORCH COLUMNS.

Made of No. 1 Poplar.   Hole bored through entire length to prevent checking.

For prices see opposite page.

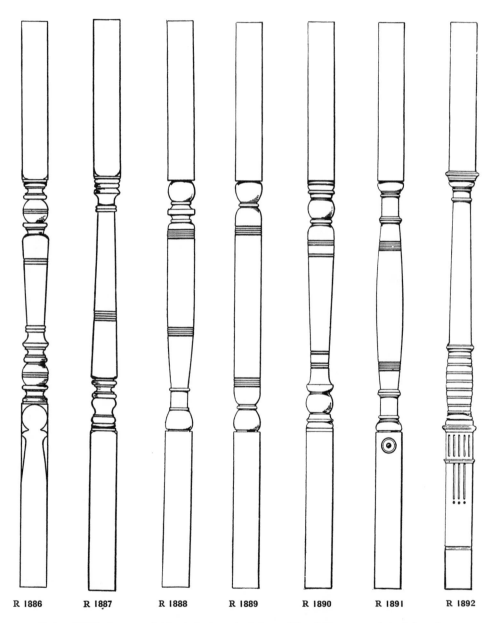

R 1886   R 1887   R 1888   R 1889   R 1890   R 1891   R 1892

Design R1887 always carried in stock of standard sizes.   Other designs are made to order only.
Our columns are smoothly turned from the best column stock to be obtained.

TURNED PORCH COLUMNS.

For designs see opposite page.

PRICES PER COLUMN.

Design	4 x 4 8 feet.	4 x 4 9 feet.	4 x 4 10 feet.	5 x 5 8 feet.	5 x 5 9 feet.	5 x 5 10 feet.	6 x 6 8 feet.	6 x 6 9 feet.	6 x 6 10 feet.
	$ cts.	$ cts.	$ cts.	$ cts.	$ cts.	$ cts.	$ cts.	$ cts.	$ cts.
R 1886	1.60	1.70	1.80	2.40	2.70	2.90	3.30	3.80	4.00
R 1887	See	our	current	discount	and	net	price	list.	
R 1888	1.60	1.70	1.80	2.40	2.70	2.90	3.30	3.80	4.00
R 1889	1.60	1.70	1.80	2.40	2.70	2.90	3.30	3.80	4.00
R 1890	1.60	1.70	1.80	2.40	2.70	2.90	3.30	3.80	4.00
R 1891	2.00	2.10	2.20	2.80	3.10	3.30	3.70	4.20	4.40
R 1892	5.20	5.40	5.50	6.00	6.20	6.50	7.00	7.30	7.60

Special prices in large quantities.

ABOVE PRICES SUBJECT TO DISCOUNT.

SAWED BALUSTERS.

MADE OF PINE OR POPLAR.

 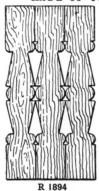 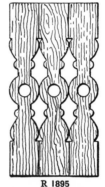 

| R 1893 | R 1894 | R 1895 | R 1896 |

All above patterns ⅞x5¾x18 to 24 inches, straight sawed, each, **12c.**
All above patterns ⅞x5¾x18 to 24 inches, rake sawed, each, **14c.**
Special prices in large quantities.

HEAVY TURNED PORCH BALUSTERS.

TURNED FROM No. I POPLAR.

| R 1900½ | R 1901½ | R 1902 | R 1903 | R 1904 | R 1905 |

2¼x2¼, 8 to 12 inches long, **12c.**; 14 x 18 inches long, **18c.**; 20 to 24 inches long, each, **24c.**
2¾x2¾, 8 to 12 inches long, **15c.**; 14 x 18 inches long, **22c.**; 20 to 24 inches long, each, **28c.**
3¾x3¾, 8 to 12 inches long, **22c.**; 14 x 18 inches long, **28c.**; 20 to 24 inches long, each, **34c.**
Special prices in large quantities.

ABOVE PRICES SUBJECT TO DISCOUNT.

TURNED DROPS.

FOR PORCHES AND BRACKETS.

Made of Pine or Poplar.

R 1906   R 1907   R 1908   R 1909   R 1910   R 1911   R 1912

Usual lengths, 4 to 6 inches.   Each, 1¾x1¾, 9c.   2¾x2¾, 15c. 3¾x3¾, 24c

DRAPERY.

Pine or Poplar.
Usually made ⅞x4 inches for porches and ⅞x6 for cornices.

⅞ x 4 per lineal foot, 10c.   R 1913   ⅞ x 6 per lineal foot 13c.

⅞ x 4 per lineal foot, 15c.   R 1914   ⅞ x 6 per lineal foot, 18c.

TURNED PORCH SPINDLES.

Prices per baluster.

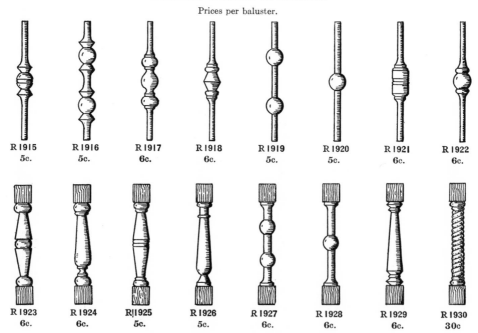

R 1915   R 1916   R 1917   R 1918   R 1919   R 1920   R 1921   R 1922
5c.   5c.   6c.   6c.   5c.   5c.   6c.   6c.

R 1923   R 1924   R 1925   R 1926   R 1927   R 1928   R 1929   R 1930
6c.   6c.   5c.   5c.   6c.   6c.   6c.   30c

ABOVE PRICES SUBJECT TO DISCOUNT.

PORCH NEWELS.

Made of No. 1 Poplar.

Prices, each.

Size of Shaft, Inches.	Height, Feet.	R 1934	R 1935	R 1937	R 1937½	R 1939	R 1939½
4 x 4	4	See our current		$1.50	$3.00		
5 x 5	4	discount		2.00	3.50	$4.00	$5.00
6 x 6	4	and		2.50	4.00	4.50	5.50
8 x 8	4	net-price list.		4.50	6.00	6.50	7.50

Special prices in large quantities.

Design R1934 always in stock in standard sizes.

ABOVE PRICES SUBJECT TO DISCOUNT.

| R 1934 | R 1935 | R 1937 | R 1937½ | R 1939 | R 1939½ |

Design R1934 always in stock in standard sizes.

ABOVE PRICES SUBJECT TO DISCOUNT.

PORCH RAILS.

Made of No. 1 Poplar.

For designs see opposite page.

R 1940. Size 2¾x3¾ inches for 1¾ balusters, per lineal foot......................$0.18
R 1941½.   "   4¾x2¾   "   1¾   "   "   " .... .32
R 1942½.   "   3¾x2¼   "   1¾   "   "   " .... .22
R 1943½.   "   2¾x1¾   "   1¾   "   "   " .... .08
R 1944½.   "   4¾x2¾   "   1¾   "   "   " .... .32
R 1945½.   "   3¾x2¾   "   1¾   "   "   " .... .26
R 1946½.   "   4¾x2¾   "   1¾   "   "   " .... .32
R 1948.   "   1¾x1¾   "   1¾   "   "   " .... .06

If above rails are wanted for heavier balusters it is not necessary to increase thickness, simply add to width of rails the difference between 1¾ balusters and the size required. Example: R1941½ is 4¾ inches wide for 1¾-inch baluster.   If made for 2¼-inch baluster the width would be 5¼ inches.

ABOVE PRICES SUBJECT TO DISCOUNT.

LIST PRICES CARVED ORNAMENTS AND ROSETTES.

Pages 142-143.

Made of pine, poplar or common hardwoods.

No.	Size.	Price each. $ cts.	No.	Size.	Price each. $ cts.
R 1166	4 x 28-inch	2.30	R 1177	5x15, ⅛-inch..........	.84
R 1167	1¾x 3 "	.66	R 1178	3x10.	.28
R 1168	1⅜x 6 "	.34	R 1179	2½-inch diameter......	.16
R 1169	3 x 31 "	1.80	R 1180	2-inch diameter........	.03
R 1170	4¼x12 "	5.40	R 1181	3½x3½.	.20
R 1171	5½x 5½"	.80	R 1182	5x5¾, 5-16-inch.	.54
R 1172	5 x 18 "	1.40	R 1183	3½x3½.	.15
R 1173	5 x 48 "	4.30	R 1184	3-inch diameter........	.12
R 1174	8½x48 "	4.30	R 1185	3-inch diameter........	.25
R 1175	7 x 48 "	6.50	R 1186	1½-inch diameter......	.02
R 1176	8½x48 "	7.00	R 1187	2½x6.	.18
			R 1188	8x14, 5-16-inch	1.00

ABOVE PRICES SUBJECT TO DISCOUNT.

PORCH RAILS.
Made of No. 1 Poplar.

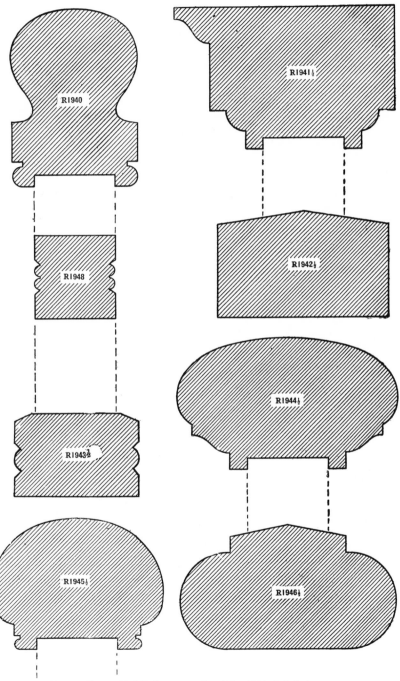

Above rails are ½ full size, proportioned for 1¾-inch balusters.
For prices see top of opposite page.

PORCH SPINDLE FRIEZE.

Usual drop 12 inches.

Per lineal foot, 70c.   R 1950½

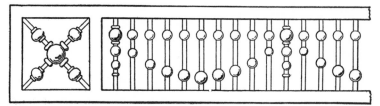

Per lineal foot, 65c.   R 1950½B

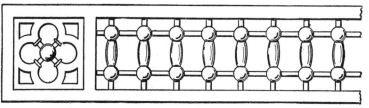

Per lineal foot, 70c.   R 1950½C

NEWEL TOPS.

For inside or outside work.

  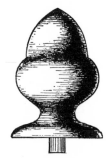

R 1950½D   R 1950½E   R 1950½G

Above designs made of pine or poplar.

Price each,	2¾ inches in diameter		....	$0.18
"	"	3¾ "	"	.24
"	"	4½ "	"	.36
"	"	5½ "	"	.40
"	"	7½ "	"	.70

ABOVE PRICES SUBJECT TO DISCOUNT.

RAFTER ENDS.

Usual size, 1¾x3¾x24 inches. Made of pine or poplar.

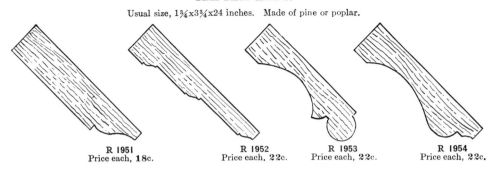

R 1951
Price each, **18c.**

R 1952
Price each, **22c.**

R 1953
Price each, **22c.**

R 1954
Price each, **22c.**

VERGE OR PORCH BRACKETS.

R 1955
Size 12x8, 2½ inches thick, each, **$2.00.**

R 1956
Size 12x8, 2½ inches thick, each, **$1.30.**

LEFT   RIGHT

OCTAGON BAY WINDOW PANELS.
Carving planted on.

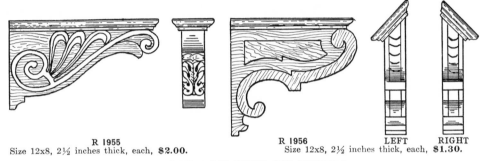

LEFT PANEL
R 1957

CENTER PANEL
R 1958

RIGHT PANEL
R 1959

Carving only for panel R1957, 12x12 inches, each, **$3.00.** Carving only for panel R1958, 24x12 inches, **$9.00.**

FANCY FRIEZE.
Made to fit on facia, 8 to 10 inches wide, of pine or poplar.

R 1960
Price of carving only per lineal foot, **90c.**
ABOVE PRICES SUBJECT TO DISCOUNT.

BRACKETS.

See designs on opposite page.

Number of design	Size inches	Thick ness in.	Price $ Cts	Size inches	Thick ness in.	Price $ Cts	Size inches	Thick ness in.	Price $ Cts	Size inches	Thick ness in.	Price $ Cts	Size inches	Thick ness in.	Price $ Cts
R1961				10x12	3½	.80	10x14	3½	.90	12x14	3½	1.00	14x18	3½	1.20
R1962	7x12	3½	.60	8x14	3½	.70	8x16	3½	.80	8x18	3½	.90	8x22	3½	1.10
R1963	14x10	1¾	.80	16x12	1¾	.80	18x14	1¾	.90	20x14	1¾	1.00	24x16	1¾	1.30
R1964	12x 8	1⅜	.22	14x10	1⅜	.24	16x12	1⅜	.28	18x12	1⅜	.32	18x14	1⅜	.36
R1965	10x12	1⅜	.22	10x14	1⅜	.24	12x14	1⅜	.28	12x16	1⅜	.32	14x18	1⅜	.36
R1966	10x12	1⅜	.22	10x14	1⅜	.24	12x14	1⅜	.28	12x16	1⅜	.32	14x18	1⅜	.36
R1967	10x12	1⅜	.22	10x14	1⅜	.24	12x14	1⅜	.28	12x16	1⅜	.32	14x18	1⅜	.36
R1968	8x10	1⅜	.20	10x12	1⅜	.20	10x14	1⅜	.22	12x12	1⅜	.22	12x14	1⅜	.22
R1969	8x10	1⅜	.22	10x12	1⅜	.22	10x14	1⅜	.24	12x12	1⅜	.24	12x14	1⅜	.24
R1969½	6x 3	1⅜	.12	8x 4	1¾	.14									
R1970	8x10	1⅜	.22	10x12	1⅜	.22	10x14	1⅜	.24	12x12	1⅜	.24	12x14	1⅜	.24
R1970½	8x 3	1¾	.18	12x 4	1¾	.24									
R1971	20x12	3½	2.20	24x12	3½	2.50	28x14	3½	3.00	32x16	3½	3.50	36x16	3½	4.00
R1971½	6x 3	1⅜	.12	8x 4	1¾	.14									
R1972	8x10	1⅜	.22	10x12	1⅜	.22	10x14	1⅜	.24	12x12	1⅜	.24	12x14	1⅜	.24
R1972½	8x10	1⅜	.12	10x12	1⅜	.14	10x14	1⅜	.16	12x12	1⅜	.18	12x14	1⅜	.20
R1973	8x10	1⅜	.22	10x12	1⅜	.22	10x14	1⅜	.24	12x12	1⅜	.24	12x14	1⅜	.24

These prices are for brackets on opposite page made (in usual sizes) of pine or poplar.

ABOVE PRICES SUBJECT TO DISCOUNT.

BRACKETS.

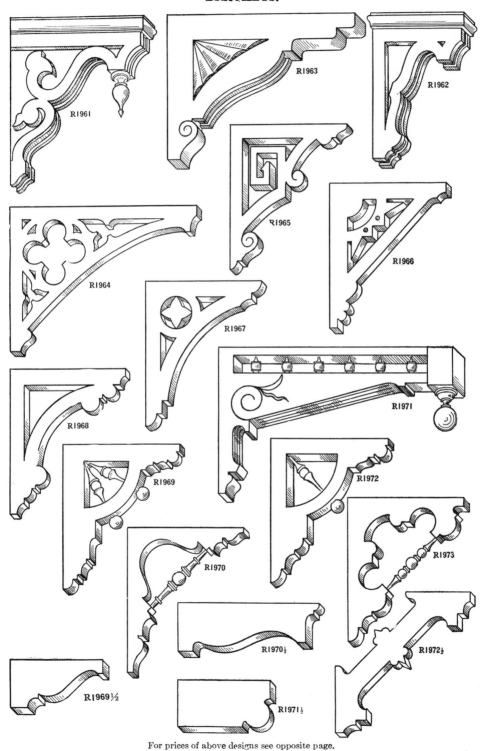

R1961 R1963 R1962 R1965 R1966 R1964 R1967 R1968 R1971 R1969 R1972 R1970 R1973 R1970½ R1972½ R1969½ R1971½

For prices of above designs see opposite page.

BRACKETS.

See designs on opposite page.

Number of design	Size inches	Thick ness in.	Price $ Cts	Size inches	Thick ness in.	Price $ Cts	Size inches	Thick ness in.	Price $ Cts	Size inches	Thick ness in.	Price $ Cts	Size inches	Thick ness in.	Price $ Cts
R1974	10x12	1⅜	.22	12x14	1⅜	.28	12x16	1⅜	.32	14x16	1⅜	.34	14x18	1⅜	.36
R1974½	10x14	1⅜	.22	12x16	1⅜	.28	14x16	1⅜	.32	14x18	1⅜	.34	14x20	1⅜	.36
R1975	10x12	1¾	.30	10x14	1¾	.36	12x16	1¾	.40	14x18	1¾	.44	14x20	1¾	.48
R1975½	6x16	1⅜	.30	6x18	1⅜	.36	6x24	1⅜	.50	6x28	1⅜	.54	6x32	1⅜	.60
R1976½	12x 8	1⅜	.22	14x10	1⅜	.24	16x10	1⅜	.28	18x12	1⅜	.32	20x14	1⅜	.40
R1977½	6x16	3½	.70	6x18	3½	.80	7x24	3½	1.00	7x28	3½	1.10	7x32	3½	1.30
R1978	12x18	3½	1.20	14x20	3½	1.50	16x24	3½	2.00	16x28	3½	2.50	18x30	3½	3.00
R1978½	14x12	3½	1.00	16x12	3½	1.10	18x14	3½	1.20	20x14	3½	1.50	22x16	3½	2.00
R1979½	12x 6	1⅜	.30	14x 6	1⅜	.32	16x 8	1⅜	.36	20x10	1⅜	.40	24x12	1⅜	.60
R1980	10x10	1⅜	.24	12x12	1⅜	.28	14x14	1⅜	.32	16x16	1⅜	.40	18x18	1⅜	.60
R1980½	4x 4	1⅜	.06												
R1981	8x 4	1¾	.30	10x 6	1¾	.34	12x 8	1¾	.40						
R1981½	4x 4	1⅜	.06												
R1982	10x12	1⅜	.22	10x14	1⅜	.24	12x12	1⅜	.24	12x14	1⅜	.28	14x16	1⅜	.36
R1982½	4x 4	1⅜	.06												
R1983	12x18	3½	1.20	14x20	3½	1.50	16x24	3½	2.00	16x28	3½	2.50	18x30	3½	3.00
R1983½	12x12	1⅜	.30	14x14	1⅜	.36	16x16	1⅜	.44	18x18	1⅜	.60	20x20	1⅜	.70
R1984½	8x14	1¾	.50	10x16	1¾	.60	10x18	1¾	.70	10x22	1¾	.80	14x24	1¾	1.00

These prices are for brackets on opposite page made (in usual sizes) of pine or poplar.

ABOVE PRICES SUBJECT TO DISCOUNT.

BRACKETS.

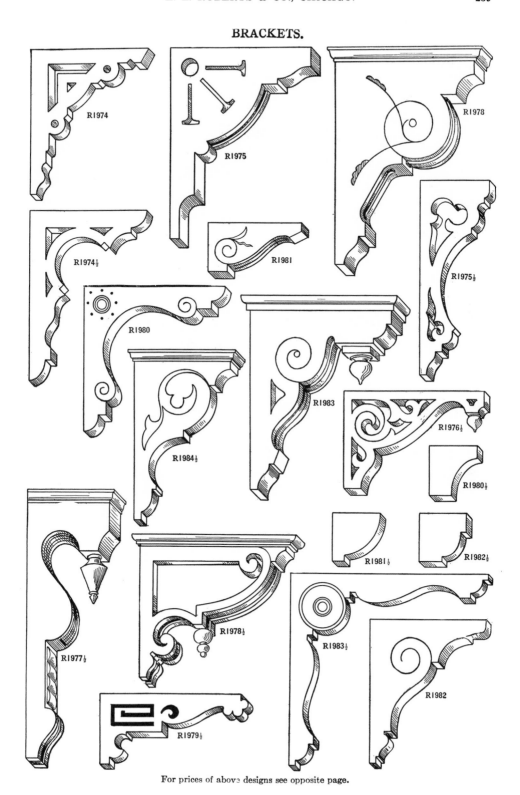

R1974

R1975

R1978

R1974½

R1981

R1975½

R1980

R1983

R1976½

R1984½

R1980½

R1977½

R1978½

R1981½

R1982½

R1983½

R1982

R1979½

For prices of above designs see opposite page.

BRACKETS.

See designs on opposite page.

Number of design	Size inches	Thick ness in.	Price $ Cts	Size inches	Thick ness in.	Price $ Cts	Size inches	Thick ness in.	Price $ Cts	Size inches	Thick ness in.	Price $ Cts	Size inches	Thick ness in.	Price $ Cts
R1986	6x16	1⅜	.30	6x18	1⅜	.36	6x24	1⅜	.50	6x28	1⅜	.54	6x32	1⅜	.60
R1987	12x 8	1⅜	.22	14x10	1⅜	.24	16x12	1⅜	.28	18x12	1⅜	.32	18x14	1⅜	.36
R1988	10x12	1⅜	.22	10x14	1⅜	.24	12x14	1⅜	.28	12x16	1⅜	.32	14x18	1⅜	.36
R1989	6x16	3½	.60	6x18	3½	.70	7x24	3½	.90	7x28	3½	1.00	7x32	3½	1.20
R1990	12x 8	1⅜	.22	14x10	1⅜	.24	16x12	1⅜	.28	18x12	1⅜	.32	18x14	1⅜	.36
R1991	12x 8	1⅜	.22	14x10	1⅜	.24	16x12	1⅜	.28	18x12	1⅜	.32	18x14	1⅜	.36
R1992	6x16	3½	.70	6x18	3½	.80	7x24	3½	1.00	7x28	3½	1.10	7x32	3½	1.40
R1993	6x16	1⅜	.30	6x18	1⅜	.36	6x24	1⅜	.50	6x28	1⅜	.54	6x32	1⅜	.60
R1994	12x 8	1⅜	.22	14x10	1⅜	.24	16x12	1⅜	.28	18x12	1⅜	.32	18x14	1⅜	.36
R1995	6x16	1⅜	.40	6x18	1⅜	.46	6x24	1⅜	.60	6x28	1⅜	.64	6x32	1⅜	.70
R1996	10x12	1⅜	.22	10x14	1⅜	.24	12x14	1⅜	.28	12x16	1⅜	.32	14x18	1⅜	.36
R1998	8x12	1⅜	.24	10x14	1⅜	.28	12x14	1⅜	.32	12x16	1⅜	.36	14x18	1⅜	.40
R2000	8x14	1⅜	.26	10x16	1⅜	.30	12x16	1⅜	.34	12x18	1⅜	.40	14x20	1⅜	.44

These prices are for brackets on opposite page made (in usual sizes) of pine or poplar.

ABOVE PRICES SUBJECT TO DISCOUNT.

BRACKETS.

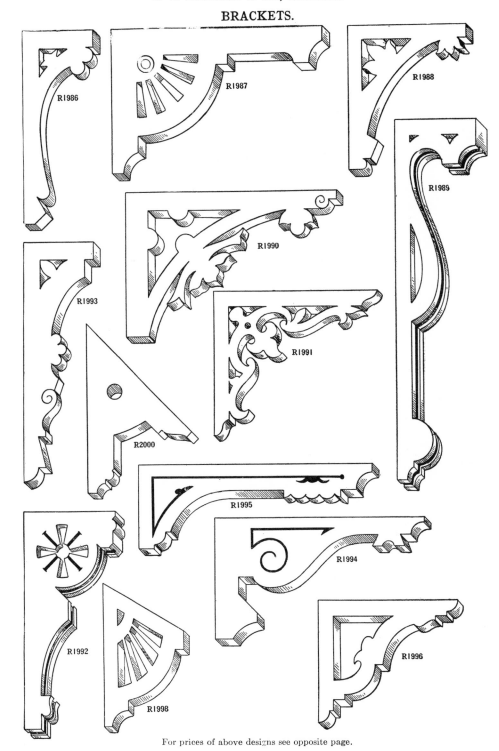

R1986

R1987

R1988

R1989

R1990

R1993

R1991

R2000

R1995

R1994

R1992

R1998

R1996

For prices of above designs see opposite page.

BRACKETS.

See designs on opposite page.

Number of design	Size inches	Thick ness in.	Price $ Cts	Size inches	Thick ness in.	Price $ Cts	Size inches	Thick ness in.	Price $ Cts	Size inches	Thick ness in.	Price $ Cts	Size inches	Thick ness in.	Price $ Cts
R2001	10x12	1⅜	.22	10x14	1⅜	.24	12x14	1⅜	.28	12x16	1⅜	.32	14x18	1⅜	.36
R2001½	6x 3	1⅜	.12	8x 4	1¾	.14									
R2002	14x14	1¾	1.00	16x16	1¾	1.20	18x18	1¾	1.50	20x20	1¾	2.00	22x22	1¾	2.50
R2002½	8x 8	1⅜	.16	10x10	1⅜	.18	12x12	1⅜	.22	12x14	1⅜	.26	14x14	1⅜	.32
R2003	14x14	1¾	.80	16x16	1¾	1.00	18x18	1¾	1.20	20x20	1¾	1.50	22x22	1¾	2.00
R2003½	12x 6	1⅜	.20	14x 6	1⅜	.22	16x 8	1⅜	.26	20x10	1⅜	.30	24x12	1⅜	.50
R2004	14x14	1¾	1.00	16x16	1¾	1.20	18x18	1¾	1.50	20x20	1¾	2.00	22x22	1⅜	2.50
R2004½	10x12	1⅜	.24	12x14	1⅜	.30									
R2005	20x12	3½	2.20	24x12	3½	2.50	28x14	3½	3.00	32x16	3½	3.50	36x16	3½	4.00
R2006	14x12	1⅜	1.80	16x12	1⅜	2.00	18x14	1⅜	2.20	20x14	1⅜	2.50	22x16	1⅜	3.00
R2007	14x16	1¾	.80	16x18	1¾	1.00	18x20	1¾	1.20	20x22	1¾	1.50	22x24	1¾	2.00
R2010	10x 6	1⅜	.34	12x 8	1⅜	.40									
R2011	12x 8	1⅜	.40	14x10	1⅜	.50	16x10	1⅜	.54	18x12	1⅜	.60	20x14	1⅜	.70

These prices are for brackets on opposite page made (in usual sizes) of pine and poplar.

ABOVE PRICES SUBJECT TO DISCOUNT

BRACKETS.

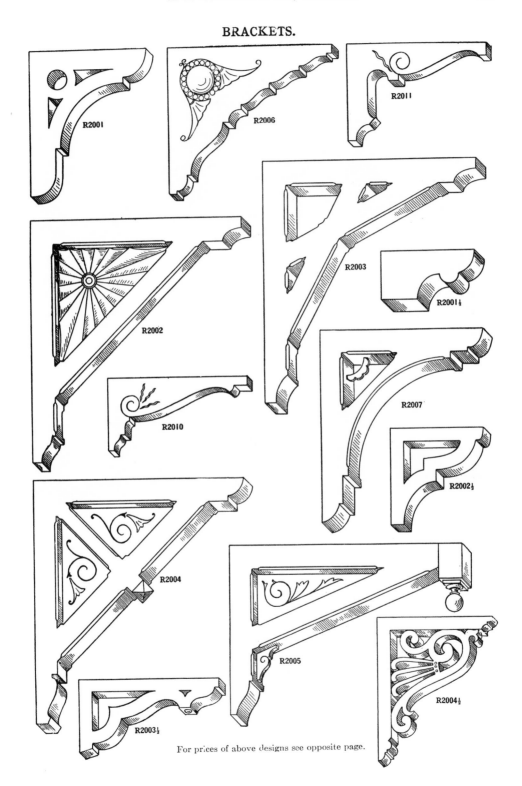

For prices of above designs see opposite page.

GABLE ORNAMENTS.
Will fit any pitch.

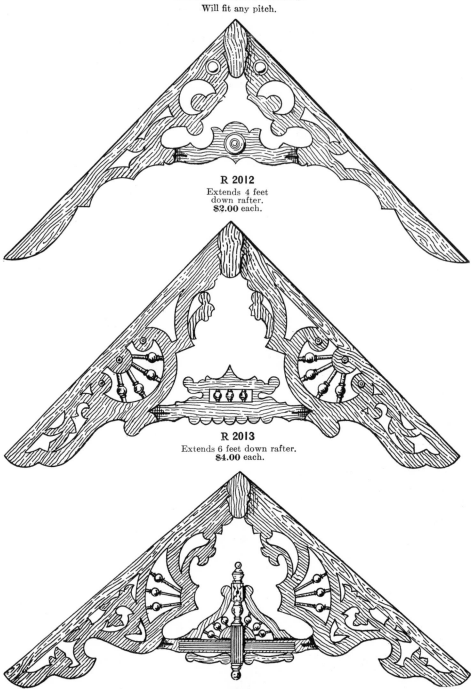

R 2012
Extends 4 feet
down rafter.
$2.00 each.

R 2013
Extends 6 feet down rafter.
$4.00 each.

R 2014
Extends 6 feet down rafter.   **$6.00** each.
ABOVE PRICES SUBJECT TO DISCOUNT.

GABLE ORNAMENTS.

Will fit any pitch.

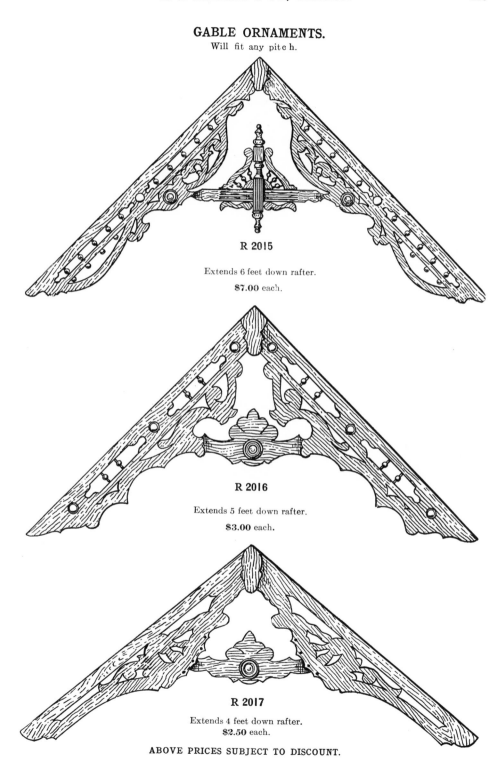

R 2015

Extends 6 feet down rafter.

$7.00 each.

R 2016

Extends 5 feet down rafter.

$3.00 each.

R 2017

Extends 4 feet down rafter.
$2.50 each.

ABOVE PRICES SUBJECT TO DISCOUNT.

PRICES OF GABLE ORNAMENTS, CRESTINGS AND FINIALS.

Shown on opposite page.

GABLE ORNAMENTS.

In ordering the gable ornaments shown on opposite page, always give the pitch of roof and the length of extension down the rafter.

Prices quoted below are the usual sizes ordered.

R2018.	To extend 6 feet down rafter..	$7.00
R2021.	" 6 " " "	7.00
R2024.	" 6 " " "	8.00
R2027.	" 6 " " "	7.00

FINIALS.

In ordering the finials shown on opposite page, always give the pitch of the roof, the length of bracket down the rafter and the height of the post in center.

Prices quoted below are for usual proportions ordered as follows:

R2022.	Posts 3¾x3¾x3 ft. 6 in. Brackets 1⅜ in. thick, extending 18 in. down roof.....$3.00
R2025.	" 3¾x3¾x3 " 6 " " 1⅜ " " 18 " " 2.50
R2028.	" 3¾x3¾x3 " 6 " " 1⅜ " " 18 " " 3.00

CRESTINGS.

For ridge finish of roofs.

In ordering the crestings shown on opposite page, always give thickness and height required and height of ends.

Prices quoted below are for the usual sizes ordered as follows:

R2019.	Cresting only, 1⅛x7½ inches per lineal foot, $0.18. End finish...........each, $0.50
R2020.	" " 1⅛x7½ " " " .20. " .... " .50
R2023.	" ' 1⅛x7½ " " " .18. " .... " .70
R2026.	" " 1⅛x7½ " " " .20. " .... " .70
R2029.	" " 1⅛x7½ " " " .18. " .... " .50
R2030.	" " 1⅛x7½ " " " .18. " .... " .50

ABOVE PRICES SUBJECT TO DISCOUNT.

GABLE ORNAMENTS, CRESTINGS AND FINIALS.

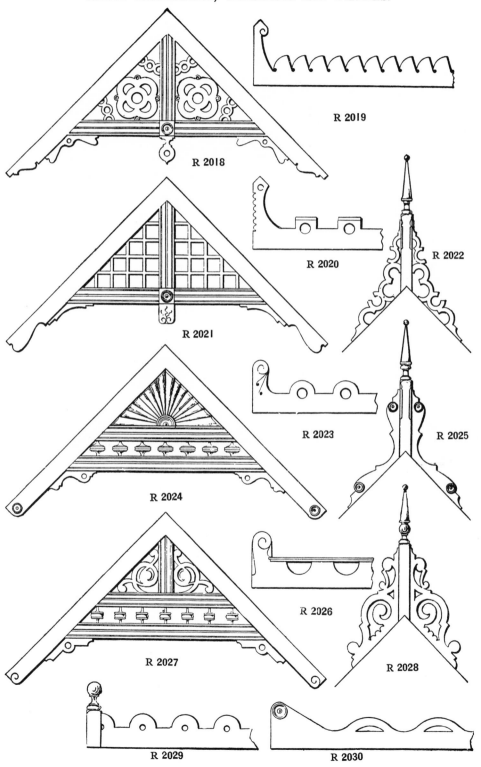

R 2018

R 2019

R 2020

R 2021

R 2022

R 2023

R 2024

R 2025

R 2026

R 2027

R 2028

R 2029

R 2030

For prices of above designs see opposite page.

VERGE BOARDS.

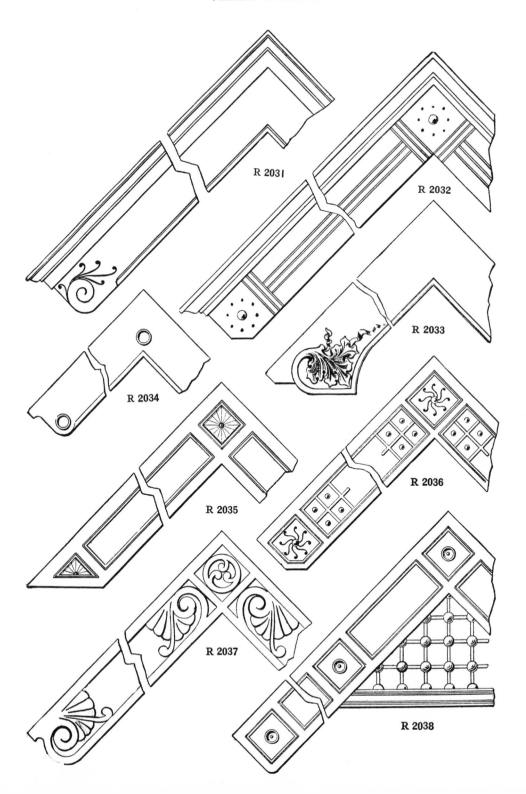

R 2031

R 2032

R 2033

R 2034

R 2035

R 2036

R 2037

R 2038

PORCH DESIGNS.

R 2039   R 2040

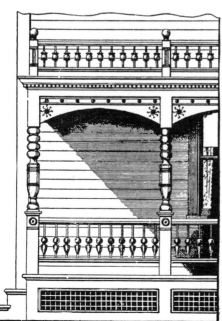

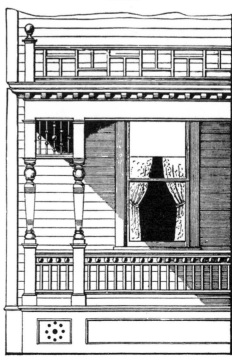

R 2041   R 2042

Send plan, giving sizes of columns and newels and spaces between columns for railing in
ordering or asking for estimate.

COMPOSITION CAPITALS.

The details and proportions of these capitals and brackets are perfect, and the material used is much more durable than wood.

The drawings on opposite page illustrate Ionic capital R2154 with necking (Empire), as applied to a column showing the wood shaft and core running through the capital supporting the entablature above. The plans of the different abacus forms as given will serve as a further illustration of the relative position of shaft and capital.

All our capitals are furnished as shown in this catalogue, each capital having a complete finish to connect with shaft. The diameter given in catalogue represents the diameter of column at neck. The height given is the exact height of capital. Always allow a trifle more height for your core so the weight will rest on shaft and not on capital, $\frac{1}{8}$ of an inch up to a 10-inch diameter; $\frac{1}{4}$ of an inch above that size will be sufficient to insure a safe application.

The thickness of our material is one inch up to a 10-inch diameter capital, making the core of a 10-inch diameter capital 8 inches, of an 8-inch capital 6 inches. Above 10 inches allow $\frac{1}{8}$ of an inch more for the thickness of material for every two inches of increased size, making core for a 14-inch diameter capital $11\frac{1}{2}$ inches, a 16-inch capital $13\frac{1}{4}$ inches, etc.

In ordering capital, give number of design and diameter of column at neck; also state material wanted, viz.: whether Exterior Composition, warranted to stand in any climate, or Interior Composition, made with grain to match any wood. (Interior Composition has a solid wood body requiring no core on column. Always state the kind of wood and finish.)

The sizes of our brackets given are:

1st. The entire width across abacus moulding.
2d. Width of face on body.
3d. Drop or length.
4th. Projection.

READ ABOVE CAREFULLY WHEN ORDERING.

For columns see pages 216 and 217.

COMPOSITION CAPITALS.

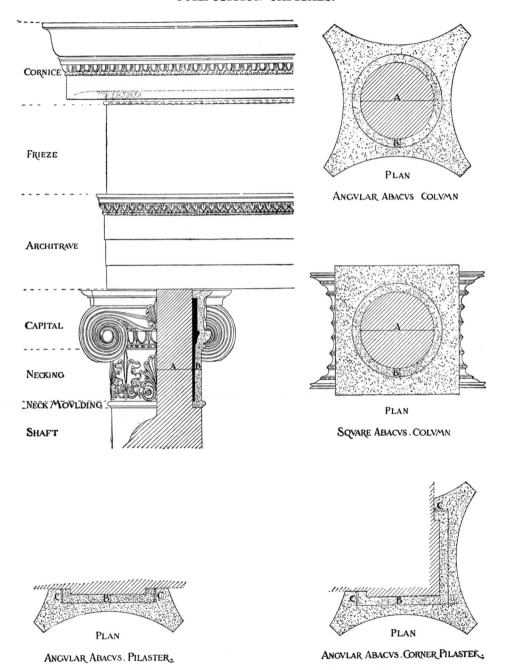

CORNICE

FRIEZE

ARCHITRAVE

CAPITAL

NECKING

NECK MOVLDING

SHAFT

PLAN

ANGVLAR ABACVS COLVMN

PLAN

SQVARE ABACVS . COLVMN

PLAN

ANGVLAR ABACVS . PILASTER.

PLAN

ANGVLAR ABACVS .CORNER PILASTER.

"A" indicates the core or extended shaft running through capital.
"B" shows thickness of composition.
"C" indicates the return of pilaster capital, which always must
be mentioned in ordering pilaster capitals.
For columns see pages 216 and 217.

COMPOSITION CAPITALS.

R 2150. Italian Renaissance Capital.

EXTERIOR.			INTERIOR.		
Diam.	Height.	Price.	Diam.	Height.	Price.
6 in.	8⅜ in.	$4.50	3 in.	4⅛ in.	$2.10
7 "	9⅝ "	5.00	3½ "	4¾ "	2.60
8 "	11 "	6.00	4 "	5½ "	3.40
9 "	12½ "	7.00	4½ "	6¼ "	3.80
10 "	13⅞ "	8.00	5 "	7 "	4.50
12 "	16¾ "	10.00	5½ "	7¾ "	5.20

R 2151. Greek Angular Ionic Capital.

EXTERIOR.			INTERIOR.		
Diam.	Height.	Price.	Diam.	Height.	Price.
6½ in.	4 in.	$4.00	3 in.	1⅞ in.	$2.00
7 "	4⅛ "	4.50	3½ "	2 3-16 "	2.40
7½ "	4¼ "	5.00	4 "	2½ "	3.00
8 "	5 "	5.50	4½ "	2 13-16 "	3.50
8½ "	5¼ "	6.00	5 "	3⅛ "	4.00
9 "	5⅝ "	6.50	5½ "	3 7-16 "	4.40
9½ "	6 "	7.00	6 "	3¾ "	5.00
10 "	6¼ "	7.50	7 "	4⅛ "	6.0C

R 2152. Roman Corinthian Capital.

EXTERIOR.			INTERIOR.		
Diam.	Height.	Price.	Diam.	Height.	Price.
6 in.	9 in.	$5.80	3 in.	4 in.	$4.00
7 "	10½ "	6.50	3½ "	4¾ "	4.70
8 "	12 "	7.00	4 "	5½ "	5.20
9 "	12½ "	8.50	4½ "	6¼ "	6.00
10 "	14⅝ "	9.50	5 "	7 "	6.50
11 "	15⅜ "	10.50	5½ "	7¾ "	8.00
12 "	16¾ "	12.00	6 "	9 "	8.60
13 "	18 "	14.00	8 "	12 "	11.60

R 2153. Greek Erechtheum Capital.

EXTERIOR.			INTERIOR.		
Diam.	Height.	Price.	Diam.	Height.	Price.
5 in.	4½ in.	$3.50	3 in.	2¾ in.	$3.40
6 "	5½ "	4.30	3½ "	3⅛ "	3.90
7 "	6⅜ "	5.30	4 "	3⅝ "	4.90
8 "	7 "	6.00	4½ "	4 "	5.40
9 "	8¼ "	7.00	5 "	4½ "	5.90
10 "	9⅛ "	8.00	5½ "	5 "	6.20
11 "	10 "	9.00	6 "	5½ "	6.80
12 "	11 "	10.00	6½ "	5⅞ "	7.50

R 2154. Empire Capital.

EXTERIOR.			INTERIOR.		
Diam.	Height.	Price.	Diam.	Height.	Price.
6½ in.	7¾ in.	$4.50	3 in.	3¾ in.	$2.00
7 "	8⅞ "	4.90	3½ "	4⅜ "	2.30
7½ "	9⅜ "	5.30	4 "	5 "	3.00
8 "	10¼ "	5.50	4½ "	5⅝ "	3.40
8½ "	10½ "	6.00	5 "	6¼ "	4.00
9 "	11½ "	7.00	5½ "	6⅞ "	4.70
9½ "	11⅞ "	7.50	6 "	7½ "	5.20
10 "	12½ "	8.00	7 "	8⅞ "	6.50

R 2155. Ionic Capital.

EXTERIOR.			INTERIOR.		
Diam.	Height.	Price.	Diam.	Height.	Price.
6½ in.	3⅝ in.	$3.70	3 in.	1¾ in.	$1.70
7 "	3¾ "	4.00	3½ "	2 "	1.90
7½ "	4¼ "	4.30	4 "	2¼ "	2.30
8 "	4⅝ "	4.50	4½ "	2½ "	2.60
8½ "	4¾ "	5.10	5 "	2⅞ "	3.40
9 "	5⅛ "	5.30	5½ "	3⅛ "	3.80
9½ "	5⅜ "	6.00	6 "	3⅜ "	4.00
10 "	5¾ "	6.50	6½ "	3⅝ "	4.50

COMPOSITION BRACKETS.

Zorzi.

R 2156

EXTERIOR.

Abacus Width.	Face Width.	Projection.	Drop.	Price.
3½ in.	3 in.	6 in.	3 in.	$1.60
4⅝ "	4 "	8 "	4 "	2.25
5¾ "	5 "	10 "	5 "	3.30
7 "	6 "	12 "	6 "	4.00
8⅛ "	7 "	14 "	7 "	5.00
9¼ "	8 "	16 "	8 "	5.50
10½ "	9 "	18 "	9 "	6.70

R 2156

INTERIOR.

Abacus Width.	Face Width.	Projection.	Drop.	Price.
3½ in.	3 in.	6 in.	3 in.	$1.80
4⅝ "	4 "	8 "	4 "	2.50
5¾ "	5 "	10 "	5 "	3.40
7 "	6 "	12 "	6 "	4.50
....	.....	.....	.....	....
....	.....	.....	.....	....
....	.....	.....	.....	....

See pages 250 and 251 in ordering. For columns see pages 216 and 217.

ABOVE PRICES SUBJECT TO DISCOUNT.

COMPOSITION CAPITALS AND BRACKETS.

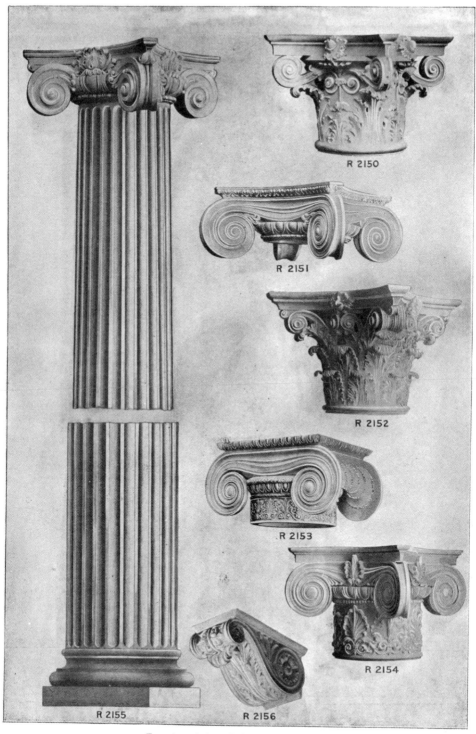

R 2150

R 2151

R 2152

.R 2153

R 2154

R 2155

R 2156

For prices of above designs see opposite page.
For columns see pages 216 and 217.

COMPOSITION PILASTER CAPITALS.

R 2160. Empire Pilaster.

EXTERIOR.			INTERIOR.		
Width.	Height.	Price.	Width.	Height.	Price.
6½ in.	7¾ in.	**$2.90**	3 in.	3¾ in.	**$1.35**
7 “	8⅞ “	**3.10**	3½ “	4⅜ “	**1.60**
7½ “	9⅜ “	**3.50**	4 “	5 “	**1.95**
8 “	10¼ “	**3.70**	4½ “	5⅝ “	**2.20**
8½ “	10½ “	**4.00**	5 “	6¼ “	**2.30**
9 “	11½ “	**4.50**	5½ “	6⅞ “	**2.80**
9½ “	11⅞ “	**5.00**	6 “	7½ “	**3.00**
10 “	12½ “	**5.20**	7 “	8⅞ “	**3.90**

R 2161. Greek Angular Ionic Pilaster.

EXTERIOR.			INTERIOR.		
Width.	Height.	Price.	Width.	Height.	Price.
6½ in.	4 in.	**$2.50**	3 in.	1⅞ in.	**$1.35**
7 “	4⅛ “	**2.90**	3½ “	2 3-16 “	**1.50**
7½ “	4¼ “	**3.10**	4 “	2½ “	**1.70**
8 “	5 “	**3.50**	4½ “	2 13-16 ‘	**2.00**
8½ “	5¼ “	**3.70**	5 “	3⅛ “	**2.30**
9 “	5⅝ “	**4.00**	5½ “	3 7-16 “	**2.60**
9½ “	6 “	**4.50**	6 “	3¾ “	**3.10**
10 “	6¼ “	**4.70**	7 “	4⅛ “	**3.60**

R 2162. Italian Renaissance Pilaster.

EXTERIOR.			INTERIOR.		
Width.	Height.	Price.	Width.	Height.	Price.
6 in.	8⅜ in.	**$2.90**	3 in.	4⅛ in.	**$1.35**
7 “	9⅝ “	**3.10**	3½ “	4¾ “	**1.70**
8 “	11 “	**3.90**	4 “	5½ “	**2.30**
9 “	12½ “	**4.40**	4½ “	6¼ “	**2.40**
10 “	13⅞ “	**5.10**	5 “	7 “	**3.10**
12 “	16¾ “	**6.40**	5½ “	7¾ “	**3.50**

R 2163. Roman Corinthian Pilaster.

EXTERIOR.			INTERIOR.		
Width.	Height.	Price.	Width.	Height.	Price.
6 in.	9 in.	**$3.50**	3 in.	4 in.	**$2.30**
7 “	10½ “	**4.00**	3½ “	4¾ “	**2.80**
8 “	12 “	**4.50**	4 “	5½ “	**3.40**
9 “	12½ “	**5.40**	4½ “	6¼ “	**3.60**
10 “	14⅝ “	**5.80**	5 ‘	7 “	**3.90**
11 “	15⅜ “	**6.40**	5½ “	7¾ “	**4.70**
12 “	16¾ “	**7.00**	6 “	9 “	**5.20**
13 “	18 “	**8.80**	8 “	12 “	**7.50**

R 2164. Greek Erechtheum Pilaster.

EXTERIOR.			INTERIOR.		
Width.	Height.	Price.	Width.	Height.	Price.
5 in.	4⅜ in.	**$1.70**	3 in.	2 in.	**$1.95**
5½ “	4¼ “	**2.25**	3½ “	2¼ “	**2.00**
6 “	5⅛ “	**2.50**	4 “	2½ “	**2.20**
7 “	4½ “	**2.90**	4½ “	3 “	**2.30**
8 “	8 “	**3.50**	5 “	3¼ “	**2.50**
9¾ “	9½ “	**3.90**	5½ “	3⅝ “	**3.40**
10 “	8 “	**4.30**	6 “	4 “	**3.90**
11 “	7⅛ “	**4.50**	6½ “	4¼ “	**4.00**

R 2165. Ionic Pilaster.

EXTERIOR.			INTERIOR.		
Width.	Height.	Price.	Width.	Height.	Price.
6½ in.	3⅝ in.	**$2.25**	3 in.	1¾ in.	**$1.05**
7 “	3¾ “	**2.40**	3½ “	2 “	**1.20**
7½ “	4¼ “	**2.60**	4 “	2¼ “	**1.35**
8 “	4⅝ “	**2.90**	4½ “	2½ “	**1.95**
8½ “	4¾ “	**3.10**	5 “	2⅞ “	**2.00**
9 “	5⅛ “	**3.50**	5½ “	3⅛ “	**2.30**
9½ “	5⅜ “	**3.70**	6 “	3⅜ “	**2.50**
10 “	5¾ “	**4.00**	6½ “	3⅝ “	**3.00**

COMPOSITION BRACKETS.

Semi-Classic.

R 2166.

EXTERIOR.

Abacus Width.	Face Width.	Projection.	Drop.	Price.
1¼ in.	1 in.	3 in.	1¼ in.	**$0.55**
1⅝ “	1¼ “	3¼ “	1½ “	**.65**
1⅞ “	1½ “	4½ “	1⅞ “	**.80**
2¼ “	1¾ “	5¼ “	2⅛ “	**1.00**
2⅝ “	2 “	6 “	2½ “	**1.10**
2⅞ “	2¼ “	6¾ “	2¾ “	**1.30**
3¼ “	2½ “	7½ “	3 “	**1.50**
3½ “	2¾ “	8¼ “	3⅜ “	**1.90**
3⅞ “	3 “	9 “	3⅝ “	**2.00**

R 2166.

INTERIOR.

Abacus Width.	Face Width.	Projection.	Drop.	Price.
1¼ in.	1 in.	3 in.	1¼ in.	**$0.55**
1⅝ “	1¼ “	3¼ “	1½ “	**.65**
1⅞ “	1½ “	4½ “	1⅞ “	**.80**
2¼ “	1¾ “	5¼ “	2⅛ “	**1.00**
2⅝ “	2 “	6 “	2½ “	**1.10**
2⅞ “	2¼ “	6¾ “	2¾ “	**1.35**
2¼ “	2½ “	7½ “	3 “	**1.85**
3½ “	2¾ “	8¼ “	3⅜ “	**1.95**
3⅞ “	3 “	9 “	3⅝ “	**2.25**

See pages 250 and 251 in ordering.
For columns see pages 216 and 217.

ABOVE PRICES SUBJECT TO DISCOUNT.

COMPOSITION PILASTER CAPITALS AND BRACKETS.

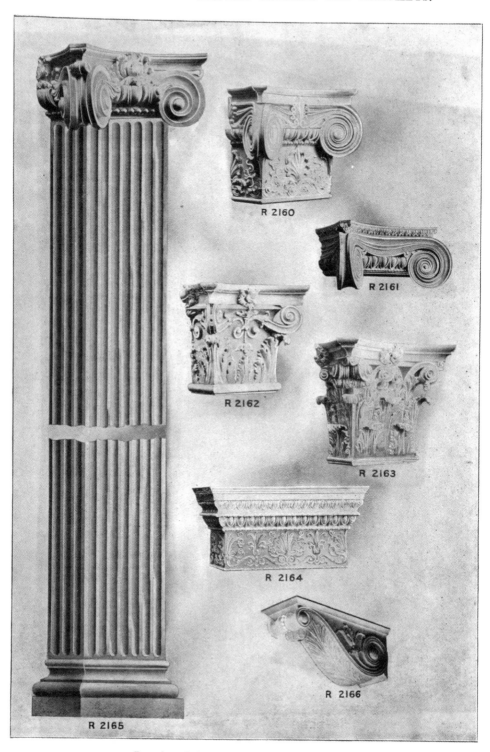

R 2160

R 2161

R 2162

R 2163

R 2164

R 2166

R 2165

For prices of above designs see opposite page.
For columns see pages 216 and 217.

DIMENSION SHINGLES.
Usually 6 inches wide.

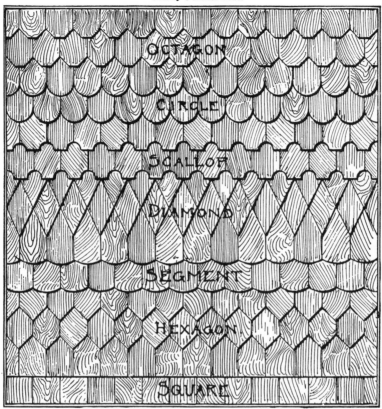

Write for prices, stating size, quantity and grade.

FENCE PICKETS.

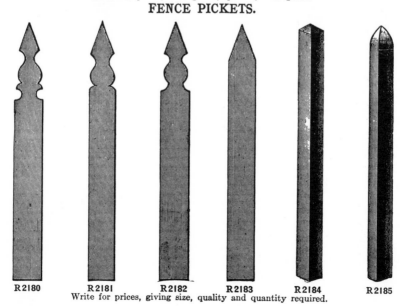

| R 2180 | R 2181 | R 2182 | R 2183 | R 2184 | R 2185 |

Write for prices, giving size, quality and quantity required.

GRILLES AND ARCHES.

In preparing the designs of grilles, and arches shown herein, care has been exercised to make the line the most complete, artistic and practical ever offered the trade.

Our long experience in manufacturing these specialties has taught us the best methods of construction. Our splendid facilities reduce the cost of production to the minimum, thereby enabling us to place in your hands a perfect article at lowest prices.

We solicit your correspondence, and will much appreciate your orders.

GRILLES.

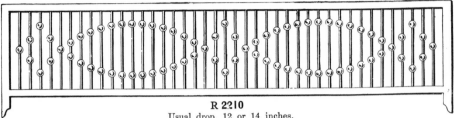

R 2210
Usual drop, 12 or 14 inches.
Not to exceed in width, 4 feet, **$4.00**; 5 feet, **$5.50**; 6 feet, **$7.00**.

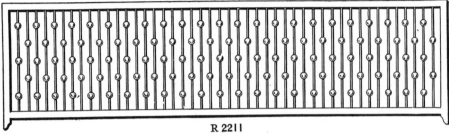

R 2211
Usual drop, 14 inches.
Not to exceed in width, 4 feet, **$5.00**; 5 feet, **$6.50**; 6 feet, **$7.50**.

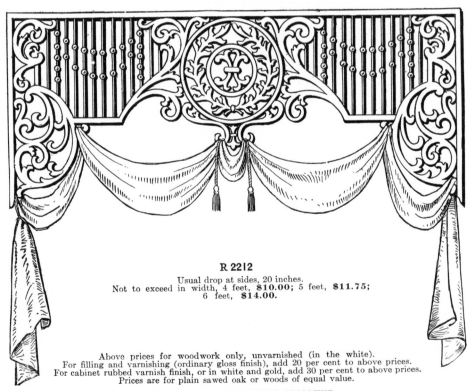

R 2212
Usual drop at sides, 20 inches.
Not to exceed in width, 4 feet, **$10.00**; 5 feet, **$11.75**;
6 feet, **$14.00**.

Above prices for woodwork only, unvarnished (in the white).
For filling and varnishing (ordinary gloss finish), add 20 per cent to above prices.
For cabinet rubbed varnish finish, or in white and gold, add 30 per cent to above prices.
Prices are for plain sawed oak or woods of equal value.

ABOVE PRICES SUBJECT TO DISCOUNT.

GRILLES.

R 2213
Usual drop, 12 or 14 inches.
Not to exceed in width, 4 feet, **$6.50**; 5 feet, **$8.00**; 6 feet, **$10.00**.

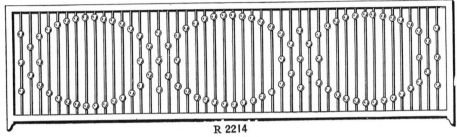

R 2214
Usual drop, 14 inches.
Not to exceed in width, 4 feet, **$4.00**; 5 feet, **$5.50**; 6 feet, **$7.00**.

R 2215
Usual drop at sides, 16 inches.
Not to exceed in width, 4 feet, **$13.50**;
5 feet, **$15.00**; 6 feet, **$17.50**.

Above prices for woodwork only, unvarnished
(in the white).
For filling and varnishing (ordinary gloss finish),
add 20 per cent to above prices.
For cabinet rubbed varnish finish, or in white and
gold, add 30 per cent to above prices.
Prices are for plain sawed oak or woods of
equal value.

ABOVE PRICES SUBJECT TO DISCOUNT.

GRILLES.

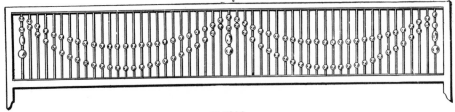

R 2216
Usual drop, 12 or 14 inches.
Not to exceed in width, 4 feet, **$4.00**; 5 feet, **$5.50**;
6 feet, **$7.00**.

R 2217
Usual drop, 12 or 14 inches.
Not to exceed in width, 4 feet, **$6.00**; 5 feet, **$7.50**;
6 feet, **$10.00**.

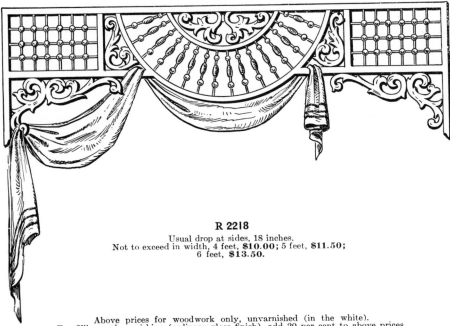

R 2218
Usual drop at sides, 18 inches.
Not to exceed in width, 4 feet, **$10.00**; 5 feet, **$11.50**;
6 feet, **$13.50**.

Above prices for woodwork only, unvarnished (in the white).
For filling and varnishing (ordinary gloss finish), add 20 per cent to above prices.
For cabinet rubbed varnish finish, or in white and gold, add 30 per cent to above prices.
Prices are for plain sawed oak or woods of equal value.

ABOVE PRICES SUBJECT TO DISCOUNT.

GRILLES.

R 2219

Usual drop, 12 or 14 inches.
Not to exceed in width, 4 feet, **$8.50**; 5 feet, **$10.00**;
6 feet, **$12.50**.

R 2220

Usual drop, 12 or 14 inches.
Not to exceed in width, 4 feet, **$6.00**; 5 feet, **$7.50**;
6 feet, **$10.00**.

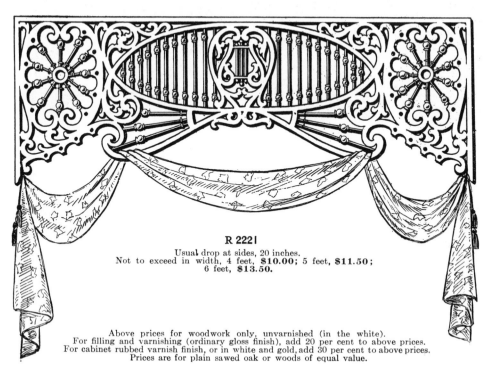

R 2221

Usual drop at sides, 20 inches.
Not to exceed in width, 4 feet, **$10.00**; 5 feet, **$11.50**;
6 feet, **$13.50**.

Above prices for woodwork only, unvarnished (in the white).
For filling and varnishing (ordinary gloss finish), add 20 per cent to above prices.
For cabinet rubbed varnish finish, or in white and gold, add 30 per cent to above prices.
Prices are for plain sawed oak or woods of equal value.

ABOVE PRICES SUBJECT TO DISCOUNT.

GRILLES.

R 2222
Usual drop, 12 or 14 inches.
Not to exceed in width, 4 feet, **$6.00**; 5 feet, **$7.50**·
6 feet, **$10.00**.

R 2223
Usual drop, 20 inches.
Not to exceed in width, 4 feet, **$10.00**; 5 feet, **$11.70**;
6 feet, **$14.00**.

Above prices for woodwork only, unvarnished (in the white).
For filling and varnishing (ordinary gloss finish), add 20 per cent to above prices.
For cabinet rubbed varnish finish, or in white and gold, add 30 per cent to above prices.
Prices are for plain sawed oak or woods of equal value.

ABOVE PRICES SUBJECT TO DISCOUNT.

GRILLES.

R 2224
Usual drop, 12 or 14 inches.
Not to exceed in width, 4 feet, **$6.00**; 5 feet, **$7.50**;
6 feet, **$10.00**.

R 2225
Usual drop at sides, 28 to 36 inches.
Not to exceed in width, 4 feet, **$19.00**; 5 feet, **$20.50**;
6 feet, **$23.00**.

Above prices for woodwork only, unvarnished (in the white).
For filling and varnishing (ordinary gloss finish), add 20 per cent to above prices.
For cabinet rubbed varnish finish, or in white and gold, add 30 per cent to above prices.
Prices are for plain sawed oak or woods of equal value.

ABOVE PRICES SUBJECT TO DISCOUNT.

GRILLES.

R 2226
Usual drop, 12 to 14 inches.
Not to exceed in width, 4 feet, **$8.50**; 5 feet, **$10.00**; 6 feet, **$12.00**.

R 2227
Usual drop, 12 to 14 inches.
Not to exceed in width, 4 feet, **$8.50**; 5 feet, **$10.00**; 6 feet, **$12.00**.

R 2228
Drop proportionate to width.
Not to exceed in width, 4 feet, **$10.00**; 5 feet, **$11.50**; 6 feet, **$13.50**.

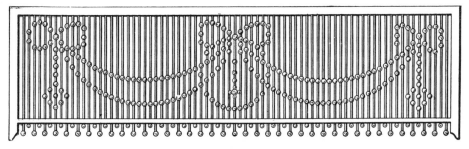

R 2229
Usual drop, 14 to 16 inches.
Not to exceed in width, 4 feet, **$7.00**; 5 feet, **$8.50**; 6 feet, **$11.00**.
Above prices for woodwork only, unvarnished (in the white).
For filling and varnishing (ordinary gloss finish), add 20 per cent to above prices
For cabinet rubbed varnish finish, or in white and gold, add 30 per cent to above prices.
Prices are for plain sawed oak or woods of equal value.

ABOVE PRICES SUBJECT TO DISCOUNT.

GRILLES.

R 2230

For Opening.

5 x 8 feet	....	$54.00
5 x 9 "	....	56.00
6 x 8 "	....	56.00
6 x 9 "	....	58.50
8 x 8 "	....	61.50
8 x 9 "	....	64.50

Above prices for woodwork only, unvarnished (in the white).
For filling and varnishing (ordinary gloss finish), add 20 per cent to above prices.
For cabinet rubbed varnish finish, or in white and gold, add 30 per cent to above prices.
Prices are for plain sawed oak or woods of equal value.

ABOVE PRICES SUBJECT TO DISCOUNT.

GRILLES.

R 2231

For Opening.

5 x 8 feet	$46.50
5 x 9 "	49.00
6 x 8 "	49.00
6 x 9 "	51.00
8 x 8 "	53.50
8 x 9 "	55.50

Above prices for woodwork only, unvarnished
(in the white).
For filling and varnishing (ordinary gloss finish), add 20 per
cent to above prices.
For cabinet rubbed varnish finish, or in white and gold, add
30 per cent to above prices.
Prices are for plain sawed oak or woods of equal value.

ABOVE PRICES SUBJECT TO DISCOUNT.

GRILLES.

2232

For Opening.

5 x 8 feet	....	$52.50
5 x 9 "	....	55.00
6 x 8 "	....	55.00
6 x 9 "	....	57.00
8 x 8 "	....	59.00
8 x 9 "	....	62.50

Above prices for woodwork only, unvarnished (in the white).
For filling and varnishing (ordinary gloss
finish), add 20 per cent to
above prices.
For cabinet rubbed varnish finish, or in
white and gold, add 30 per cent
to above prices.
Prices are for plain sawed oak or woods of
equal value.

ABOVE PRICES SUBJECT TO DISCOUNT.

GRILLES.

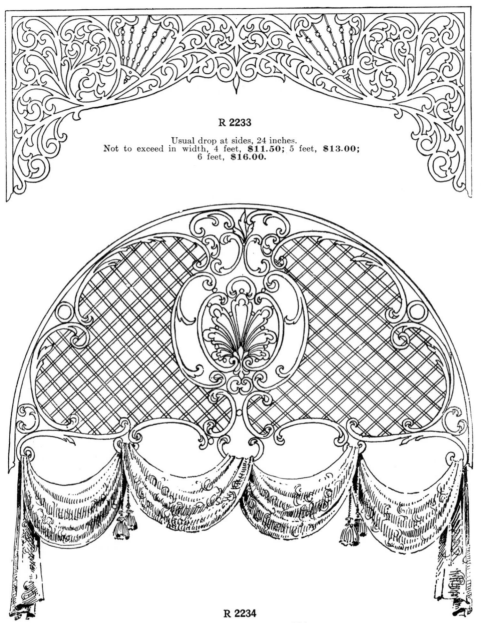

R 2233

Usual drop at sides, 24 inches.
Not to exceed in width, 4 feet, **$11.50**; 5 feet, **$13.00**;
6 feet, **$16.00**.

R 2234

Usual drop, one-half the width.
Not to exceed in width, 4 feet, **$13.00**; 5 feet, **$14.50**;
6 feet, **$19.00**.

Above prices for woodwork only, unvarnished (in the white).
For filling and varnishing (ordinary gloss finish), add 20 per cent to above prices.
For cabinet rubbed varnish finish, or in white and gold, add 30 per cent to above prices.
Prices are for plain sawed oak or woods of equal value.

ABOVE PRICES SUBJECT TO DISCOUNT.

GRILLES.

R 2235
Usual drop, 14 to 16 inches.
Not to exceed in width. 4 feet, **$10.00**; 5 feet, **$11.50**; 6 feet, **$13.50.**

R 2236

For Opening.

5 x 8 feet................	**$49.50**
5 x 9 "	**51.00**
6 x 8 "	**51.00**
6 x 9 "	**53.50**
8 x 8 "	**55.50**
8 x 9 "	**58.50**

Above prices for woodwork only, unvarnished (in the white).
For filling and varnishing (ordinary gloss finish), add 20 per cent to above prices.
For cabinet rubbed varnish finish, or in white and gold, add 30 per cent to above prices.
Prices are for plain sawed oak or woods of equal value.

ABOVE PRICES SUBJECT TO DISCOUNT.

GRILLES.

R 2237

Usual drop, 14 to 16 inches.
Not to exceed in width,
4 feet, $11.50; 5 feet, $13.00;
6 feet, $15.00.

R 2238

Usual drop, 24 inches at side.
Not to exceed in width, 4 feet, $11.50; 5 feet, $14.00;
6 feet, $15.00.

Above prices for woodwork only, unvarnished (in the white).
For filling and varnishing (ordinary gloss finish), add 20 per cent to above prices.
For cabinet rubbed varnish finish, or in white and gold, add 30 per cent to above prices.
Prices are for plain sawed oak or woods of equal value.
ABOVE PRICES SUBJECT TO DISCOUNT.

GRILLES.

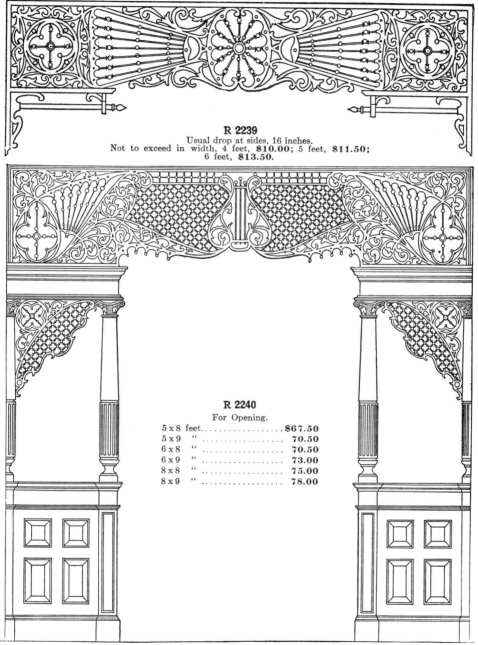

R 2239

Usual drop at sides, 16 inches.
Not to exceed in width, 4 feet, **$10.00**; 5 feet, **$11.50**;
6 feet, **$13.50**.

R 2240

For Opening.

5 x 8 feet	....	$67.50
5 x 9 "	....	70.50
6 x 8 "	....	70.50
6 x 9 "	....	73.00
8 x 8 "	....	75.00
8 x 9 "	....	78.00

Above prices for woodwork only, unvarnished (in the white).
For filling and varnishing (ordinary gloss finish), add 20 per cent to above prices.
For cabinet rubbed varnish finish, or in white and gold, add 30 per cent to above prices.
Prices are for plain sawed oak or woods of equal value.
ABOVE PRICES SUBJECT TO DISCOUNT.

GRILLES.

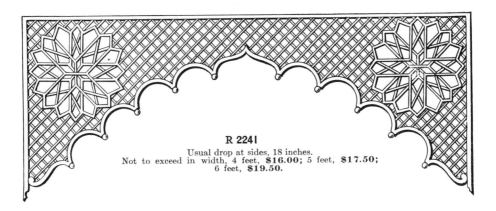

R 2241
Usual drop at sides, 18 inches.
Not to exceed in width, 4 feet, **\$16.00**; 5 feet, **\$17.50**;
6 feet, **\$19.50**.

R 2242
Usual drop at sides, 24 inches.
Not to exceed in width, 4 feet, **\$14.00**; 5 feet, **\$14.50**;
6 feet, **\$16.50**.

Above prices for woodwork only, unvarnished (in the white).
For filling and varnishing (ordinary gloss finish), add 20 per cent to above prices.
For cabinet rubbed varnish finish, or in white and gold, add 30 per cent to above prices.
Prices are for plain sawed oak or woods of equal value.

ABOVE PRICES SUBJECT TO DISCOUNT.

GRILLES.

R 2243

For Opening.

5 x 8 feet	$39.00
5 x 9 "	41.50
6 x 8 "	45.00
6 x 9 "	45.00
8 x 8 "	47.50
8 x 9 "	49.50

Above prices for woodwork only, unvarnished (in the white).
For filling and varnishing (ordinary gloss finish),
add 20 per cent to above prices.
For cabinet rubbed varnish finish, or in white and gold,
add 30 per cent to above prices.
Prices are for plain sawed oak or woods of equal value.

ABOVE PRICES SUBJECT TO DISCOUNT.

GRILLES.

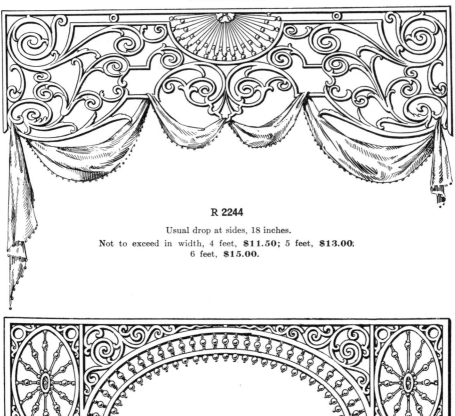

R 2244

Usual drop at sides, 18 inches.
Not to exceed in width, 4 feet, **$11.50;** 5 feet, **$13.00;**
6 feet, **$15.00.**

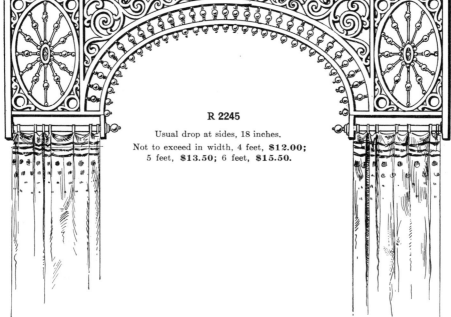

R 2245

Usual drop at sides, 18 inches.
Not to exceed in width, 4 feet, **$12.00;**
5 feet, **$13.50;** 6 feet, **$15.50.**

Above prices for woodwork only, unvarnished (in the white).
For filling and varnishing (ordinary gloss finish), add 20 per cent to above prices.
For cabinet rubbed varnish finish, or in white and gold, add 30 per cent to above prices.
Prices are for plain sawed oak or woods of equal value.
ABOVE PRICES SUBJECT TO DISCOUNT.

GRILLES.

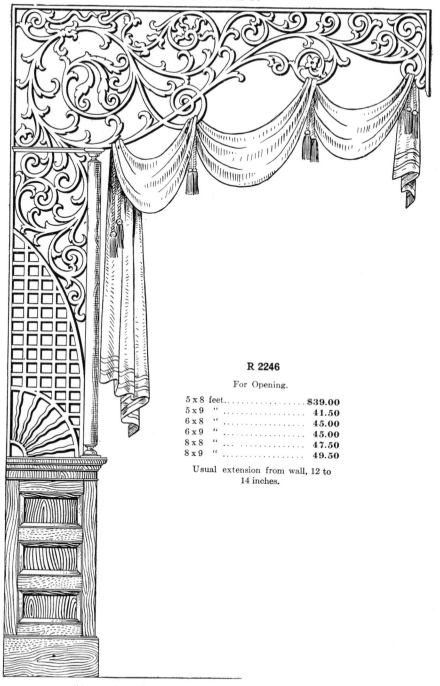

R 2246

For Opening.

5 x 8 feet	....	$39.00
5 x 9 "	....	41.50
6 x 8 "	....	45.00
6 x 9 "	....	45.00
8 x 8 "	....	47.50
8 x 9 "	....	49.50

Usual extension from wall, 12 to 14 inches.

Above prices for woodwork only, unvarnished (in the white).
For filling and varnishing (ordinary gloss finish), add 20 per cent to above prices.
For cabinet rubbed varnish finish, or in white and gold, add 30 per cent to above prices.
Prices are for plain sawed oak or woods of equal value.
ABOVE PRICES SUBJECT TO DISCOUNT.

GRILLES.

R 2247

Usual drop, 14 inches. Not to exceed in width, 4 feet, **$10.50**; 5 feet, **$12.00**; 6 feet, **$14.50**.

R 2248

Usual drop, 14 inches. . Not to exceed in width, 4 feet, **$10.50**; 5 feet, **$12.00**; 6 feet, **$14.50**.

R 2249

Usual drop at sides, 20 inches.
Not to exceed in width, 4 feet, **$11.50**;
5 feet, **$13.00**; 6 feet, **$15.00**.

Above prices for woodwork only, unvarnished (in the white).
For filling and varnishing (ordinary gloss finish), add 20 per cent to above prices.
For cabinet rubbed varnish finish, or in white and gold, add 30 per cent to above prices.
Prices are for plain sawed oak or woods of equal value.
ABOVE PRICES SUBJECT TO DISCOUNT.

GRILLES.

R 2250

For Opening.

5 x 8 feet	....	$46.50
5 x 9 "	....	49.00
6 x 8 "	....	49.00
6 x 9 "	....	51.00
8 x 8 "	....	53.50
8 x 9 "	....	55.50

Above prices for woodwork only, unvarnished (in the white).
For filling and varnishing (ordinary gloss finish), add 20 per cent to above prices.
For cabinet rubbed varnish finish, or in white and gold, add 30 per cent to above prices.
Prices are for plain sawed oak or woods of equal value.
ABOVE PRICES SUBJECT TO DISCOUNT.

GRILLES.

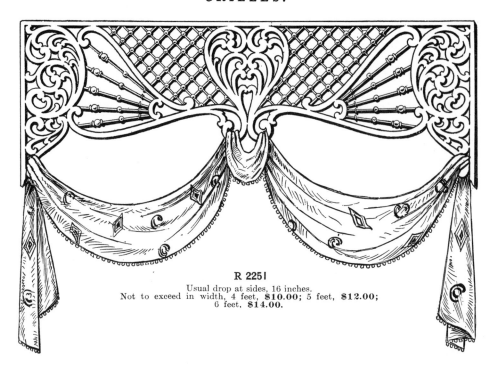

R 2251

Usual drop at sides, 16 inches.
Not to exceed in width, 4 feet, **$10.00**; 5 feet, **$12.00**;
6 feet, **$14.00**.

R 2252

Usual drop at sides, 16 inches.
Not to exceed in width, 4 feet, **$11.50**; 5 feet, **$13.00**;
6 feet, **$15.00**.

Above prices for woodwork only, unvarnished (in the white).
For filling and varnishing (ordinary gloss finish), add 20 per cent to above prices.
For cabinet rubbed varnish finish, or in white and gold, add 30 per cent to above prices.
Prices are for plain sawed oak or woods of equal value.

ABOVE PRICES SUBJECT TO DISCOUNT.

GRILLES.

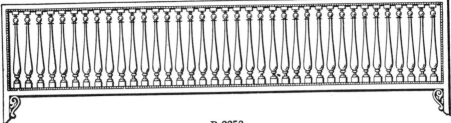

R 2253
Usual drop, 12 to 14 inches.
Not to exceed in width, 4 feet, **$9.00;** 5 feet **$10.50;** 6 feet, **$12.00.**

R 2254
Usual drop at sides, 16 inches.
Not to exceed in width, 4 feet, **$12.00;** 5 feet, **$13.50;**
6 feet, **$16.00.**

R 2255
Usual height at sides, 18 inches.
This is for screen at back of show window. Lettering can be altered to suit your requirements.
Not to exceed in width, 4 feet, **$14.50;** 5 feet, **$16.00;** 6 feet, **$18.00.**
Above prices for woodwork only, unvarnished (in the white).
For filling and varnishing (ordinary gloss finish), add 20 per cent to above prices.
For cabinet rubbed varnish finish, or in white and gold, add 30 per cent to above prices.
Prices are for plain sawed oak or woods of equal value.
ABOVE PRICES SUBJECT TO DISCOUNT.

GRILLES.

R 2256
18 x18
$5.50

R 2257
For openings not to exceed in width, 3 feet,
$9.00

R 2258
For openings not to exceed in
width, 3 feet, **$8.50**

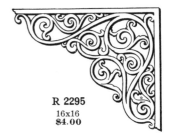

R 2295
16x16
$4.00

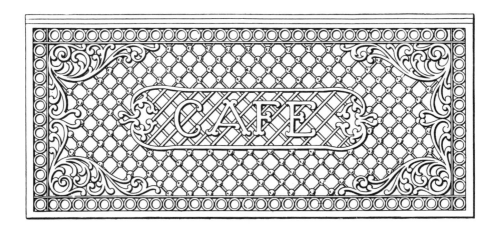

R 2260
Usual height, 18 inches.
This is for screen at back of show window or in doorway. Lettering can be altered to suit your requirements.
Not to exceed in width, 4 feet, **$17.50**; 5 feet, **$19.00**;
6 feet, **$21.00**.

Above prices for woodwork only, unvarnished (in the white).
For filling and varnishing (ordinary gloss finish), add 20 per cent to above prices.
For cabinet rubbed varnish finish, or in white and gold, add 30 per cent to above prices.
Prices are for plain sawed oak or woods of equal value.

ABOVE PRICES SUBJECT TO DISCOUNT.

GRILLES.

R 226i

For Opening.

5 x 8 feet	....	$51.00
5 x 9 "	....	53.50
6 x 8 "	....	53.50
6 x 9 "	....	55.50
8 x 8 "	....	58.00
8 x 9 "	....	60.00

Above prices for woodwork only, unvarnished (in the white).
For filling and varnishing (ordinary gloss finish), add 20 per cent to above prices.
For cabinet rubbed varnish finish, or in white and gold, add 30 per cent to above prices.
Prices are for plain sawed oak or woods of equal value.

ABOVE PRICES SUBJECT TO DISCOUNT.

GRILLES.

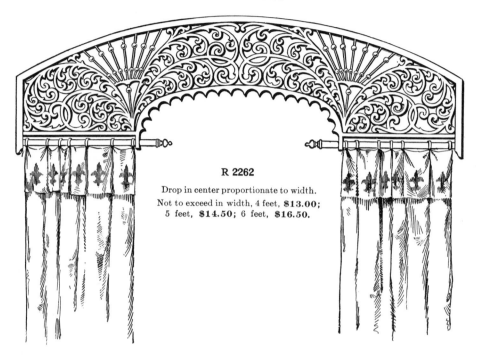

R 2262

Drop in center proportionate to width.

Not to exceed in width, 4 feet, **$13.00**;
5 feet, **$14.50**; 6 feet, **$16.50**.

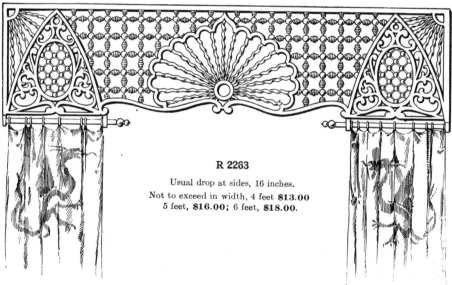

R 2263

Usual drop at sides, 16 inches.

Not to exceed in width, 4 feet **$13.00**
5 feet, **$16.00**; 6 feet, **$18.00**.

Above prices for woodwork only, unvarnished (in the white).
For filling and varnishing (ordinary gloss finish), add 20 per cent to above prices.
For cabinet rubbed varnish finish, or in white and gold, add 30 per cent to above prices.
Prices are for plain sawed oak or woods of equal value.

ABOVE PRICES SUBJECT TO DISCOUNT.

GRILLES.

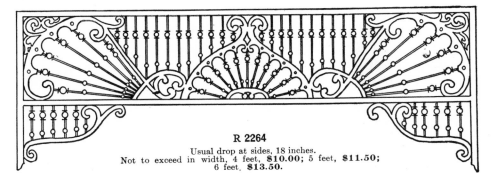

R 2264

Usual drop at sides, 18 inches.
Not to exceed in width, 4 feet, **$10.00**; 5 feet, **$11.50**;
6 feet, **$13.50**.

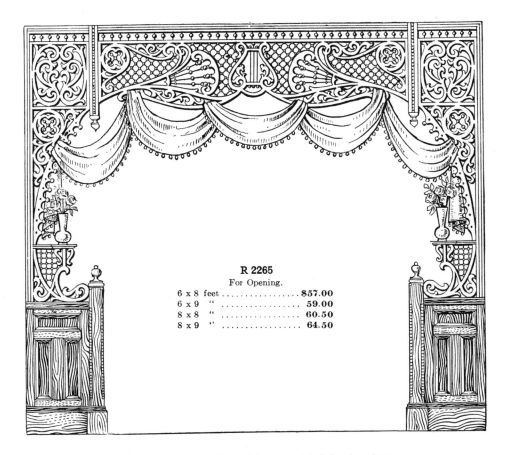

R 2265

For Opening.

6 x 8 feet	**$57.00**
6 x 9 "	**59.00**
8 x 8 "	**60.50**
8 x 9 "	**64.50**

Above prices for woodwork only, unvarnished (in the white).
For filling and varnishing (ordinary gloss finish), add 20 per cent to above prices.
For cabinet rubbed varnish finish, or in white and gold, add 30 per cent to above prices.
Prices are for plain sawed oak or woods of equal value.

ABOVE PRICES SUBJECT TO DISCOUNT.

GRILLES.

R 2266

Drop in center proportionate to width.

Not to exceed in width, 4 feet, **$10.00**; 5 feet, **$11.50**;
6 feet, **$13.50**.

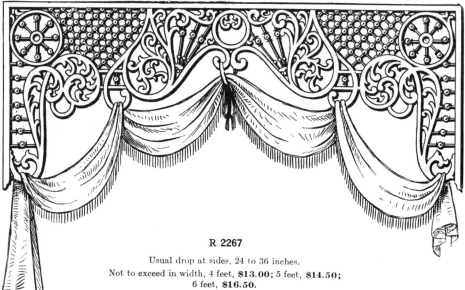

R 2267

Usual drop at sides, 24 to 36 inches.

Not to exceed in width, 4 feet, **$13.00**; 5 feet, **$14.50**;
6 feet, **$16.50**.

Above prices for woodwork only, unvarnished (in the white).
For filling and varnishing (ordinary gloss finish), add 20 per cent to above prices.
For cabinet rubbed varnish finish, or in white and gold, add 30 per cent to above prices.
Prices are for plain sawed oak or woods of equal value.
ABOVE PRICES SUBJECT TO DISCOUNT.

GRILLES.

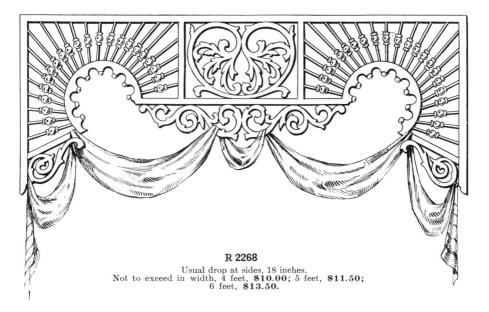

R 2268
Usual drop at sides, 18 inches.
Not to exceed in width, 4 feet, **$10.00**; 5 feet, **$11.50**;
6 feet, **$13.50**.

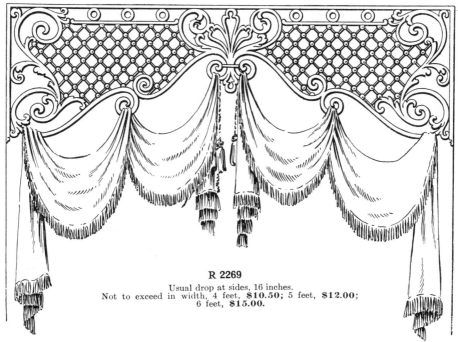

R 2269
Usual drop at sides, 16 inches.
Not to exceed in width, 4 feet, **$10.50**; 5 feet, **$12.00**;
6 feet, **$15.00**.

Above prices for woodwork only, unvarnished (in the white).
For filling and varnishing (ordinary gloss finish), add 20 per cent to above prices.
For cabinet rubbed varnish finish, or in white and gold, add 30 per cent to above prices.
Prices are for plain sawed oak or woods of equal value.

ABOVE PRICES SUBJECT TO DISCOUNT.

GRILLES.

R 2270

Usual drop at sides, 20 inches.
Not to exceed in width, 4 feet, **$11.50**; 5 feet, **$13.50**;
6 feet, **$15.00**.

R 2271

Usual drop at sides, 16 inches.
Not to exceed in width, 4 feet, **$13.50**; 5 feet, **$14.50**;
6 feet **$16.50**.

Above prices for woodwork only, unvarnished (in the white).
For filling and varnishing (ordinary gloss finish), add 20 per cent to above prices.
For cabinet rubbed varnish finish, or in white and gold, add 30 per cent to above prices.
Prices are for plain sawed oak or woods of equal value.

ABOVE PRICES SUBJECT TO DISCOUNT.

GRILLES.

R 2272

Usual drop at sides, 16 inches.
Not to exceed in width, 4 feet, **$11.50**;
5 feet, **$13.50**; 6 feet, **$15.00**.

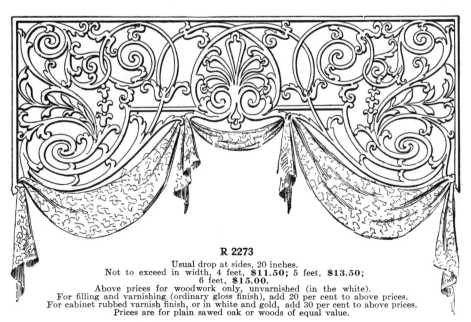

R 2273

Usual drop at sides, 20 inches.
Not to exceed in width, 4 feet, **$11.50**; 5 feet, **$13.50**;
6 feet, **$15.00**.
Above prices for woodwork only, unvarnished (in the white).
For filling and varnishing (ordinary gloss finish), add 20 per cent to above prices.
For cabinet rubbed varnish finish, or in white and gold, add 30 per cent to above prices.
Prices are for plain sawed oak or woods of equal value.

ABOVE PRICES SUBJECT TO DISCOUNT.

GRILLES.

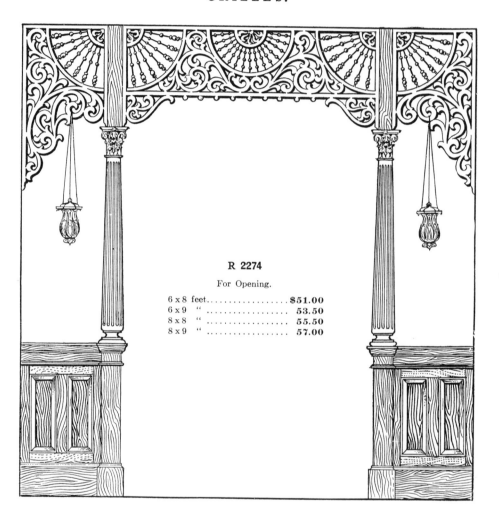

R 2274

For Opening.

6 x 8 feet..................	$51.00
6 x 9 "	53.50
8 x 8 "	55.50
8 x 9 "	57.00

Above prices for woodwork only, unvarnished (in the white).
For filling and varnishing (ordinary gloss finish), add 20 per cent to above prices.
For cabinet rubbed varnish finish, or in white and gold, add 30 per cent to above prices.
Prices are for plain sawed oak or woods of equal value.

ABOVE PRICES SUBJECT TO DISCOUNT.

GRILLES.

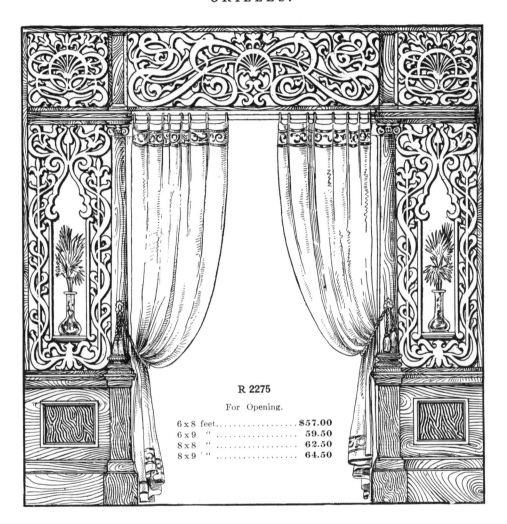

R 2275

For Opening.

6 x 8 feet	$57.00
6 x 9 "	59.50
8 x 8 "	62.50
8 x 9 "	64.50

Above prices for woodwork only, unvarnished (in the white).
For filling and varnishing (ordinary gloss finish), add 20 per cent to above prices.
For cabinet rubbed varnish finish, or in white and gold, add 30 per cent to above prices.
Prices are for plain sawed oak or woods of equal value.

ABOVE PRICES SUBJECT TO DISCOUNT.

GRILLES.

R 2276

For Opening.

6 x 8 feet	....	$64.00
6 x 9 "	....	66.00
8 x 8 "	....	68.00
8 x 9 "	....	72.00

Above prices for woodwork only, unvarnished (in the white).
For filling and varnishing (ordinary gloss finish), add 20 per cent to above prices.
For cabinet rubbed varnish finish, or in white and gold, add 30 per cent to above prices.
Prices are for plain sawed oak or woods of equal value.

ABOVE PRICES SUBJECT TO DISCOUNT.

GRILLES.

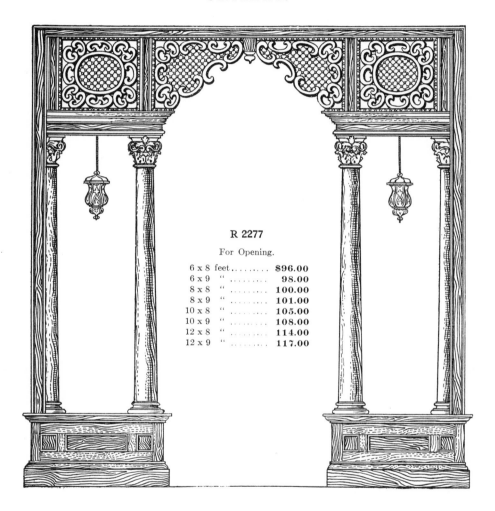

R 2277

For Opening.

6 x 8 feet.........	**$96.00**
6 x 9 "	**98.00**
8 x 8 "	**100.00**
8 x 9 "	**101.00**
10 x 8 "	**105.00**
10 x 9 "	**108.00**
12 x 8 "	**114.00**
12 x 9 "	**117.00**

Above prices for woodwork only, unvarnished (in the white).
For filling and varnishing (ordinary gloss finish), add 20 per cent to above prices.
For cabinet rubbed varnish finish, or in white and gold, add 30 per cent to above prices.
Prices are for plain sawed oak or woods of equal value.

ABOVE PRICES SUBJECT TO DISCOUNT.

CASED OPENING,

WITH COLUMNS.

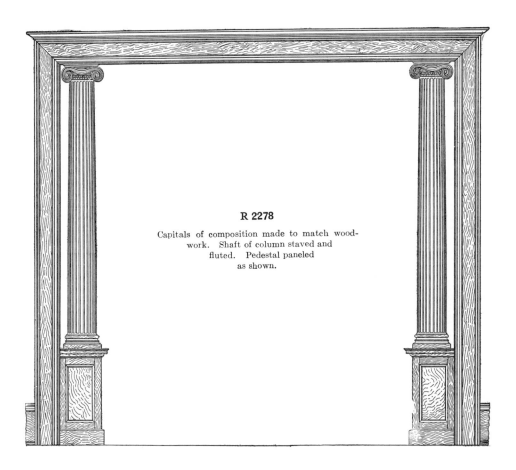

R 2278

Capitals of composition made to match woodwork. Shaft of column staved and
fluted. Pedestal paneled
as shown.

Jambs of opening must be as wide as widest part of pedestal.
The trim around each side of jambs must match the other trim in rooms connected by opening.
Prices quoted upon receipt of size of opening, width of jambs, designs of trim and kind of wood wanted.

HARDWOOD MANTELS.

On the following pages we show our complete line of mantels and fittings. We use only thoroughly kiln dried lumber of selected figure, and the goods are made by the best mechanics to be found anywhere. Do not confound these high-grade goods with the many so called **cheap** lines of goods now on the market. A mantel is an article of furniture and should be well made and finished. Our goods will please the most critical buyer.

FINISH. Oak mantels can be finished natural, antique, golden, weathered and old English or Flemish colors. Golden oak is very popular and unless ordered otherwise we will ship in this color. Birch mantels are finished in natural or to imitate mahogany or cherry. Samples mailed free upon request. If mantel is to match other finish in color, send sample and we will furnish same color.

SIZE. All stock mantels are five feet wide, which is the regular standard size. (Always state width of mantel and your grate selection in order.) Special sizes, smaller or larger than five feet wide, are made to order at extra price. Our mantels are carried in stock (in the white) and have to be filled and varnished to order. This process usually requires two weeks time.

TILES. Our stock consists of the latest and most artistic colors or shades, such as ivory, cream, beautiful tints of green, old rose and delft blue. Also a full assortment of mottled onyx colors. If no preference is specified in your order, we select and ship colors that best harmonize with mantel and wood. Samples mailed free.

GRATES. On pages 296 to 300, we give a complete description of the different kinds of coal, wood and gas grates supplied with our mantels. Every grate is thoroughly fitted, finished and constructed to burn economically and cleanly, requiring little care to obtain a cheerful and satisfactory fire with all the beautiful features of an open fire-place. Kindly specify grate wanted.

SPECIALS. Fancy woods, such as birdseye or curly maple, curly birch, genuine mahogany, white and gold, etc., also special sizes made to order at reasonable prices on application.

Cement, fire clay and fire brick are not sent, as the same can be bought in your town for less than the freight would amount to.

Tile facings for mantels are mounted in slabs (when so ordered) at **$4.00** per set extra, subject to mantel discount.

Full and complete plans for setting tile accompany every shipment.

We also furnish tiles for bath room floors, wainscotings, store floors and for all other purposes. Send for designs and prices stating quantity required.

For general instructions see pages 294 and 295.

DIRECTIONS FOR SETTING WOOD MANTELS, TILE AND FIRE-PLACES.

See illustration on opposite page.

See that your chimney is well built and sound, and an arch is turned for the hearth. Put all the tile to soak in clean water. They may remain there an hour or more and then be laid out to drip. In the box with the tile will be found a diagram showing how the hearth is to be laid out. See illustration on opposite page. Place the mantel against the wall and mark out the hearth. Take careful measurements of the profile of mantel, the tile opening, etc., also mark the chimney where the screws go through the mantel to hold it in place, and remove the mantel. Cut out the floor to the proper size and lay in the concrete or the foundation to within an inch of the floor level. The concrete may be made of gravel and common cement. (Some prefer to lay in common brick; if this is done the brick must be well soaked before laying the cement and tile on them.) Examine the diagram and lay out the hearth on the floor convenient enough to be picked up piece by piece and put in place. When the concrete has set, mix some Portland cement (one-third cement and two-thirds clean sharp sand) and place this on the concrete thick enough to raise the tile one-eighth inch above the floor. When you have the cement in smooth and level, lay the tile on it, commencing on the outside as per diagram. After the tile are all laid in and fitted nicely to place, wedge them all around to keep them from spreading and hammer them down lightly with a wood block or a smooth piece of board to the level of the floor. When you have got them all nicely in place, level and evenly spaced, mix a little of the Portland cement quite thin and wash it over the surface, working it into the joints where needed. After this has partially set wipe the tile perfectly clean with sawdust or shavings or whatever you have handy. All of the cement should be cleaned off, as it is very difficult to remove it after it has set. Drill and plug the chimney where the screws take hold to fasten the mantel.

As an assistance to you in the above work, study well the illustration on opposite page.

You have already got the profile, etc., of the mantel. Now lay up the piers, then take the iron arch-bar, lay it across from pier to pier and build the arch on them, making it high enough to fill the opening and a trifle over. Now, the arch-bar is as high as the frame, and the piers far enough apart to allow the fire-brick to go in and the frame to fit all around. Set the grate into the fire-place to get the proper angle, and build the fire-place of the fire-brick as shown, leaving about three-quarters of an inch play all around the grate. Use fire-clay to lay up the fire-brick with. Cut the fire-brick on the sides so as to allow the back brick to rest against them, and draw in the sides to fit the damper. Fill in behind the inclining back with bats and mortar. All this has been done leaving a space of seven-eighths of an inch from the face of the masonry to the profile of the mantel in which to put the cement and tile for the facing, except where the edge of the fire-brick is caught by the frame. Set the metal frame in place, blocking it away from the face of the masonry where necessary, and anchor it to the masonry with the wires. Mix Portland cement for the facing, half and half with clean sharp sand, and set on the facing tile as shown on plan in box with tile, breaking joints and setting the tile so that no opening will show between them and the frame or mantel, using care to keep them plumb and the surface even, finishing the work same as in the hearth.

Drive some wood plugs into the chimney where the screws go through the mantel, and when the mason and tile work is perfectly dry, screw the mantel to place, using the wood buttons to cover up the screw holes.

"Tiles can be cut, if it is necessary, by scratching the enamel with a hard sharp steel instrument, like a cold chisel or sharpened file, and then striking them on the back, opposite the scratch, with a light hammer. The edges can be ground smooth, if wished, on a fire-brick."

The profile is the projection of the tile facing of mantel from face to chimney and represents the distance the face of tiling must be set from face of chimney.

See illustration on opposite page.

SECTION ILLUSTRATING INSTRUCTIONS ON OPPOSITE PAGE.

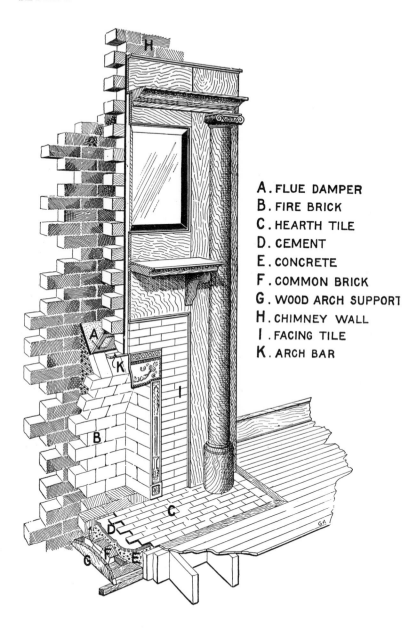

A. FLUE DAMPER
B. FIRE BRICK
C. HEARTH TILE
D. CEMENT
E. CONCRETE
F. COMMON BRICK
G. WOOD ARCH SUPPORT
H. CHIMNEY WALL
I. FACING TILE
K. ARCH BAR

Note.—All our hearths are sent out the width of the mantel ordered and the depth shown under each design. We make extra charge for larger hearths. A plan is enclosed in the box with the title for both facing and hearth, showing exact position of each piece and the number of pieces required. The hearths are always laid out before being packed so no shortage will occur.

COMBINATION GRATES FOR WOOD MANTELS.

This grate consisting of steel frame oxidized triple brass or copper plated, with black basket grate and ash screen.

Size 24½ in. x 30¼ in...... **$5.50**
"   30½ " x 30¼ " **8.00**

Add for extra parts if wanted:
Summer front **$2.50**
Flue damper **1.90**
Blower **1.00**
Arch bar .... **.50**

The 24½ in. frame has grate 20 inches wide and 8 inches deep. The 30½ inch frame has grate 24 inches wide and 8 inches deep.

R 2280
Combination Grate, without Summer Front.

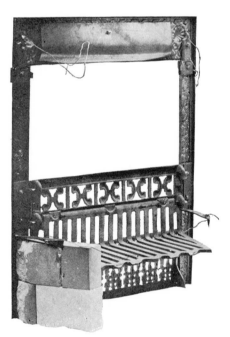

Grate, Sectional View.

The above illustrates Combination Grate in position, with anchor support resting on brick, the same passing under lugs which support basket.

Note.—This grate does not include fire brick, as same can be bought in your town for less than the freight would amount to. The small grate requires 35 and the large grate 42 fire brick.

R 2280
Combination Grate, with Summer Front.

This grate is unexcelled for burning wood and soft coal; the basket or fire pot is heavy cast iron, very serviceable; the steel frame has projecting canopy at top. The summer piece is of ornamental steel, cannot break and as it is light in weight is easily put in place; not at all like the heavy cast iron fronts.

ABOVE PRICES SUBJECT TO DISCOUNT.

CLUB HOUSE GRATES FOR WOOD MANTELS.

This grate consisting of ornamental steel frame, oxidized triple brass or copper plated, Club House basket grate with dumping bottom, ash screen, flue damper and arch bar.

Size 24½ in. x 30¼ in...... $ 9.50
"   30½ " x 30¼ " 13.00

Add for extra parts if wanted.
Summer front $3.25
Blower 1.00
The 24½ in. frame has grate 20 inches wide and 12 inches deep. The 30½ in. frame has grate 24 inches wide and 12 inches deep.

R 2281
Club House Grate.

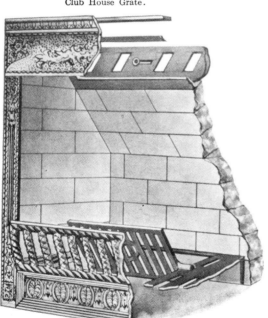

This grate is a good burner for hard or soft coal and wood. The grate dump and bottom is of heavy cast iron. The steel frame has canopy at top.

Note.— Price does not include fire brick, as same can be bought in your town for less than the freight charges would amount to. The small grate requires 35 and the large grate 42 fire brick.

R 2281.
Club House Grate.
Side view showing flue damper, dumping bottom, arch bar and fire brick.

ABOVE PRICES SUBJECT TO DISCOUNT.

GAS GRATES FOR WOOD MANTELS.

This grate consisting of complete asbestos gas grate and summer piece of heavy steel oxidized brass or copper plated.

Size 24½ in. x30¼ in........ ...$13.00
 "   30½ " x30¼ " 16.0C

R 2282
Gas Grate Open.

This grate is fitted with our latest improved five row steel burners, spreading one continuous sheet of fire over the asbestos back, and radiating at least one-third more heat than can be produced by any other gas grate with the same amount of gas. It has projecting canopy top, also gas valve, mixer and copper reflectors. Grate is all put together complete, ready for use.

Economy, cleanliness and beauty are features that have been admitted by all who have used them; each grate produces the greatest possible heat for the gas consumed, the combustion being as near perfect as it is possible to get in a grate. Burns any and all kinds of gas—natural, artificial, gasoline gas, etc. Is more economical than coal. Try one and be convinced.

Note.—Please be particular to specify kind of gas you intend to burn in a grate when ordering same

R 2282
Gas Grate Closed

ABOVE PRICES SUBJECT TO DISCOUNT

COMPLETE SET GRATES FOR WOOD MANTELS.

R 2283
Complete Set Grate Open.

This grate consisting of steel frame, oxidized triple brass or copper plated, basket grate with shaking bottom, fire brick back, double draft flue dampers, ash screen and handsome summer piece.

Size 24½ in. x30¼ in........**$20.00**
" 30½ " x30¼ " **23.00**

The 24½ in. frame has fire pot 20 inches wide and 12 inches deep. The 30½ in. frame has fire pot 24 inches wide and 12 inches deep.

This double damper set grate is unsurpassed in appearance, durability and general utility; it has heavy fire clay lining on back and the sides are of heavy iron. It is all in one piece ready for fastening in place and does not require the services of skilled workman to set. The top damper is operated by rod from face of frame.

R 2283
Complete Set Grate Closed.

Bottom View Grate.

Shaking and dumping attachment. A practical, useful device for separating the ashes and dead cinders from live coals; used in this set grate and furnished without extra charge.

While this grate costs more than an ordinary grate, yet you more than save the difference in consumption of fuel during the first season in use.

For beauty, durability and economy it has no equal.

ABOVE PRICES SUBJECT TO DISCOUNT.

COMPLETE SET GRATES FOR WOOD MANTELS.

R 2284
Complete Set Grate Open.

This grate consisting of cast iron frame, oxidized triple brass or copper plated, basket grate with shaking bottom, full fire brick lined, double draft flue dampers, sliding ash screen and handsome summer piece.

Size 24½x30¼ inches.........**$26.00**
"   30½x30¼   " **29.00**

The 24½ in. frame has fire pot 20 inches wide and 12 inches deep. The 30½ in. frame has fire pot 24 inches wide and 12 inches deep.

This double damper set grate is unsurpassed in appearance, durability and general utility; it has heavy fire clay linings on sides and back; is all in one piece ready for fastening in place and does not require the services of skilled workman to set.

Sectional View of Set Grate.

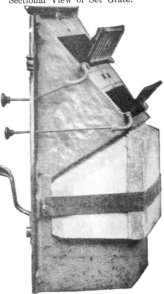

Side view showing double damper attachment and fire clay brick linings entirely surrounding fire pot.

Note.—We call your special attention to the side view, showing arrangement of the two dampers and the heavy fire clay brick linings. The shaking and dumping attachment is furnished with each grate without extra charge; has damper slide in basket front, which can be closed completely to control fire and prevent dust when shaking.

While this grate costs more than an ordinary grate, yet you more than save the difference in consumption of fuel during the first season in use.

For beauty, durability and economy it has no equal.

(For cut showing Bottom View Grate, see page 299.)

Shaking and dumping attachment. A practical, useful device for separating the ashes and dead cinders from live coals; used in this set grate and furnished without extra charge.

R 2284
Complete Set Grate Closed.

ABOVE PRICES SUBJECT TO DISCOUNT.

HARDWOOD MANTELS.

R 2302

Quartered Oak or Birch.
Width 5 ft.   Height 4 ft. 8 in.   Profile 4⅛ in.   Tile opening 42x39 inches.
Price of woodwork finished with colored enamel tile for facing 42x39 inches, and hearths 60x18 inches,
$32.00.
For price complete add to above your grate selection, pages 296 to 300.
This mantel takes a grate frame 24½x30¼ inches.

ABOVE PRICES SUBJECT TO DISCOUNT.

HARDWOOD MANTELS.

R 2305½

Oak or Birch.

Width 5 ft.　　Height 6 ft. 1 in.　　Profile 1 $\frac{3}{16}$ in.

Tile opening 36x36 inches.　French bevel plate mirror 28x16 inches.

Price of woodwork finished, with colored enamel tile for facing, 36x36 inches, and hearth 60x18 **inches,**

$38.00.

For price complete add to above your grate selection, pages 296 to 300.

This mantle takes a grate frame 24½x30¼ inches.

ABOVE PRICES SUBJECT TO DISCOUNT.

HARDWOOD MANTELS.

R 2306½

Quartered Oak or Birch.

Width 5 ft.   Height 6 ft. 4 in.   Profile 1⅞ in.

Tile opening 36 in. wide by 36 in. high.   French bevel plate mirror 36x18 inches.

Price of woodwork finished, with colored enamel tile for facing 36x36 inches and hearth 60x18 inches.

$43.00.

For price complete add to above your grate selection, pages 296 to 300.

This mantel takes a grate frame 24½x30¼ inches.

ABOVE PRICES SUBJECT TO DISCOUNT.

HARDWOOD MANTELS.

R 2307½

Oak or Birch.

Width 5 ft.   Height 6 ft. 4 in.   Profile 1⅞ in.

Tile opening 36 inches wide by 36 inches high.   French bevel plate mirror 36x18 inches.

Price of woodwork finished, with colored enamel tile for facing 36x36 inches and hearth 60x18 inches,

$40.00.

For price complete add to above your grate selection, pages 296 to 300.

This mantel takes grate frame 24½x30¼ inches.

ABOVE PRICES SUBJECT TO DISCOUNT.

HARDWOOD MANTELS.

R 2308½

Oak or Birch.

Width 5 ft.   Height 6 ft. 4 in.   Profile 2 in.

Veneered columns.   Tile opening 36x36 inches.   French bevel plate mirror 36x18 inches.

Price of woodwork finished, with colored enamel tile for facing 36x36 inches, and hearth 60x18 inches

$40.00.

For price complete add to above your grate selection, pages 296 to 300.

This mantel takes a grate frame 24½x30¼ inches.

ABOVE PRICES SUBJECT TO DISCOUNT.

HARDWOOD MANTELS.

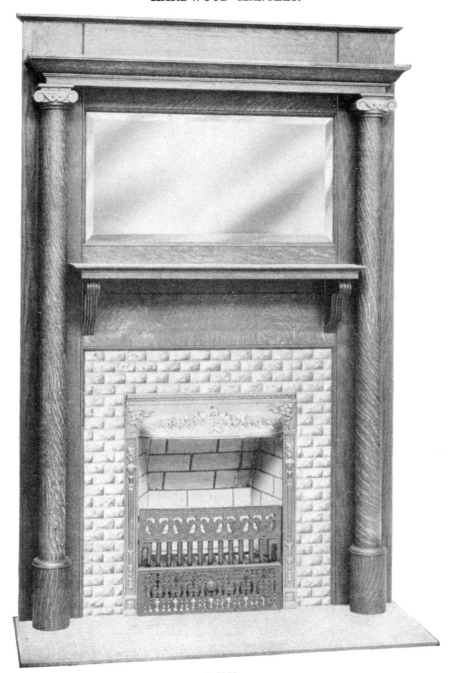

R 2309

Oak or Birch.

Width 5 ft.　Height 6 ft. 10 in.　Profile 2 in.

Veneered columns.　Tile opening 36x36.　French bevel plate mirror 36x18 inches.

Price of woodwork finished, with colored enamel tile for facing 36x36 inches, and hearth 60x18 inches,

$56.00.

For price complete add to above your grate selection　pages 296 to 300.

This mantel takes a grate frame 24½x30¼ inches.

ABOVE PRICES SUBJECT TO DISCOUNT.

HARDWOOD MANTELS.

R 2310
Quartered Oak or Birch.
Width 5 ft.   Height 6 ft. 10 in.   Profile 2⅞ in.
Tile opening 36x39 inches.   French bevel plate mirror 36x18 inches.   Beautifully curved veneered
pilasters.   Highly polished finish.   Price of woodwork finished, with
colored enamel tile for facing 36x39 inches, and
hearth 60x21 inches.
$72.00.
For price complete add to above your grate selection, pages 296 to 300.
This mantel takes grate frame 24½x30¼ inches.
ABOVE PRICES SUBJECT TO DISCOUNT.

HARDWOOD MANTELS.

R 2311
Quartered Oak or Birch.
Width 5 ft.   Height 7 ft. ½ in.   Profile 3⅞ in.
Tile opening 42 inches wide and 39 inches high.   French bevel plate mirror 32x18.
Fluted columns.   Highly polished finish.
Price of woodwork finished with colored enamel tile for facing 42x39 inches, and hearth 60x21 inches,
$74.00.
For price complete add to above your grate selection, pages 296 to 300.
This mantel takes a grate frame 24½x30¼ inches.
ABOVE PRICES SUBJECT TO DISCOUNT.

HARDWOOD MANTELS.

R 2312
Quartered Oak or Birch.
Width 5 ft.   Height 6 ft. 10 in.   Profile 1⅝ in.
Tile opening 42 inches wide by 39 inches high.   French bevel plate mirror 36x18 inches.
Veneered columns.   Highly polished finish.
Price of woodwork finished, with colored enamel tile for facing 42x39 inches, and hearth 60x21 inches,
$72.00.
For price complete add to above your grate selection, pages 296 to 300.
This mantel takes a grate frame 30½x30¼ inches.
ABOVE PRICES SUBJECT TO DISCOUNT.

HARDWOOD MANTELS.

R 2313

Quartered Oak or Birch.
Width 5 ft.   Height 6 ft. 10 in.   Profile 1⅝ in.
Tile opening 42 inches wide by 39 inches high.   French bevel plate mirror 36x18 inches.
Veneered columns.   Highly polished finish.
Price of woodwork finished, with colored enamel tile for facing 42x39 inches, and hearth 60x21 inches,
$72.00.
For price complete add to above your grate selection, pages 296 to 300.
This mantel takes a grate frame 24½x30¼ inches.
ABOVE PRICES SUBJECT TO DISCOUNT.

HARDWOOD MANTELS.

R 2314

Quartered Oak or Birch.
Width 5 ft.   Height 7 ft. 6 in.   Profile 2⅞ in.
Tile opening 42 inches wide by 42 inches high.   French bevel plate mirror 36x18 inches.
Splendid fluted pilasters.   Highly polished finish.
Price of woodwork finished, with colored enamel tile for facing 42x42 inches, and hearth 60x21 inches
$78.00.
For price complete add to above your grate selection, pages 296 to 300.
This mantel takes a grate frame 30½x30¼ inches.
ABOVE PRICES SUBJECT TO DISCOUNT.

HARDWOOD MANTELS.

R 2315

Quartered Oak or Birch.

Width 5 ft.   Height 7 ft. 3 in.   Profile $3\frac{1}{4}$ in.

Tile opening 40 inches wide by 39 inches high.   French bevel plate mirror 40x18 inches.

Beautiful fluted columns.   Highly polished finish.

Price of woodwork finished, with colored enamel tile facing 42x39 inches, and hearth 60x21 inches,

$84.00.

For price complete add to above your grate selection, pages 296 to 300.

This mantel takes a grate frame $30\frac{1}{2}$x$30\frac{1}{4}$ inches.

ABOVE PRICES SUBJECT TO DISCOUNT.

HARDWOOD MANTELS.

R 2316
Quartered Oak or Birch.
Width 5 ft.   Height 7 ft 2 in.   Profile 1⅝ in.
Tile opening 42 inches wide by 39 inches high.   French bevel plate mirror 36x18 inches
Massive veneered columns.   Highly polished finish.
Price of woodwork finished, with colored enamel tile facing 42x39 inches, and hearth 60x21 inches,
$86.00.
For price complete add to above your grate selection, pages 296 to 300.
This mantel takes a grate frame 24½x30¼ inches.
ABOVE PRICES SUBJECT TO DISCOUNT.

HARDWOOD MANTELS.

R 2316½

Quartered Oak or Birch.
Width 5 ft.   Height 7 ft. 1 in.   Profile 1⅝ in.
Tile opening 42x42 inches.   Plain French plate mirror to shelf 36x18 inches.
Columns massive and veneered throughout.   Highly polished finish.
Price of woodwork finished, with colored enamel tile facing 42x42 inches, and hearth **60x21 inches,**
$122.00.
For price complete add to above your grate selection, pages 296 to 300.
This mantel takes a grate frame 30½x30¼ inches.
ABOVE PRICES SUBJECT TO DISCOUNT.

HARDWOOD MANTELS.

R 2317

Quartered Oak or Birch.

Width 5 ft. Height 7 ft. 9½ in. Profile 1⅝ in.

Tile opening 42 inches wide by 39 inches high. Plain French plate mirror to shelf 40x22 inches.

Large and imposing veneered columns and heavy shelf. Highly polished finish.

Price of woodwork finished, with colored enamel tile for facing 42x39 inches, and hearth 60x21 inches,

$128.00.

For price complete add to above your grate selection, pages 296 to 300.

This mantel takes a grate frame 30½x30¼ inches.

ABOVE PRICES SUBJECT TO DISCOUNT.

HARDWOOD MANTELS.

R 2317½

Quartered Oak or Birch.
Width 5 ft.   Height 5 ft. 1 in.   Profile 3¼ in.
Tile opening 42 inches wide by 42 inches high.   Polished finish.
Price of woodwork finished with colored enamel tile facing 42x42 inches, and hearth 60x21 inches,

$56.00.

Black iron fireplace frame for above, extra............$4.50
Cast iron (black finish) fireplace lining, for above, extra.... 9.00
Gas log 18 inches long, as in cut, for above, extra 14.00

For cheaper fireplace lining see opposite page.
For other designs of andirons see page 323.
For coal or gas grates for above see pages 296 to 300.

ABOVE PRICES SUBJECT TO DISCOUNT.

HARDWOOD MANTELS.

R 2317¾

Quartered Oak or Birch.
Width 5 ft.   Height 8 ft. 4 in.   Profile 2⅝ in.   Highly polished.
Tile opening 42 inches wide by 48 inches high.
Price of woodwork finished, with colored enamel tile facing 42x48 inches, and hearth 60x24 inches,
$200.00.
Brass or copper plated fireplace frames for above, extra............**$4.50**
Steel fireplace lining, black finish, as in cut, extra.................**5.00**
Gas log 18 inches long for above, as in cut, extra..................**14.00**
Polished cast brass andirons for above, as in cut, extra............**50.00**
For coal burning grate see pages 296 to 300.   For cheaper andirons see page 323.
This mantel also made 5 feet 6 inches and 6 feet wide at extra price.
ABOVE PRICES SUBJECT TO DISCOUNT.

HARDWOOD CONSOLS.

R 2318
Oak or Birch.
Price complete, as shown, for parlor or reception hall,
$102.00.
Width 4 feet 7½ inches.   Height 7 feet 5½ inches.   French beveled plate mirror 36x56 inches.
Made to match mantel R2309 but will look well with any other design.
ABOVE PRICES SUBJECT TO DISCOUNT.

HARDWOOD CONSOLS.

R 2319
Quartered Oak or Birch.
Price complete, as shown, for parlor or reception hall, highly polished finish,
$126.00.
Width 5 feet.   Height 8 feet.   French beveled plate mirror 40x60 inches.
An elegant article in every respect.
ABOVE PRICES SUBJECT TO DISCOUNT.

MANTEL ACCESSORIES.

R 2320

WROUGHT IRON FIRE SET.

28 inches high.

Price, complete, as shown...............................$7.00

R 2321

WROUGHT IRON FINISHED FENDER.

6½ inches high.

Price, 35 or 41 inches long.........................$ 9.50
Price, 47 or 53 inches long......................... 11.50

These fenders and fire sets add much to the appearance of the fireplace and are very useful.

ABOVE PRICES SUBJECT TO DISCOUNT.

MANTEL ACCESSORIES.

R 2322

POLISHED BRASS FIRE SET.

26 inches high.

Price, complete, as shown $11.00

R 2323

POLISHED BRASS FENDER.

6 inches high.

Price, 35 or 41 inches long $11.50
Price, 47 or 53 inches long 14.00

No first class fireplace is complete without a fender and fire set.   They put on the finishing touch.

ABOVE PRICES SUBJECT TO DISCOUNT.

MANTEL ACCESSORIES.

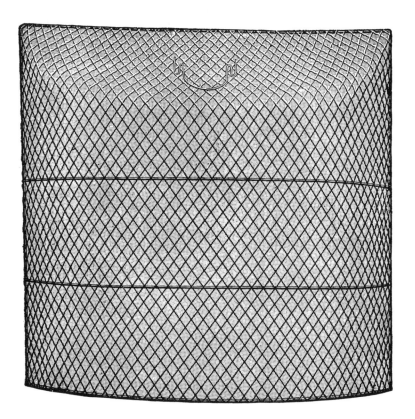

R 2324

WIRE SPARK GUARDS.

Heavy coppered screen with fine wire lining.

Price, 24x30 inches....................................$3.00
Price, 30x30 inches....................................4.00

These guards remove the last element of danger from an open fireplace. They keep sparks in their proper place and children from harm.

ABOVE PRICES SUBJECT TO DISCOUNT.

MANTEL ACCESSORIES.

WROUGHT IRON ANDIRONS.

All hand forged.

R 2325

22¼ inches high.
Per pair...........**$10.00**

**COMBINATION BRASS AND
IRON ANDIRONS.**

Antique brass finish.

R 2325½

24 inches high.
Per pair.........**$9.25**

These andirons can be used for either gas log or real wood fire.
They are splendidly made and will last a lifetime.

ABOVE PRICES SUBJECT TO DISCOUNT.

MANTEL ACCESSORIES.

R 2326

ASH PIT COVER.
11 inches long; 9 inches wide.
Price, each, **$1.00.**

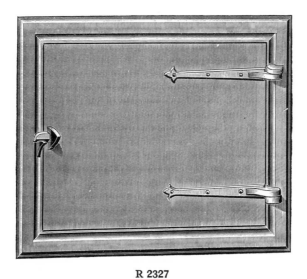

R 2327

ASH PIT DOORS.
13 inches wide; 10½ inches high.
Price, each, **$2.50.**

The addition of an ash pit while building the chimney is of trifling expense, and saves much time and trouble in caring for the fireplace.

ABOVE PRICES SUBJECT TO DISCOUNT.

PARQUETRY FLOORS.

These floors are not a fad, they have been in use in Europe for centuries. With a little care they will last a lifetime. Carpets are more expensive, require more labor to keep clean and are very unhealthy. A servant of average intelligence can keep parquetry floors as if they were newly laid with but little effort. A hardwood floor is absolutely "Hygienic"; ask your physician about it. New homes are rarely built without parquetry floors, and they are rapidly replacing carpets in the older buildings. They are 5-16 inches thick, less than the ordinary threshold, so they can be laid in one room over the old floor and not interfere with the other rooms or doorways. Anyone familiar with the use of a saw, hammer and varnish brush can lay and finish them. Send us a plan of your rooms with exact measurements, as on page 329, and select your design. We can then make you exact estimate of cost and a working plan will be sent with the invoice for the goods showing just where each piece is to be laid. See directions for laying and finishing, pages 326 and 327.

PARQUETRY FLOORS.

DIRECTIONS FOR LAYING.

LAYING WOOD CARPET. Start at the wall, removing the quarter round, then measure out into the room from the wall the width of the first breadth of carpet, and tack down the strips marked "A" in the following cut. Measure your space thus framed for the center, to make certain it will contain other breadths, as planned, be sure that the corners turned by this strip are square, lay and brad the breadths in center of room, then put down the outside breadth, bringing it up to the strip first laid. The quarter round should cover the rows of brads next the wall.

NAILING WOOD CARPET. Drive the brads in rows about 9 inches apart, placing a brad at each edge of each slat, as shown in this cut:

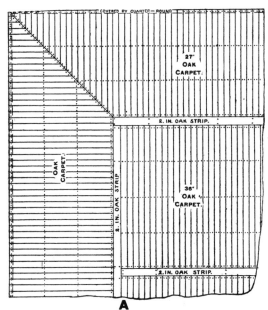

Use a 1¼-inch No. 15 wire brad. After the whole has been bradded down, go over and with a punch not larger than the head of the brad, sink each brad 1-16-inch below the surface of the wood.

SMOOTHING OFF. After the brads are all driven and countersunk, go over the floor carefully, and wherever any of the joints are found uneven, make smooth with a steel scraper in the hands as shown. Any hammer marks indenting the wood should be scraped out, as they will show when the polish is on.

LAYING PARQUETRY. The pattern fields are usually laid beginning at the center of the room. First find the border line, and tacking down a strip to frame in the center or field, start in center of the room and work out to the sides and ends until the border line is met, when the strip can be taken up and the border laid in its place, filling out to the wall as planned.

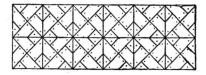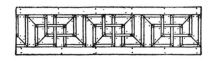

NAILING PARQUETRY. Brads are driven to suit the pattern. Each piece of wood in the pattern, unless very small, should be securely nailed down and countersunk for scraping.

PARQUETRY FLOORS.

DIRECTIONS FOR FINISHING.

SANDING. After the floor is scraped, go over the entire surface with No. 1½ sandpaper, first with the grain and then across the grain. It will be found easy to do this by placing a half dozen sheets of the sandpaper under the weighted brush, which are held in place by being tacked at the sides of the brush block.

FILLING. Clean off the floor carefully to remove all dust and grit from sanding, apply our Paste Wood Filler to the surface of the wood with a brush, going over no more surface at a time than will admit being cleaned off before hardening. After the filler has set, rub off with excelsior or cloth, rubbing across the grain when practicable. Allow the filler twelve hours, at least, to dry.

PUTTYING. Go over the entire floor and putty up each nail hole to match the wood, then sand again lightly to clean the surface of filler and putty marks.

VARNISH FINISH. Wipe the floor off thoroughly and apply a coat of Floor Varnish with a brush; allow it twelve hours or more to dry, second or third coat, according to the finish desired.

WAX FINISH. After one coat of Floor Varnish sand the surface, wipe off and apply a coat of the Wax with a rag, spreading it out thin in all directions. Allow it about half an hour to dry, then take a stiff brush (one of our weighted ones preferred, see page 325), and rub the floor across first, and with the grain afterward. A piece of dry cloth, felt or carpet placed under the brush, will give the finishing gloss.

CAUTION. Never use soap or water in cleaning hardwood floors. Take up ordinary dust and dirt with a soft cloth wrapped around a broom. Where badly soiled, clean with a soft cloth dipped in turpentine—touch up with wax or varnish.

FINISHING MATERIALS.

Specially Prepared for Our Floors.

FILLER, Wax and Varnish complete for each 100 square feet of surface..........................$2.25

ITEMIZED PRICE LIST OF FINISHING MATERIALS.

HARD WAX FINISH, in self-sealing cans, 1, 2, 4 and 8 lbs., per lb................................. **60c**

PASTE WOOD FILLER, in cans, 2, 5 and 10 lbs., per lb...................................... **20c**

FLOOR VARNISH.   Quarts..........**$1.25**.   Half-gallons..........**$1.90**.   Gallons..........**$3.60**
An under coat for wax, or a finish in itself complete.

WEIGHTED FLOOR BRUSHES, 25 lbs., each, as shown in cut on page 325...................**$4.00**
Used for sanding new floors when laid, and keeping the floors polished.

ABOVE PRICES SUBJECT TO DISCOUNT.

PARQUETRY STRIPS,

5-16 INCH THICK,

Are used in connection with wood carpet, priced below, or the fields or borders
of any designs on the following pages.

	Woods Used.	Width, Inches.	Price, Cts. per ft.	Width, Inches.	Price, Cts. per ft.
	Oak........	1½	1¼	2	1½
	Mahogany ...	1½	4	2	7
	Cherry......	1½	2	2	3
	Dark Oak....	1½	1¾	2	2
	Walnut......	1½	2	2	3
	Maple	1½	1¾	2	2

WOOD CARPET.

5-16 INCH THICK.

This flooring material is made of hardwood strips, 1½ inches wide, glued to heavy cotton cloth. It is made
in widths of 27 inches and 36 inches and in sections containing 4 yards. Any quantity can be taken by simply
slitting the cloth between the slats. The widths can be ripped to 6, 9, 12 or 18 inches, to be used as borders or
margins next the walls, at a slight additional cost for cutting.

PRICE LIST OF WOOD CARPET.

Price per lineal yard.	Width.	Price.	Width.	Price.
All oak, quartered white....................	27 inches.	$1.00	36 inches.	$1.20
Oak with walnut or cherry.................	27 "	1.20	36 "	1.45
All walnut or cherry.......................	27 "	1.80	36 "	2.15
All oak diagonal	24 "	1.90	36 "	....

ABOVE PRICES SUBJECT TO DISCOUNT.

HARDWOOD FLOORS.

3-8 INCH THICK.

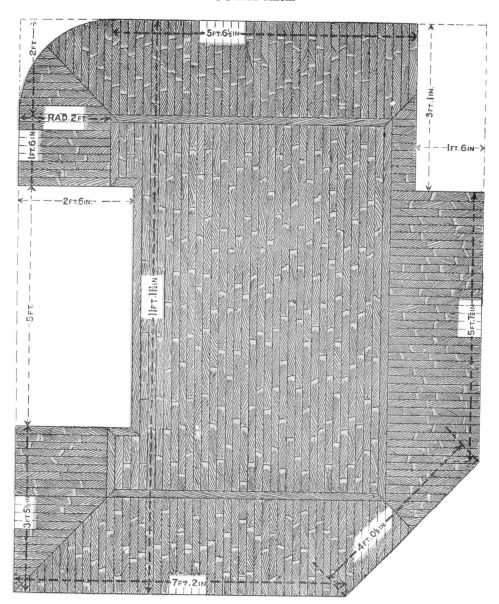

DESIGN R 2380

Adapted to room of any shape { Plain Oak, per square foot, **10c.**
{ Quar. " " " " **12c.**

This design is made of **3-8 x 2** inch face, tongued, grooved and end matched clear red or white oak flooring, with a square-edged **2** inch strip to divide border from field.

This is the cheapest form of ornamental floor.

Always send exact measurements and plan as shown above, also location and width of all door openings.

ABOVE PRICES SUBJECT TO DISCOUNT.

PARQUETRY BORDERS.

5-16 INCH THICK.

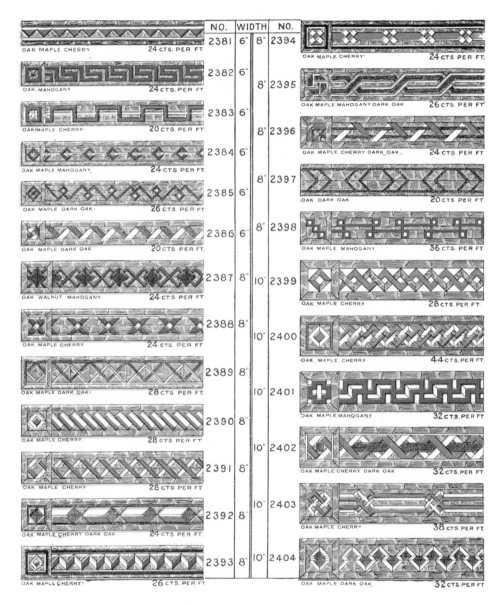

NO.	WIDTH	NO.
2381	6"	8" 2394
2382	6"	
2383	6"	8" 2395
2384	6"	8" 2396
2385	6"	8" 2397
2386	6"	8" 2398
2387	8"	10" 2399
2388	8"	10" 2400
2389	8"	10" 2401
2390	8"	10" 2402
2391	8"	10" 2403
2392	8"	10" 2404
2393	8"	

Above prices are per lineal foot.

Can be used with **3-8** inch tongued and grooved flooring, as on pages **332** and **333**, or with any parquetry design on following pages.

ABOVE PRICES SUBJECT TO DISCOUNT.

PARQUETRY BORDERS.

5-16 INCH THICK.

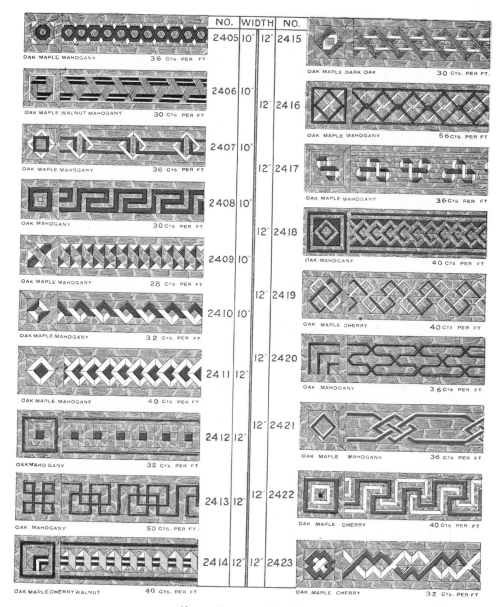

NO.	WIDTH	WIDTH	NO.
2405	10"	12"	2415
2406	10"	12"	2416
2407	10"	12"	2417
2408	10"	12"	2418
2409	10"	12"	2419
2410	10"	12"	2420
2411	12"	12"	2421
2412	12"	12"	2422
2413	12"	12"	2423
2414	12"		

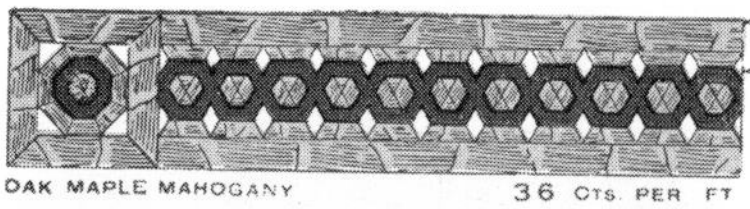
OAK MAPLE MAHOGANY 36 CTS. PER FT

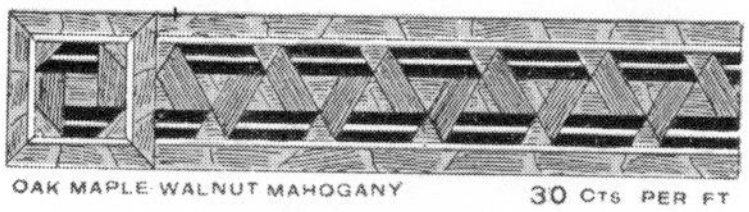
OAK MAPLE WALNUT MAHOGANY 30 CTS. PER FT

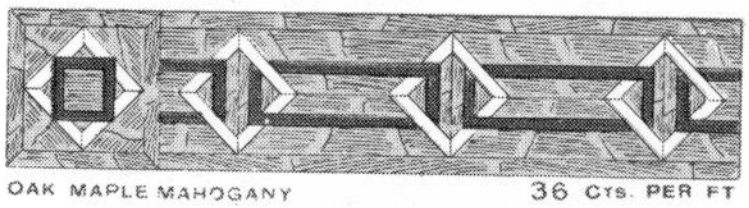
OAK MAPLE MAHOGANY 36 CTS. PER FT

OAK MAHOGANY 30 CTS. PER FT

OAK MAPLE MAHOGANY 28 CTS. PER FT

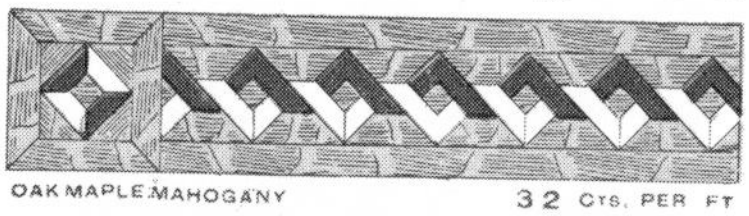
OAK MAPLE MAHOGANY 32 CTS. PER FT

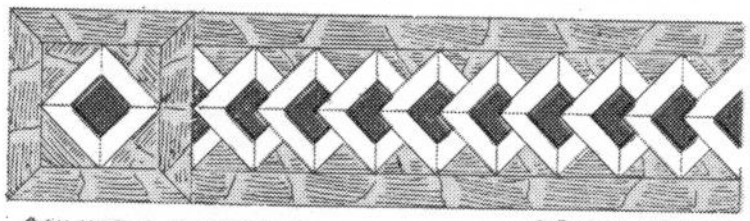
OAK MAPLE MAHOGANY 40 CTS. PER FT

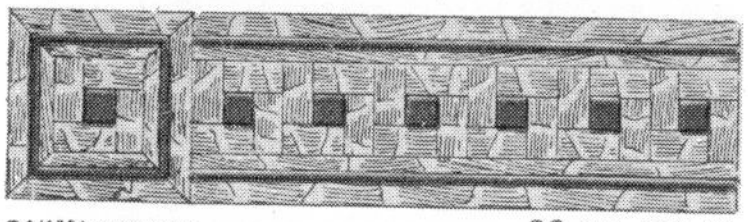
OAK MAHOGANY 32 CTS. PER FT

OAK MAHOGANY 50 CTS. PER FT.

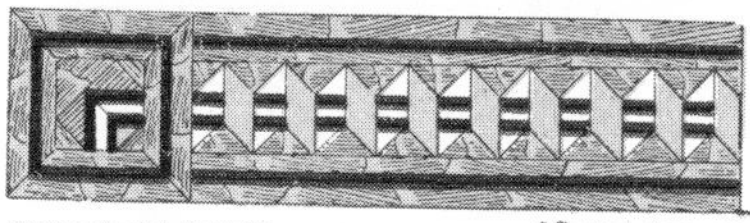
OAK MAPLE CHERRY WALNUT 40 CTS. PER FT

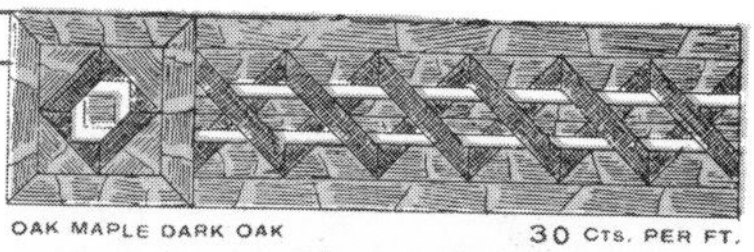
OAK MAPLE DARK OAK 30 CTS. PER FT.

OAK MAPLE MAHOGANY 56 CTS. PER FT

OAK MAPLE MAHOGANY 36 CTS. PER FT

OAK MAHOGANY 40 CTS. PER FT

OAK MAPLE CHERRY 40 CTS. PER FT

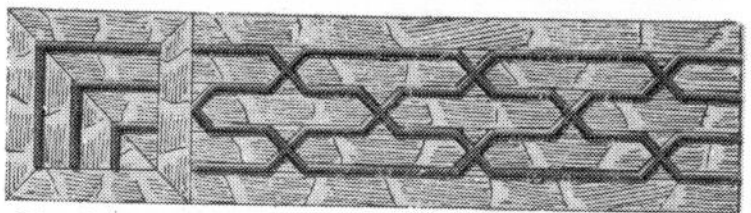
OAK MAHOGANY 36 CTS. PER FT.

OAK MAPLE MAHOGANY 36 CTS. PER FT

OAK MAPLE CHERRY 40 CTS. PER FT

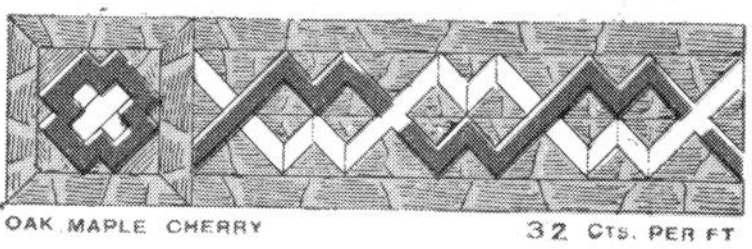
OAK MAPLE CHERRY 32 CTS. PER FT

Above prices are per lineal foot.

Can be used with **3-8** inch tongued and grooved flooring, as on pages **332** and **333**, or with any parquetry design on following pages.

ABOVE PRICES SUBJECT TO DISCOUNT.

PARQUETRY FLOORS.

5-16 INCH THICK.

DESIGN R 2424

Adapted to room of any shape.   Per square foot, **18c.**
Above price is for room containing not less than **200** square feet.   On smaller rooms will make net estimate.
The center or field is made of tongued and grooved **3-8** inch flooring.
Always send exact measurements and plan as shown on page **329.**
Allow **10** per cent. for waste in figuring square feet in a floor.
ABOVE PRICES SUBJECT TO DISCOUNT.

PARQUETRY FLOORS.
5-16 INCH THICK.

DESIGN R 2425
Adapted to rooms of any shape. Per square foot, **18c.**
Above price is for rooms containing not less than **200** square feet. On smaller rooms will make net estimate.
The center or field is made of tongued and grooved **3-8** inch flooring.
Always send exact measurements and plan as shown on page **329.**
Allow **10** per cent. for waste in figuring square feet in a floor.
ABOVE PRICES SUBJECT TO DISCOUNT.

PARQUETRY FLOORS.

5-16 INCH THICK.

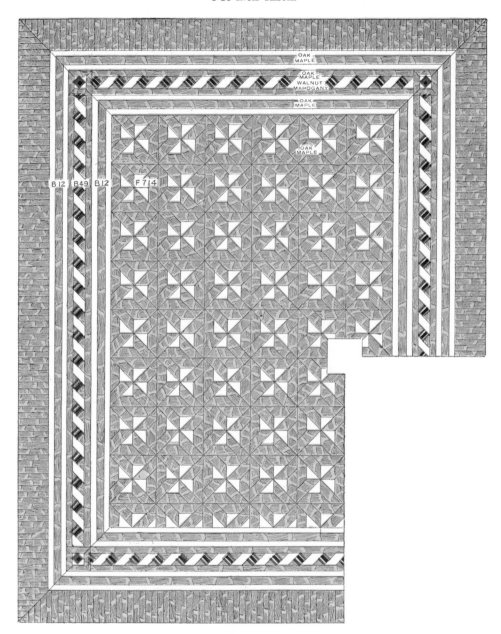

DESIGN R 2426
Adapted to room of any shape. Per square foot, 28c.
Above price is for room containing not less than **200** square feet. On smaller rooms will make net estimate.
Always send exact measurements and plan as shown on page **329**.
Allow **10** per cent. waste in figuring square feet in a floor.
ABOVE PRICES SUBJECT TO DISCOUNT.

PARQUETRY FLOORS.

5-16 INCH THICK.

DESIGN R 2427
Adapted to room of any shape. Per square foot, **23c.**
Above price is for room containing not less than **200** square feet. On smaller rooms will make net estimate.
Always send exact measurements and plan as shown on page **329.**
Allow **10** per cent. for waste in figuring square feet in a floor.
ABOVE PRICES SUBJECT TO DISCOUNT.

PARQUETRY FLOORS.

5-16 INCH THICK.

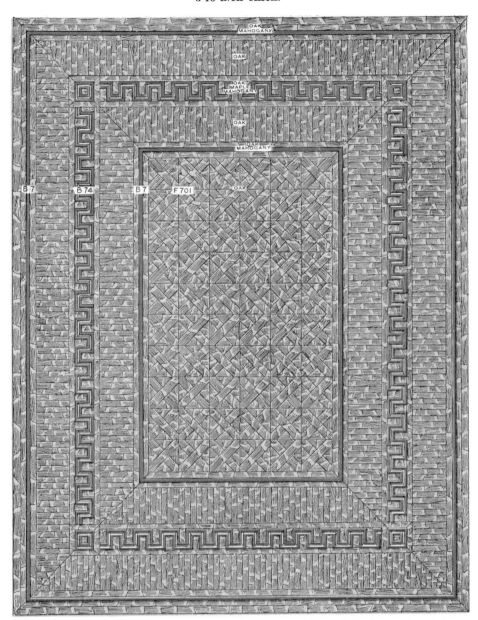

DESIGN R 2428
Adapted to room of any shape. Per square foot, 28c.
Above price is for room containing not less than **200** square feet. On smaller rooms will make net estimate.
Always send exact measurements and plan as shown on page **329**.
Allow **10** per cent. for waste in figuring square feet in a floor.

ABOVE PRICES SUBJECT TO DISCOUNT.

PARQUETRY FLOORS.

5-16 INCH THICK.

DESIGN R 2429

Adapted to room of any shape. Per square foot. **40c.**

Above price is for room containing not less than **200** square feet. On smaller rooms will make net estimate.
Always send exact measurements and plan as shown on page **329.**
Allow **10** per cent. for waste in figuring square feet in a floor.

ABOVE PRICES SUBJECT TO DISCOUNT.

PARQUETRY FLOORS.
5-16 INCH THICK.

DESIGN R 2430
Adapted to room of any shape. Per square foot, **21c.**

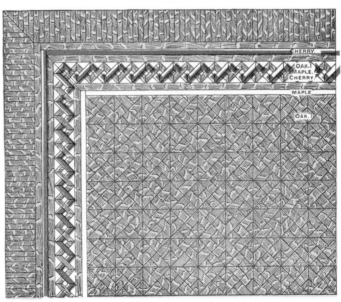

DESIGN R 2431
Adapted to room of any shape. Per square foot, **26¾c.**
Above prices for rooms containing not less than **200** square feet.   On smaller rooms will make net estimate.
Always send exact measurements and plan as shown on page **329**.
Allow **10** per cent. for waste in figuring square feet in a floor.
ABOVE PRICES SUBJECT TO DISCOUNT.

PARQUETRY FLOORS.

5-16 INCH THICK.

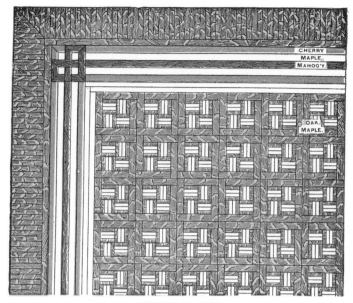

DESIGN R 2432

Adapted to room of any shape.   Per square foot, 23½c.

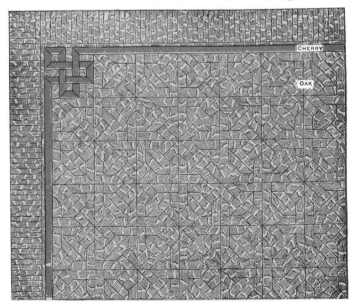

DESIGN R 2433

Adapted to room of any shape.   Per square foot, 26c.

Above prices for room containing not less than **200** square feet.   On smaller rooms will make net estimate.

Always send exact measurements and plan as shown on page **329**.

Allow **10** per cent. for waste in figuring square feet in a floor.

ABOVE PRICES SUBJECT TO DISCOUNT.

PARQUETRY FLOORS.

5-16 INCH THICK.

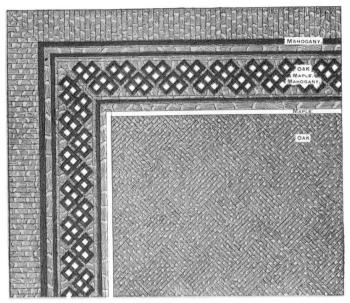

DESIGN R 2434

Adapted to room of any shape.   Per square foot, **34c.**

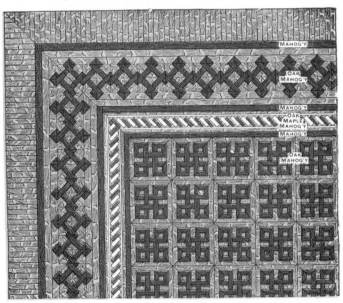

DESIGN R 2435

Adapted to room of any shape.   Per square foot, **40c.**

Above prices for rooms containing not less than **200** square feet. On smaller rooms will make net estimate.

Always send exact measurements and plan as shown on page **329.**

Allow **10** per cent. for waste in figuring square feet in a floor.

ABOVE PRICES SUBJECT TO DISCOUNT.

CHINA CLOSETS.

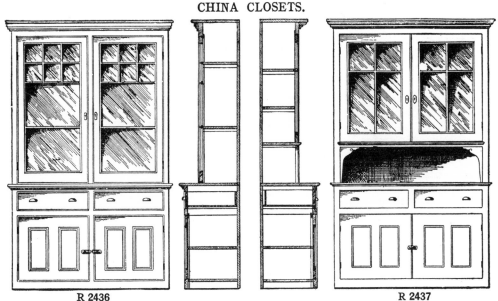

R 2436   R 2437

In writing for price give opening to fill and depth of shelves.   Also state if open or glazed doors.

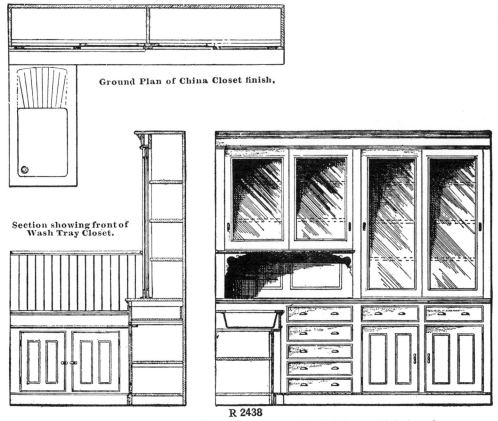

Ground Plan of China Closet finish.

Section showing front of
Wash Tray Closet.

R 2438

In asking price give opening to fill, depth of shelves, style of glazing and kind of wood.
See other designs, pages 342 and 343.

MEDICINE CASES AND SIDEBOARDS.

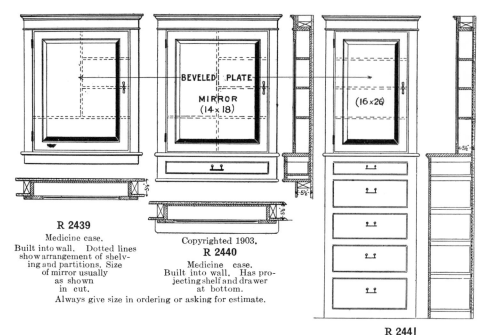

R 2439

Medicine case.

Built into wall. Dotted lines show arrangement of shelving and partitions. Size of mirror usually as shown in cut.

Always give size in ordering or asking for estimate.

Copyrighted 1903.

R 2440

Medicine case.

Built into wall. Has projecting shelf and drawer at bottom.

R 2441

R 2441. Medicine and towel closet combined. Built into wall. Lower part containing drawers projects out into room. Width usually as indicated by size of glass. Height same as doors of room. Always give size in ordering or asking for estimate.

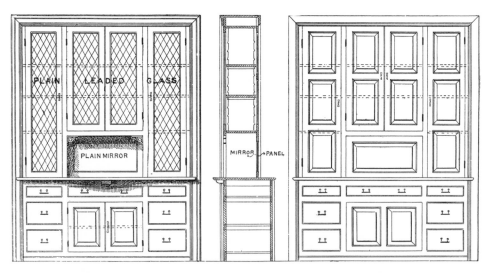

R 2442

Dining Room Elevation.

Copyrighted 1903.

R 2443

Kitchen or Pantry Elevation.

Designs R2442 and R2443 can be used separately, but are designed as one case, showing in dining-room on one side and kitchen or pantry on other side. The drawers are double acting, pulling from either side. The doors open from either side, saving many steps and making a handsome case. The finish is usually made to match the trim of the room in which it is placed. Always give complete measurements in ordering or asking for estimate.

PANTRY FIXTURES, LINEN CLOSETS AND SIDEBOARDS.

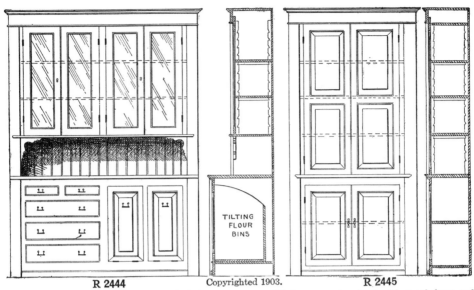

Copyrighted 1903.

R 2444

Pantry closet with glass doors, adjustable shelving, drawers, and two tilting flour bins.

R 2445

Kitchen or pantry closet with panel doors and adjustable shelving.

Always give complete measurements in ordering or asking for estimate.

Copyrighted 1903.

R 2446

Sideboard or china closet. A handsome and complete case with leaded glass doors, mirrors at back and sides of counter shelf.

R 2447

Linen closet with panel doors, adjustable shelving above and drawers below.

The finish is usually made to match trim of room in which it is placed.
Always give complete measurements in ordering or asking for estimate.

CLOCK AND MANTEL SHELVES.

Made of white pine, yellow pine or poplar, at prices named below.

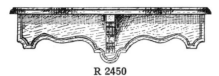

R 2450
16 inches long.
Price each, **$0.70.**

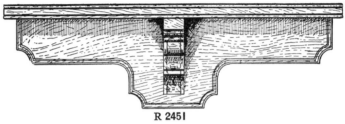

R 2451
36 inches long.
Price each, **$1.20.**

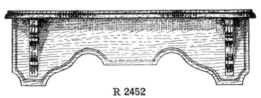

R 2452
30 inches long.
Price each, **$1.10.**

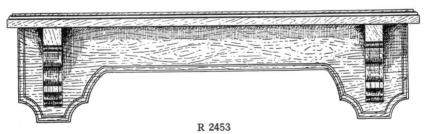

R 2453
48 inches long.
Price each, **$2.00.**
Special prices in quantity.
Will quote also in hardwoods on receipt of specifications.

ABOVE PRICES SUBJECT TO DISCOUNT.

ORNAMENTAL GLASS.

Beautiful effects in glass are now produced by many processes. The following pages exhibit a complete line of new and original designs for all classes of buildings. Two entirely new features have been added to the large assortment: Battenberg lace effects on glass, pages 354 and 355, and leaded white and clear glass, page 366. We make a specialty of church and society windows, and show a number of emblems, in proper coloring, on page 379. We will also furnish special designs in water colors upon receipt of complete specifications. Our leaded glass is designed by artists, and constructed in the most approved manner by skilled workmen. We use only best qualities of glass and materials.

All goods are carefully packed and boxed
to prevent damage in transit.

CUT GLASS DESIGNS.
On double strength glass.

R 2500

R 2502

R 2503

These designs carried in stock in following sizes only
22x30 and 24x32 inches, **$3.50** each; 26x34, 24x36 and 28x36, **$4 00** each.
All other sizes, **90c.** per square foot.
Special prices on large quantities.
ABOVE PRICES SUBJECT TO DISCOUNT.

CUT GLASS DESIGNS.
On double strength glass.

R 2504

R 2505

R 2506

R 2507

These designs carried in stock in following sizes only:
22x30 and 24x32 inches, at **$3.50** each; 26x34, 24x36 and 28x36 inches, at **$4.00** each.
All other sizes **90c** per square foot.
Special prices on large quantities.
ABOVE PRICES SUBJECT TO DISCOUNT.

SPECIAL GLASS DESIGNS.

R 2508
$1.50 per square foot.
On double strength glass.
Letters **15c.** each, net, extra.

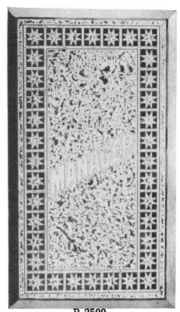

R 2509
$1.50 per square foot.
On double strength glass.
Letters **15c.** each, net, extra.

R 2510
On double strength glass.

R 2511
$1.50 per square foot.
On heavy beveled Florentine glass.

Design R2510 carried in stock in following sizes only:
22x30 and 24x32 inches, at **$3.50** each; 26x34, 24x36 and 28x36 inches, at **$4.00** each.
All other sizes **90c** per square foot.
Special prices on large quantities.
ABOVE PRICES SUBJECT TO DISCOUNT.

SPECIAL GLASS DESIGNS.

R 2512
On double strength glass.
$1.50 per square foot.

R 2513
On double strength glass.
$1.50 per square foot.

R 2514
On double strength glass.
$1.30 per square foot.

R 2515
On double strength glass.
$1.30 per square foot.

Letters 30c each, extra.

ABOVE PRICES SUBJECT TO DISCOUNT.

CUT GLASS DESIGNS.
On double strength glass.

R 2516½
$1.30 per square foot.

R 2517
$1.30 per square foot.

R 2518
$1.30 per square foot.

R 2519
$1.30 per square foot.
One-half of the above design can be used
for a narrow light.

ABOVE PRICES SUBJECT TO DISCOUNT.

CUT GLASS DESIGNS.

On double strength glass.

R 2520
$1.10 per square foot.

R 2521
$1.10 per square foot.

R 2522
$1.30 per square foot.

R 2523
$1.20 per square foot.

ABOVE PRICES SUBJECT TO DISCOUNT

CUT GLASS DESIGNS.
On double strength glass.

R 2524
$1.30 per square foot.

R 2526
$1.30 per square foot.

R 2527
$1.50 per square foot.

R 2530
$1.20 per square foot.

ABOVE PRICES SUBJECT TO DISCOUNT.

GEOMETRIC CHIPPED LIGHTS.
On double strength glass.

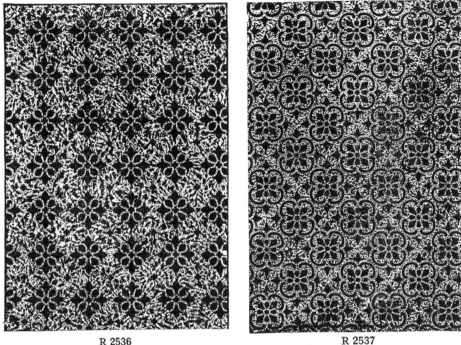

R 2536
70 cents per square foot.

R 2537
70 cents per square foot.

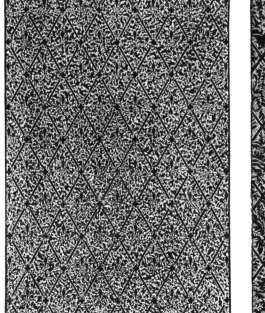

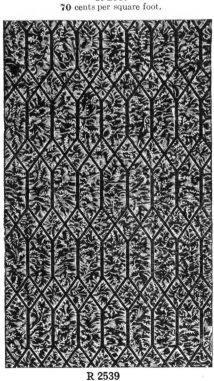

R 2538
70 cents per square foot.

R 2539
70 cents per square foot.

ABOVE PRICES SUBJECT TO DISCOUNT.

BATTENBERG LACE DESIGNS.

On double strength glass.

R 3078
90c per square foot.

R 3079
90c per square foot.

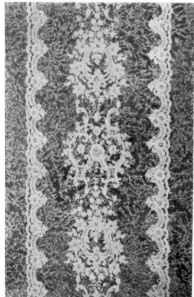

R 3080
90c per square foot.

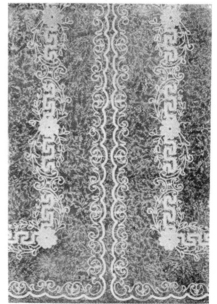

R 3081
90c per square foot.

Splendid reproductions of Battenberg lace designs, produced by photographic process direct
from the original lace to the glass.
They make new and handsome decorative door lights.
Special prices in large quantities.
ABOVE PRICES SUBJECT TO DISCOUNT.

BATTENBERG LACE DESIGNS.

On double strength glass.

R 3082 R 3083

R 3084 R 3085

These designs carried in stock in following size only:
22x30 and 24x32 inches, **$3.50** each; 26x34, 24x36 and 28x36 inches, **$4.00** each.
All other designs 90 cents per square foot.
Special prices in large quantities.
ABOVE PRICES SUBJECT TO DISCOUNT.

LEADED CLEAR GLASS.

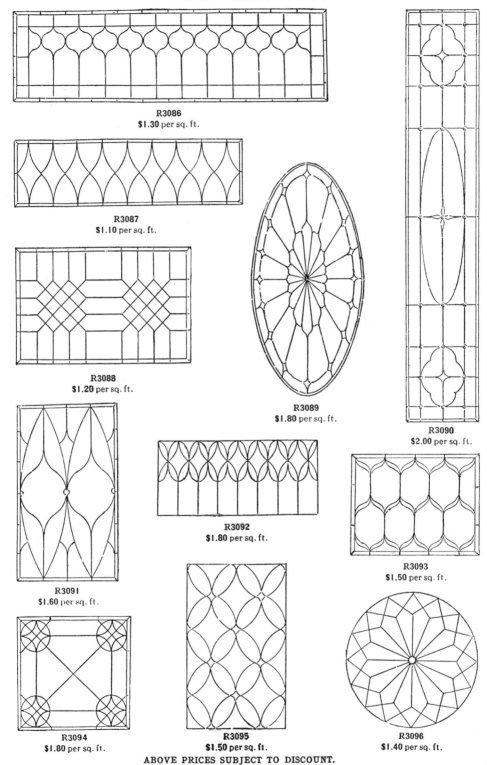

R3086
$1.30 per sq. ft.

R3087
$1.10 per sq. ft.

R3088
$1.20 per sq. ft.

R3089
$1.80 per sq. ft.

R3090
$2.00 per sq. ft.

R3091
$1.60 per sq. ft.

R3092
$1.80 per sq. ft.

R3093
$1.50 per sq. ft.

R3094
$1.80 per sq. ft.

R3095
$1.50 per sq. ft.

R3096
$1.40 per sq. ft.

ABOVE PRICES SUBJECT TO DISCOUNT.

LEADED CLEAR GLASS.

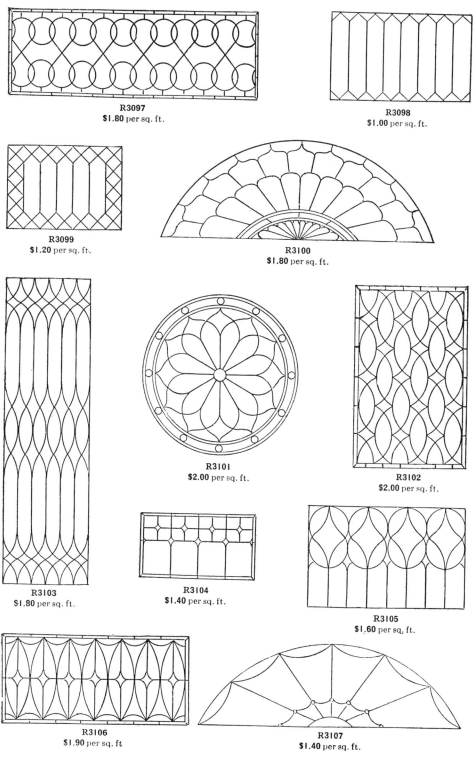

R3097
$1.80 per sq. ft.

R3098
$1.00 per sq. ft.

R3099
$1.20 per sq. ft.

R3100
$1.80 per sq. ft.

R3101
$2.00 per sq. ft.

R3102
$2.00 per sq. ft.

R3103
$1.80 per sq. ft.

R3104
$1.40 per sq. ft.

R3105
$1.60 per sq. ft.

R3106
$1.90 per sq. ft

R3107
$1.40 per sq. ft.

ABOVE PRICES SUBJECT TO DISCOUNT

LEADED ART GLASS.

R3108
$1.80 per sq. ft.

R3109
$1.50 per sq. ft.

R3110
$2.00 per sq ft

R3111
$3.00 per sq. ft.

R3112
$1.50 per sq. ft.

R3113
$2.70 per sq. ft.

R3114
$1.80 per sq. tt.

R3115
$2.70 per sq ft.

R3116
$1.10 per sq. ft.

R3117
$1.60 per sq. ft.

Designs R3110 R3117 are carried in stock.   40 x 14 and 44 x 16 inches at special prices.
See window designs page 61.   All other sizes as priced above.
ABOVE PRICES SUBJECT TO DISCOUNT.

LEADED ART GLASS.

R3118
$3.00 per sq. ft.

R3119
$2.00 per sq. ft

R3120
$2.30 per sq. ft.

R3121
$2.00 per sq. ft.

R3122
$4.00 per sq. ft.

R3123
$1.80 per sq. ft.

R3124
$3.00 per sq. ft.

R3125
$2.40 per sq. ft.

R3126
$2.30 per sq. ft.

R3127
$1.80 per sq. ft.

R3128
$2.00 per sq. ft.

R3129
$2.00 per sq. ft.

R3130 $2.00 per sq. tt.

R3131
$2.30 per sq. ft.

R3132
$2.30 per sq. ft.

ABOVE PRICES SUBJECT TO DISCOUNT.

LEADED BEVELED PLATE GLASS.

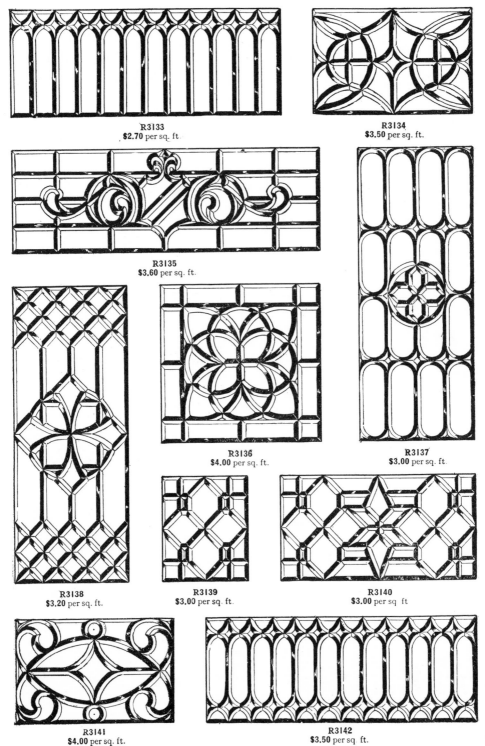

R3133
$2.70 per sq. ft.

R3134
$3.50 per sq. ft.

R3135
$3.60 per sq. ft.

R3136
$4.00 per sq. ft.

R3137
$3.00 per sq. ft.

R3138
$3.20 per sq. ft.

R3139
$3.00 per sq. ft.

R3140
$3.00 per sq ft

R3141
$4.00 per sq. ft.

R3142
$3.50 per sq. ft.

If set in copper bars add to above prices 20 per cent.
ABOVE PRICES SUBJECT TO DISCOUNT.

LEADED BEVELED PLATE GLASS.

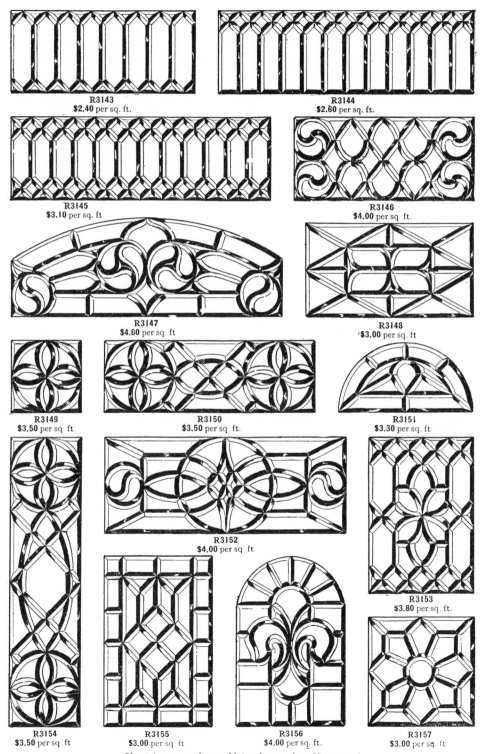

R3143
$2.40 per sq. ft.

R3144
$2.60 per sq. ft.

R3145
$3.10 per sq. ft

R3146
$4.00 per sq. ft.

R3147
$4.00 per sq ft

R3148
'$3.00 per sq. ft

R3149
$3.50 per sq. ft.

R3150
$3.50 per sq. ft.

R3151
$3.30 per sq. ft

R3152
$4.00 per sq ft

R3153
$3.80 per sq. ft.

R3154
$3.50 per sq. ft

R3155
$3.00 per sq ft

R3156
$4.00 per sq. ft.

R3157
$3.00 per sq. ft

If set in copper bars add to above prices 20 per cent.
ABOVE PRICES SUBJECT TO DISCOUNT.

LEADED ART GLASS.

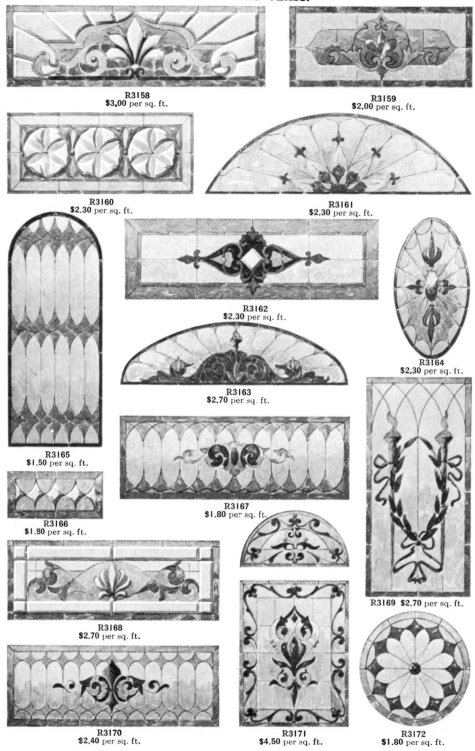

R3158
$3.00 per sq. ft.

R3159
$2.00 per sq. ft.

R3160
$2.30 per sq. ft.

R3161
$2.30 per sq. ft.

R3162
$2.30 per sq. ft.

R3163
$2.70 per sq. ft.

R3164
$2.30 per sq. ft.

R3165
$1.50 per sq. ft.

R3166
$1.80 per sq. ft.

R3167
$1.80 per sq. ft.

R3168
$2.70 per sq. ft.

R3169 $2.70 per sq. ft.

R3170
$2.40 per sq. ft.

R3171
$4.50 per sq. ft.

R3172
$1.80 per sq. ft.

ABOVE PRICES SUBJECT TO DISCOUNT.

LEADED ART GLASS.

R3173
$3.00 per sq. ft.

R3174
$5.00 per sq. ft.

R3175
$1.80 per sq. ft

R3176
$1.80 per sq. ft.

R3177
$1.80 per sq. ft.

R3178
$4.50 per sq. ft.

R3179
$5.20 per sq. ft.

R3180
$3.00 per sq. ft.

R3181
$3.00 per sq. ft.

R3182
$2.00 per sq. ft.

R3183
$2.50 per sq. ft.

R3184
$2.70 per sq. ft.

ABOVE PRICES SUBJECT TO DISCOUNT.

MITER CUT PLATE GLASS.

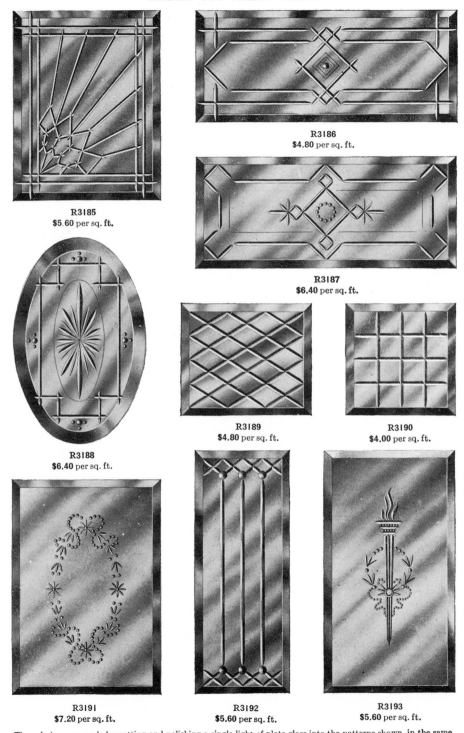

R3185
$5.60 per sq. ft.

R3186
$4.80 per sq. ft.

R3187
$6.40 per sq. ft.

R3188
$6.40 per sq. ft.

R3189
$4.80 per sq. ft.

R3190
$4.00 per sq. ft.

R3191
$7.20 per sq. ft.

R3192
$5.60 per sq. ft.

R3193
$5.60 per sq. ft.

These designs are made by cutting and polishing a single light of plate glass into the patterns shown, in the same manner that cut glass table ware is made. It is artistic and brilliant in its effect.

ABOVE PRICES SUBJECT TO DISCOUNT.

LEADED ART GLASS.

R3194
$5.00 per sq. ft.

R3195
$2.30 per sq. ft.

R3196 $4.50 per sq. ft.

R3197
$3.60 per sq. ft.

R3198
$4.50 per sq. ft.

R3199 $2.70 per sq. ft.

R3200
$4.20 per sq. ft.

R3201
$4.20 per sq. ft.

R3202
$3.00 per sq. ft.

R3203
$4.20 per sq. ft.

R3204
$4.20 per sq. ft.

R3205
$2.70 per sq. ft.

Designs R3200, R3201, R3203 and R3204 are designed for triple windows with transoms or can be used
separately with good effect.
ABOVE PRICES SUBJECT TO DISCOUNT.

LEADED WHITE AND CLEAR GLASS.

R3206
$2.00 per sq. ft.

R3207
$2.50 per sq. ft.

R3208
$2.00 per sq. ft.

R3209
$2.70 per sq. ft.

R3210
$3.00 per sq. ft.

R3211
$2.00 per sq. ft.

R3212
$1.80 per sq. ft.

R3213
$1.80 per sq. ft.

R3214
$2.30 per sq. ft.

R3215
$3.50 per sq. ft.

R3216
$2.30 per sq. ft.

R3217
$3.50 per sq. ft.

The above designs are made of clear double strength, white moss and white ondoyant glass, no colors of any kind being used. Where delicate effects are wanted they make a charming effect.

ABOVE PRICES SUBJECT TO DISCOUNT.

LEADED ART GLASS.

R3218 $2.50 per sq. ft.

R3219
$3.00 per sq. ft.

R3220
$2.50 per sq. ft.

R3221
$2.50 per sq. ft.

R3222
$2.50 per sq. ft.

R3223
$3.60 per sq. ft.

R3225
$3.00 per sq. ft.

R3226
$1.80 per sq. ft.

R3224
$3.00 per sq. ft.

R3227
$2.50 per sq. ft.

R3228
$2.70 per sq. ft.

R3229
$2.50 per sq. ft.

R3230
$2.50 per sq. ft.

R3231
$1.80 per sq. ft.

R3232
$1.80 per sq. ft.

R3233
$3.00 per sq. ft.

R3234
$2.50 per sq. ft.

R3235
$3.00 per sq. ft.

ABOVE PRICES SUBJECT TO DISCOUNT.

LEADED BEVELED PLATE GLASS.

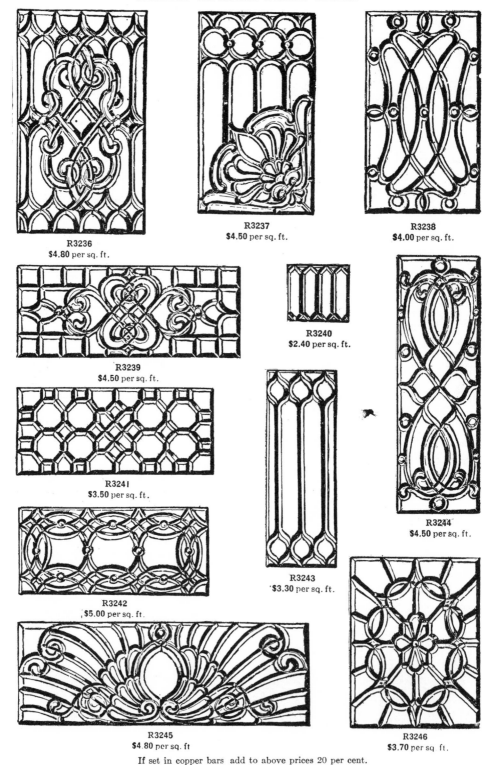

R3236
$4.80 per sq. ft.

R3237
$4.50 per sq. ft.

R3238
$4.00 per sq. ft.

R3239
$4.50 per sq. ft.

R3240
$2.40 per sq. ft.

R3241
$3.50 per sq. ft.

R3242
$5.00 per sq. ft.

R3243
$3.30 per sq. ft.

R3244
$4.50 per sq. ft.

R3245
$4.80 per sq. ft

R3246
$3.70 per sq. ft.

If set in copper bars add to above prices 20 per cent.
ABOVE PRICES SUBJECT TO DISCOUNT.

LEADED BEVELED PLATE GLASS.

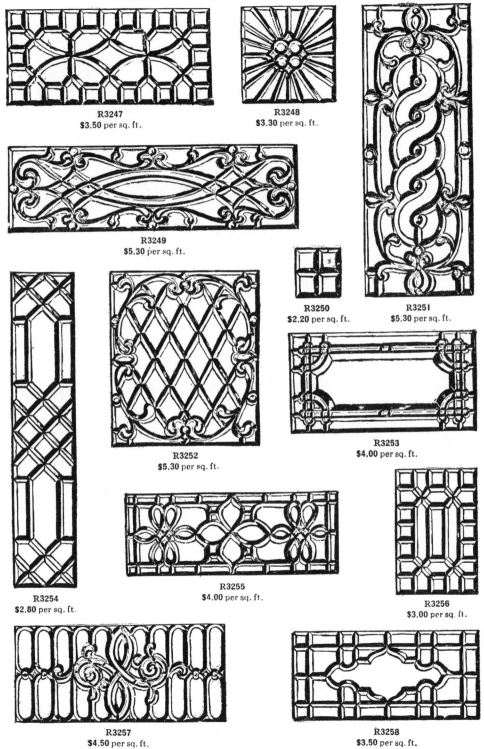

R3247
$3.50 per sq. ft.

R3248
$3.30 per sq. ft.

R3249
$5.30 per sq. ft.

R3250
$2.20 per sq. ft.

R3251
$5.30 per sq. ft.

R3252
$5.30 per sq. ft.

R3253
$4.00 per sq. ft.

R3254
$2.80 per sq. ft.

R3255
$4.00 per sq. ft.

R3256
$3.00 per sq. ft.

R3257
$4.50 per sq. ft.

R3258
$3.50 per sq. ft.

If set in copper bars add to above prices 20 per cent.

ABOVE PRICES SUBJECT TO DISCOUNT.

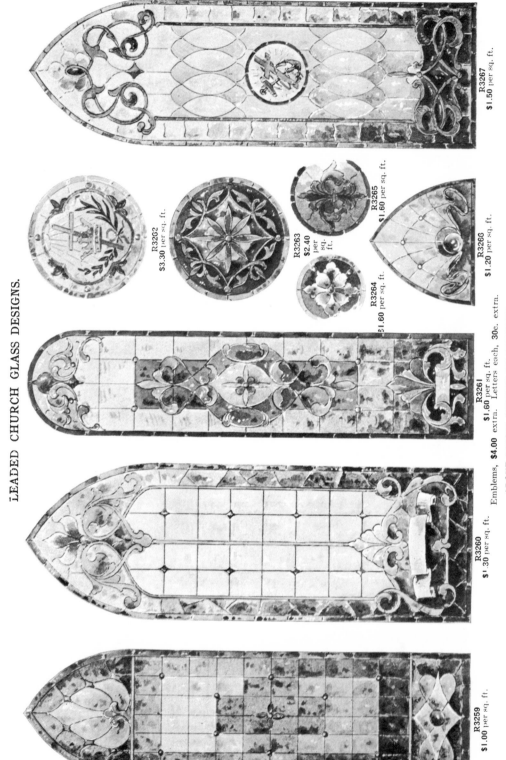

LEADED CHURCH GLASS DESIGNS.

R3267
$1.50 per sq. ft.

R3262
$3.30 per sq. ft.

R3263
$2.40 per sq. ft.

R3264
$1.60 per sq. ft.

R3265
$1.60 per sq. ft.

R3266
$1.20 per sq. ft.

R3261
$1.60 per sq. ft. Emblems, $4.00 extra. Letters each, 30c. extra.

R3260
$1.30 per sq. ft.

R3259
$1.00 per sq. ft.

ABOVE PRICES SUBJECT TO DISCOUNT.

CHURCH WINDOWS.

WITH WOOD BARS.

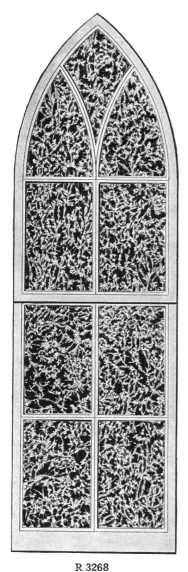

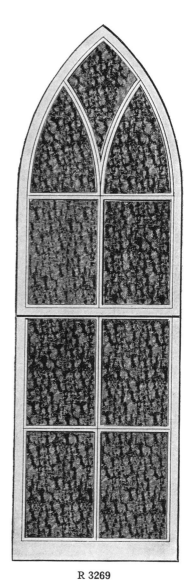

R 3268

Glazed with R3297.

R 3269

Glazed with R3299

Give exact width, total height in center, thickness of window and style of glazing in ordering or asking for estimate, also read note at bottom of page 54.

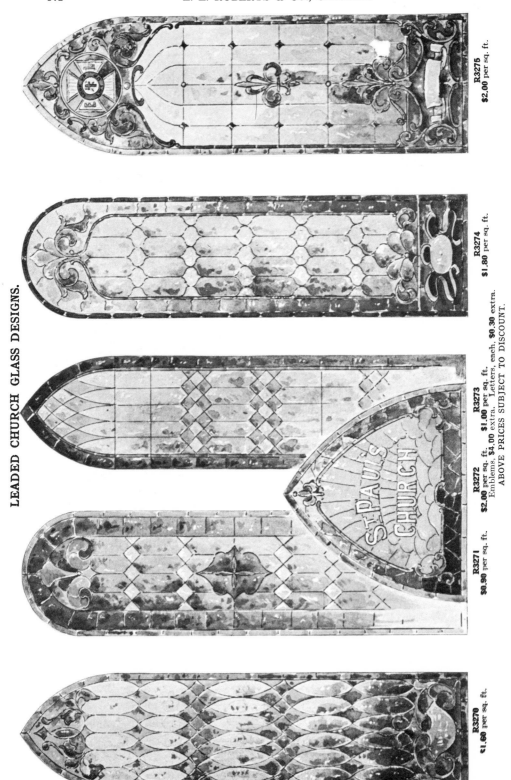

LEADED CHURCH GLASS DESIGNS.

R3275
$2.00 per sq. ft.

R3274
$1.80 per sq. ft.

R3273
$1.00 per sq. ft.

R3272
$2.00 per sq. ft.

R3271
$0.90 per sq. ft.

R3270
$1.60 per sq. ft.

Emblems, $4.00 extra. Letters, each, $0.30 extra.
ABOVE PRICES SUBJECT TO DISCOUNT.

CHURCH WINDOWS.

WITH WOOD BARS.

R 3276

Center glazed with R3298, border
assorted colors.

R 3277

Center glazed with R3299, border
assorted colors.

Give exact width, total height in center, thickness of window and style
of glazing in ordering or asking for estimate, also
read note at bottom of page 54.

LEADED CHURCH GLASS DESIGN.

R3278
$1.20 per sq. ft.
Emblems, **$4.00** each, extra.

R3279
$1.70 per sq. ft.
Letters, **$0.30** each, extra.   These designs can be used singly or in a triple opening as shown.

R3278
$1.20 per sq. ft.

ABOVE PRICES SUBJECT TO DISCOUNT.

CHURCH WINDOWS.

WITH WOOD BARS.

R 3280

Center glazed with R3296, border
assorted colors.

R 3281

Center glazed with R3297, border
assorted colors,

Give exact width, total height in center, thickness of window and style
of glazing in ordering or asking for estimate, also
read note at bottom of page 54.

LEADED CHURCH GLASS DESIGNS.

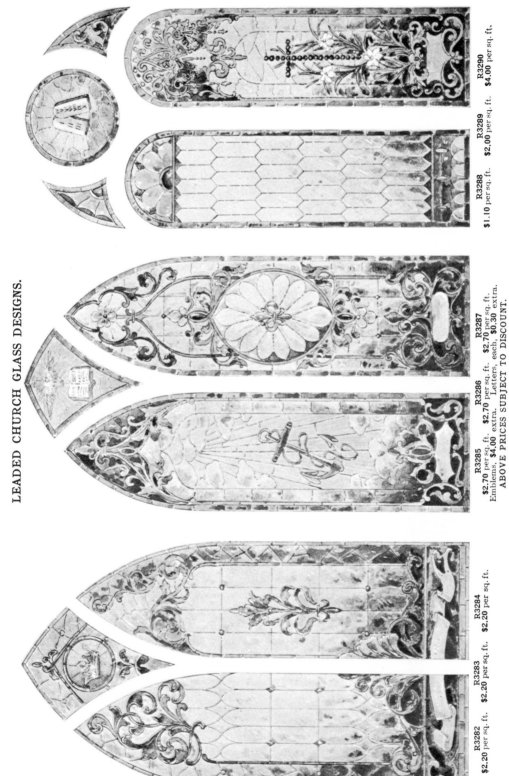

R3290 $4.00 per sq. ft.

R3289 $2.00 per sq. ft.

R3288 $1.10 per sq. ft.

R3287 $2.70 per sq. ft.

R3286 $2.70 per sq. ft.

R3285 $2.70 per sq. ft. Emblems, $4.00 extra. Letters, each, $0.30 extra.
ABOVE PRICES SUBJECT TO DISCOUNT.

R3284 $2.20 per sq. ft.

R3283 $2.20 per sq. ft.

R3282 $2.20 per sq. ft.

LEADED CHURCH GLASS DESIGNS.

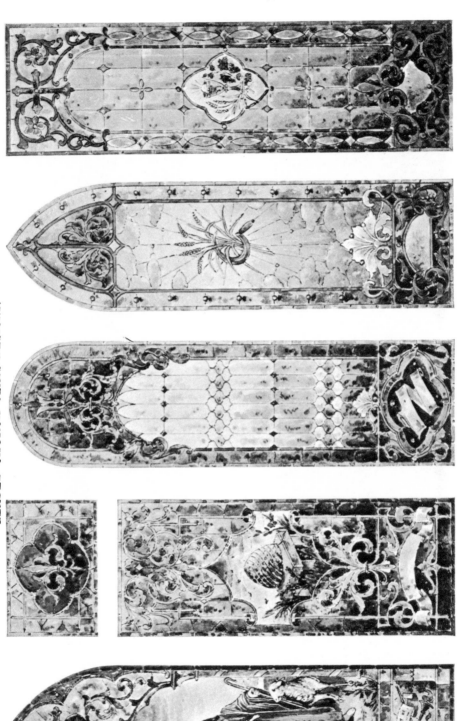

R3295
$2.40 per sq. ft.

R3294
$2.40 per sq. ft.   Ordinary sized emblem, $4.00 extra.

R3293
$2.40 per sq. ft.   Painted emblem in R3292, $40.00 extra.

R3292
$3.40 per sq. ft.   Painted figure in R3291, $150.00 extra.

R3291
$3.00 per sq. ft.
Letters, each, $0.30 extra.

ABOVE PRICES SUBJECT TO DISCOUNT.

FIGURED GLASS.

FOR DOORS, PARTITIONS AND CHURCH WINDOWS.

R 3296
Enameled Glass.
40 cents per square foot.

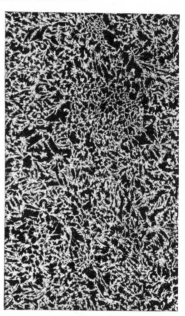

R 3297
Chipped Glass.
50 cents per square foot.

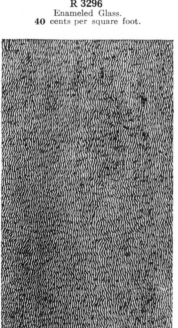

R 3298
Ondoyant Glass.
40 cents per square foot.

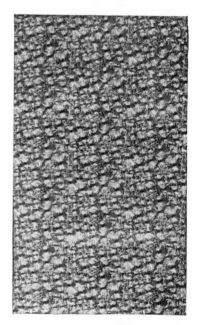

R 3299
Florentine Glass.
50 cents per square foot.

This glass carried in stock 30 inches in width and under.   The enameled, chipped and Florentine
are white, the ondoyant, both white and colored.
Special prices in large quantities.

ABOVE PRICES SUBJECT TO DISCOUNT.

HAND PAINTED EMBLEMS FOR CHURCH AND SOCIETY WINDOWS.

R3300	R3301	R3302
R3303	R3304	R3305
R3306	R3307	R3308
R3309	R3310	R3311

These emblems are usually made 12 inches in diameter and inserted in large windows as shown in design R3267. Prices each, **$4.00**. Will make estimate on larger sizes.

ABOVE PRICES SUBJECT TO DISCOUNT.

CHURCH DOORS.

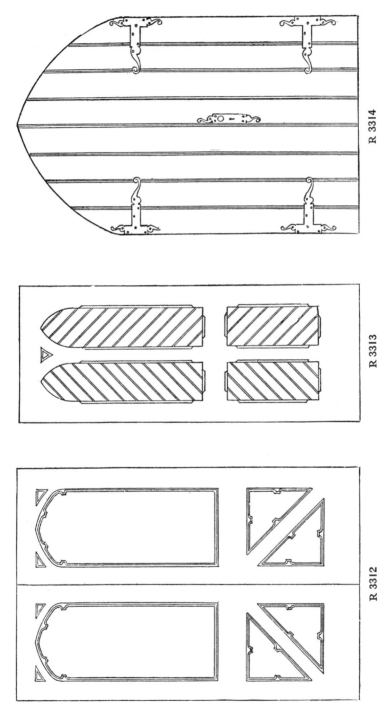

R 3314

R 3313

R 3312

Send sizes, thickness, kind of wood and full information in ordering or asking for estimate.

ALTAR RAILING.

PRICES FOR PLAIN RED OR WHITE OAK.
USUAL HEIGHT, TWO FEET.

R 3497

Railing, per lineal foot, **$6.00.**   Posts, each, **$6.00.**

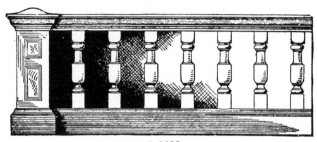

R 3498

Railing, per lineal foot **$3.50.**   Posts, each, **$7.00.**

R 3499

Railing, per lineal foot, **$7.50.**   Posts, each, **$6.00.**

ABOVE PRICES SUBJECT TO DISCOUNT.

OFFICE DESKS.

R 3600

R3600. 54 inches long; 36 inches wide; 50 inches high; weight, packed for shipment, 355 lbs., Price. $116.00
R3601. 60 "   "   36   "   "   50   "   "   "   "   "   "   375 "   "   126.00
R3602. 66 "   "   36   "   "   50   "   "   "   "   "   "   395 "   "   138.00
R3603. 72 "   "   36   "   "   50 "   "   "   "   "   "   415 "   "   152.00

Splendidly figured quartered golden oak, highy polished, extension slides, full
paneled and finished back, built up writing bed, indexed letter file,
convenient drawers of all sizes, wooden pigeon-hole boxes,
carved handle to drawers, elegant hardware and
a place for everything.

A desk suitable for the finest office at
moderate price.
Priced in mahogany upon request.

ABOVE PRICES SUBJECT TO DISCOUNT.

OFFICE DESKS.

R 3604

R3604.	50 inches long;	35 inches wide;	50 inches high; weight, packed for shipment,	295 lbs., Price, $	71.00
R3605.	54 "	" 35 "	" 50 " " " " " "	310 " "	78.00
R3606.	60 "	" 35 "	" 50 " " " " " "	325 " "	88.00
R3607.	66 "	" 35 "	" 50 " " " " " "	340 " "	97.00
R3608.	72 "	" 35 "	" 50 " " " " " "	355 " "	107.00

Selected quartered golden oak, polish finish, extension slides, full paneled and
finished back, built up writing bed, carved handles to drawers,
ball bearing casters, a splendid desk in
every partcular.

EXTRAS.

Cardboard Filing Boxes to fit above Pigeon Holes. Each, $0.30
Wood Front "   "   "   "   "   "   " 0.50
All Wood   "   "   "   "   "   "   " 0.75
Drop Front "   "   "   "   "   "   1.00

ABOVE PRICES SUBJECT TO DISCOUNT.

OFFICE DESKS.

R 3609

R3609. 50 inches long; 35 inches wide; 50 inches high; weight packed for shipment, 260 lbs.,   Price, **$54.00**
R3610. 54 "   " 35 "   " 50 "   "   "   "   "   280 "   "   59.00
R3611. 60 "   " 35 "   " 50 "   "   "   "   "   "   300 "   "   64.00

Plain golden oak, polished finish, full paneled and finished back, **built up** writing
bed, large center drawer and ball bearing casters.
A substantial and elegant desk at low price.
For prices of filing boxes to fit above pigeon holes see bottom of page 383.

ABOVE PRICES SUBJECT TO DISCOUNT.

OFFICE DESKS.

R 3612

R3612.	48 inches long; 30 inches wide; 49 inches high; weight, packed for shipment, 210 lbs.,											Price, $41.00
R3613.	54 "	"	30 "	"	49 "	"	"	"	"	"	"	225 "	" 45.00
R3614.	60 "	"	30 "	"	49 "	"	"	"	"	"	"	235 "	" 49.00

Plain golden oak, extension slides, partitioned cupboard on right side for large
books, ball bearing casters and good hardware.
A great bargain in low priced goods.

EXTRAS.

For finished oak panel in center, add to above price, $2.50.
For prices of filing boxes to fit above pigeon holes see bottom of page 383.

ABOVE PRICES SUBJECT TO DISCOUNT.

OFFICE DESKS.

R 3615

R3615.   42 inches long; 30 inches wide; 45 inches high; weight, packed for shipment, **160** lbs.

Price.............. **$33.00**

Plain golden oak, extension slide, ball bearing casters.   A well made desk for limited space.
For prices of filing boxes to fit above pigeon holes, see bottom of page 383.

R 3616

R3616.	50 inches long; 35 inches wide; weight, packed for shipment, 180 lbs.								Price, $35.00
R3617.	54 "	" 35 "	"	"	"	"	"	190 "	"	39.00
R3618.	60 "	" 35 "	"	"	"	"	"	200 "	"	42.00
R3619.	54 "	" 48 "	"	(Double Desk) "	"	255 "	"	57.00
R3620.	60 "	" 48 "	"	"	"	"	"	275 "	"	64.00

Plain golden oak, polished finish, large center drawer, ball bearing casters.
Double desks alike on both sides.
A splendid article in every particular.

ABOVE PRICES SUBJECT TO DISCOUNT.

OFFICE DESKS.

R 3621

R3621.	72 inches long; 34 inches wide; weight, packed for shipment, 175 lbs.							Price,	**$35.00**
R3622.	96 "	"	34 "	"	"		210 "	"	**43.00**
R3623.	72 "	"	54 "	"	(Double Desk) "	"	235 "	"	**52.00**
R3624.	96 "	"	54 "	"	"	"	300 "	"	**65.00**

Plain golden oak, rubbed finish, a well made and durable desk.

R 3625

R3625.	72 inches long; 34 inches wide; weight, packed for shipment, 275 lbs....Price,	**$105.00**
R3626.	96 "	"	34 "	"	"	350 ".... " **130.00**

Cashier's desk. Plain golden oak, rubbed finish, one cash drawer with Yale lock,
chipped glass screen, open in center, with shelf on outside.
An elegant fixture for store or office.

ABOVE PRICES SUBJECT TO DISCOUNT.

TYPEWRITER DESKS.

R 3627

Plain golden oak, gloss finish, 3 feet long, 2 feet 6 inches wide, extension
slide, paneled finished back.
A complete flat top desk when closed.
Keeps machine free from dust.
Weight, packed for shipment, 125 lbs.

Price, $37.00

R 3628

Plain golden oak, gloss finish, 4 feet long, 2 feet 6 inches wide, extension
slides, paneled finished back.
A complete flat top desk when closed.
Keeps machine free from dust when not in use.
Weight, packed for shipment, 160 lbs.

Price, $43.00

ABOVE PRICES SUBJECT TO DISCOUNT.

OFFICE CHAIRS AND STOOLS.

R 3629

Golden oak, weight, packed for shipment, 65 lbs.
A good pivot chair for medium priced desk.
Price, with wooden seat.................$ 9.00
"   "   cane   " 10.00

R 3630

Golden oak, weight, packed for shipment, 75 lbs.
A splendid highly polished pivot chair for
high grade desk.
Price................................$16.00

R 3631

Golden oak, weight, packed for shipment, 30 lbs.
A well made and durable stool with
adjustable pivot top.
Price with wooden seat....................$5.50
"   "   cane   " 6.00

R 3632

Golden oak, weight, packed for shipment, 30 lbs.
A comfortable and durable stool with
adjustable pivot top.
Price with wooden seat....................$7.50
"   "   cane   " 8.00

ABOVE PRICES SUBJECT TO DISCOUNT.

BUILDING AND ROOFING PAPERS.

ROBERTS.

Rosin sized sheathing, **30** lbs. to the roll.

EUREKA.

Rosin sized sheathing, **20** lbs. to the roll.

Each roll contains **500** square feet.
These papers are made especially for our trade.
They are strictly felt filled and therefore better adapted to with-
stand moisture and cold than the ordinary
pulp filled stock.

We can also make prompt shipment of the following
at market prices:

PLAIN BOARD	**700** square feet to **100** pounds.
TARRED BOARD	**600** " " " **100** "
INODOROUS BOARD	**600** " " " **100** "
TARRED FELT	**650** " " " **100** "
THREADED FELT	**500** " " to the roll.
DEADENING FELT	**1½** pounds to the square yard.
CARPET LININGS	**50** yards to the roll.

VULCANITE ASPHALT ROOFING.

Coated both sides with Silicate.

No painting required. Will last a lifetime.
Guaranteed to contain no coal tar.
Positively the best roofing on the market.
Carried in stock in three weights. Light, Heavy and Extra Heavy.
Each roll will cover **100** square feet.
Send for samples and book of information.

THREE-PLY BLACK DIAMOND ROOFING.

We are also prepared to ship quickly this well known roofing with
all supplies for finishing complete.
Each roll will cover **100** square feet.
Prices quoted on application.
Special prices for orders of **25** rolls or over.

OFFICIAL

·CHICAGO MOULDING BOOK
(ILLUSTRATED)

SHOWING FULL FINISHED SIZE OF

MOULDINGS

WITH EXACT SIZE AND LIST PRICE PER ONE HUNDRED LINEAL FEET MARKED ON EACH

ADOPTED MAY 2, 1901

MOULDINGS.

Our mouldings are smoothly manufactured from thoroughly seasoned stock and are strictly up to grade.

———

See pages 144 to 165 for special hardwood moulding designs in actual colors.

Pressed, Turned and Roped Mouldings, Pages 211 to 214.

List Prices as given are per 100 lineal feet.

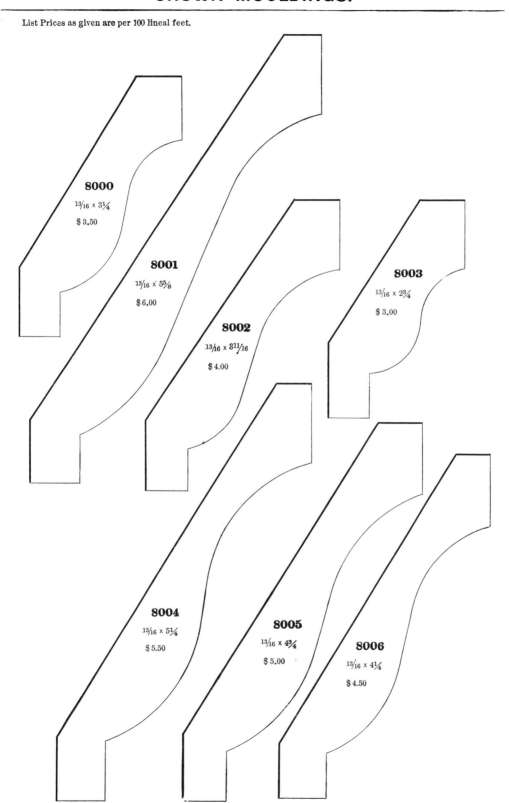

8000

$13/16 \times 3\frac{1}{4}$

$ 3.50

8001

$13/16 \times 5\frac{5}{8}$

$ 6.00

8002

$13/16 \times 3\frac{11}{16}$

$ 4.00

8003

$13/16 \times 2\frac{3}{4}$

$ 3.00

8004

$13/16 \times 5\frac{1}{4}$

$ 5.50

8005

$13/16 \times 4\frac{3}{4}$

$ 5.00

8006

$13/16 \times 4\frac{1}{4}$

$ 4.50

List Prices as given are per 100 lineal feet.

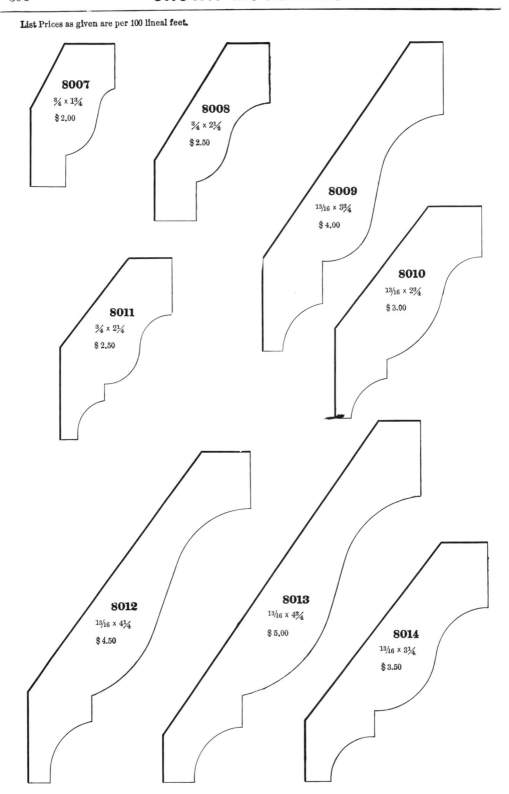

8007
¾ x 1¾
$ 2.00

8008
¾ x 2¼
$ 2.50

8009
13/16 x 3¾
$ 4.00

8010
13/16 x 2¾
$ 3.00

8011
¾ x 2¼
$ 2.50

8012
13/16 x 4¼
$ 4.50

8013
13/16 x 4¾
$ 5.00

8014
13/16 x 3¼
$ 3.50

List Prices as given are per 100 lineal feet.

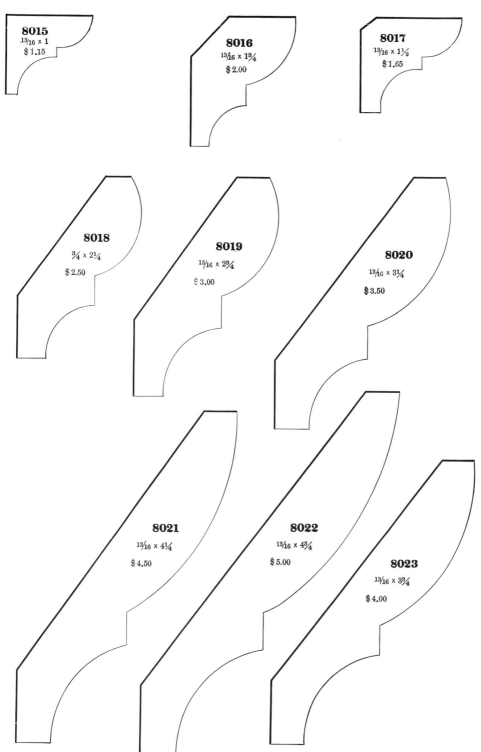

8015
$\frac{13}{16} \times 1$
$ 1.15

8016
$\frac{13}{16} \times 1\frac{3}{4}$
$ 2.00

8017
$\frac{13}{16} \times 1\frac{1}{2}$
$ 1.65

8018
$\frac{3}{4} \times 2\frac{1}{4}$
$ 2.50

8019
$\frac{13}{16} \times 2\frac{3}{4}$
$ 3.00

8020
$\frac{13}{16} \times 3\frac{1}{4}$
$ 3.50

8021
$\frac{13}{16} \times 4\frac{1}{4}$
$ 4.50

8022
$\frac{13}{16} \times 4\frac{3}{4}$
$ 5.00

8023
$\frac{13}{16} \times 3\frac{3}{4}$
$ 4.00

List Prices as given are per 100 lineal feet.

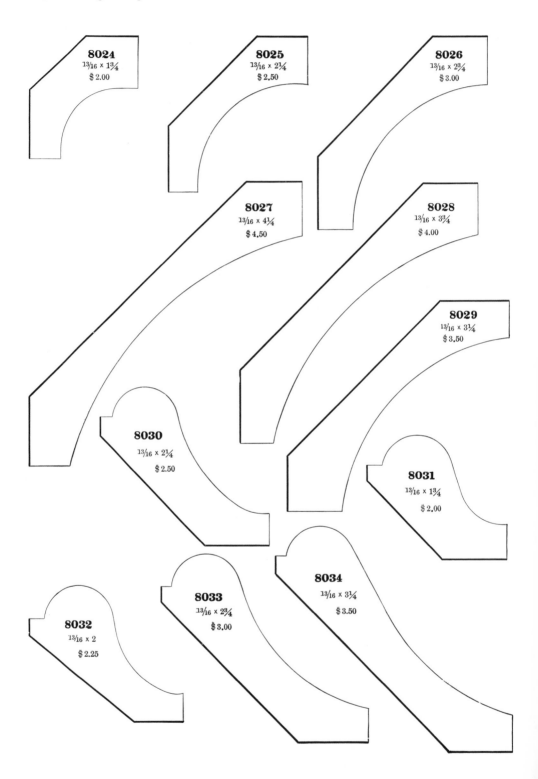

8024
13/16 x 1¾
$ 2.00

8025
13/16 x 2¼
$ 2.50

8026
13/16 x 2¾
$ 3.00

8027
13/16 x 4¼
$ 4.50

8028
13/16 x 3¾
$ 4.00

8029
13/16 x 3¼
$ 3.50

8030
13/16 x 2¼
$ 2.50

8031
13/16 x 1¾
$ 2.00

8032
13/16 x 2
$ 2.25

8033
13/16 x 2¾
$ 3.00

8034
13/16 x 3¼
$ 3.50

List Prices as given are per 100 lineal feet.

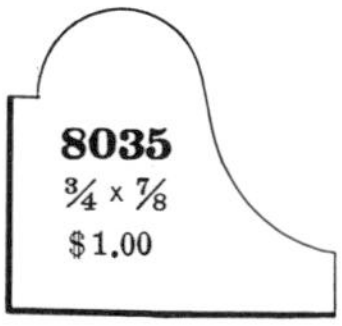

8035
¾ x ⅞
$1.00

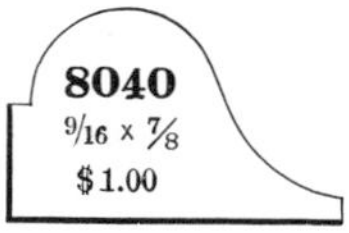

8040
9/16 x ⅞
$1.00

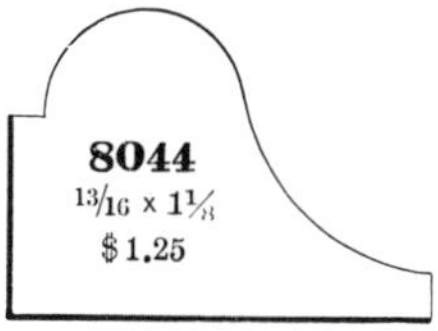

8044
13/16 x 1⅛
$1.25

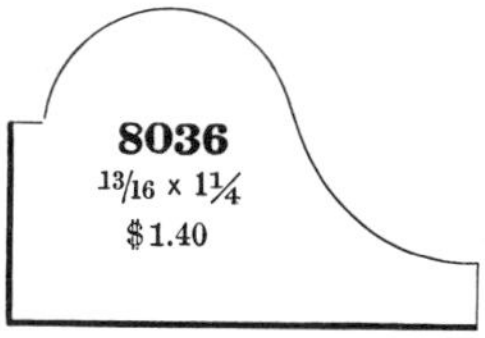

8036
13/16 x 1¼
$1.40

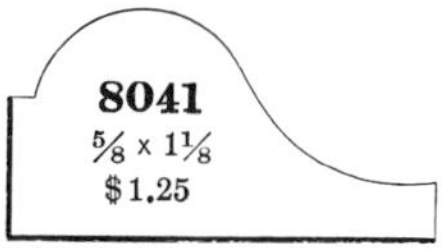

8041
⅝ x 1⅛
$1.25

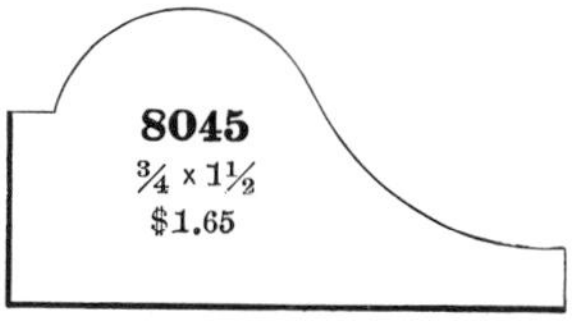

8045
¾ x 1½
$1.65

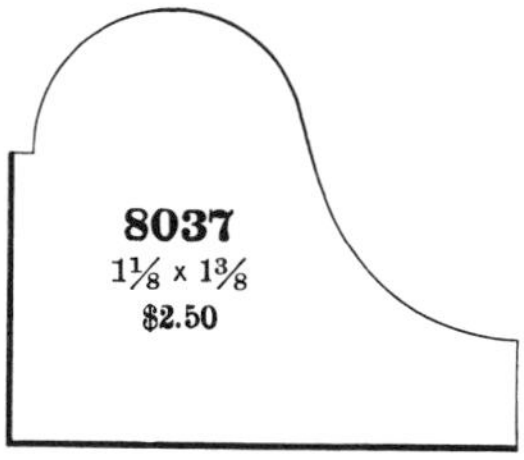

8037
1⅛ x 1⅜
$2.50

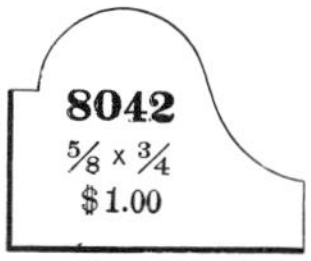

8042
⅝ x ¾
$1.00

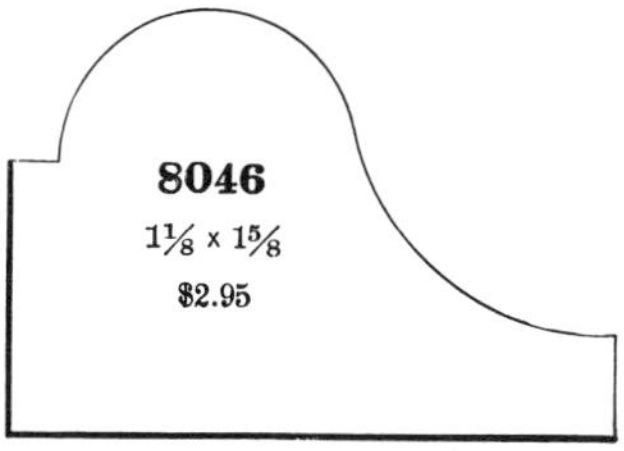

8046
1⅛ x 1⅝
$2.95

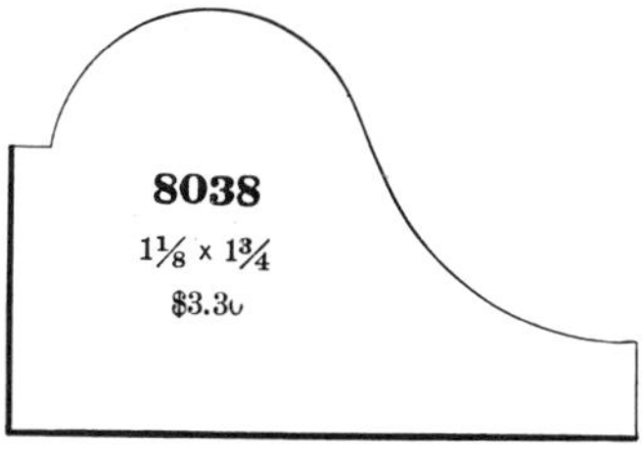

8038
1⅛ x 1¾
$3.30

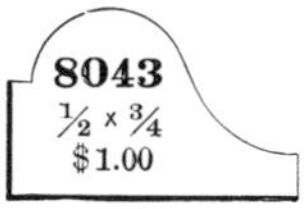

8043
½ x ¾
$1.00

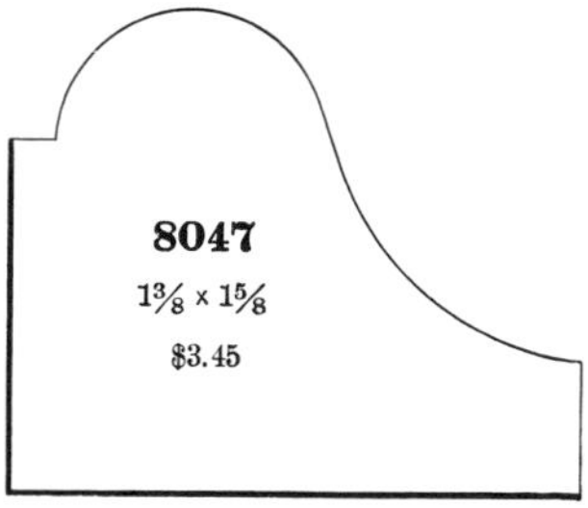

8047
1⅜ x 1⅝
$3.45

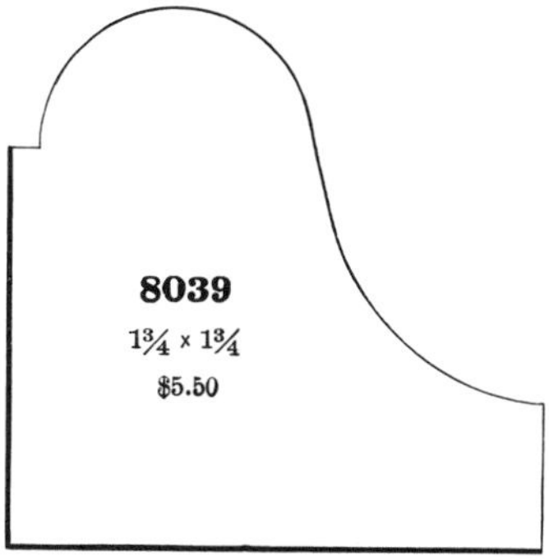

8039
1¾ x 1¾
$5.50

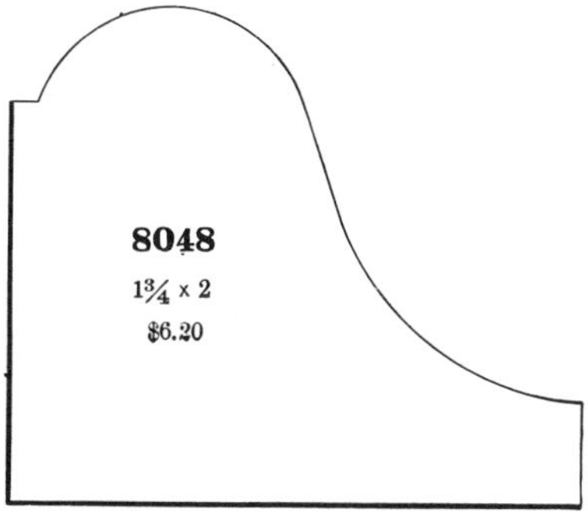

8048
1¾ x 2
$6.20

List Prices as given are per 100 lineal feet.

8049
1⅝ × 1⅝
$4.85

8054
13/16 × 1
$1.15

8058
⅜ × ⅝
$1.00

8050
1¼ × 1¼
$2.75

8055
1⅜
$3.30

8059
½ × ⅞
$1.00

8051
1 × 1
$1.70

8056
1⅝
$4.85

8060
¾ × ⅞
$1.00

8052
¾ × ¾
$1.00

8061
13/16 × 1⅛
$1.25

8057
1⅝
$4.85

8062
13/16 × 1¾
$2.00

8053
⅝ × ⅝
$1.00

List Prices as given are per 100 lineal feet.

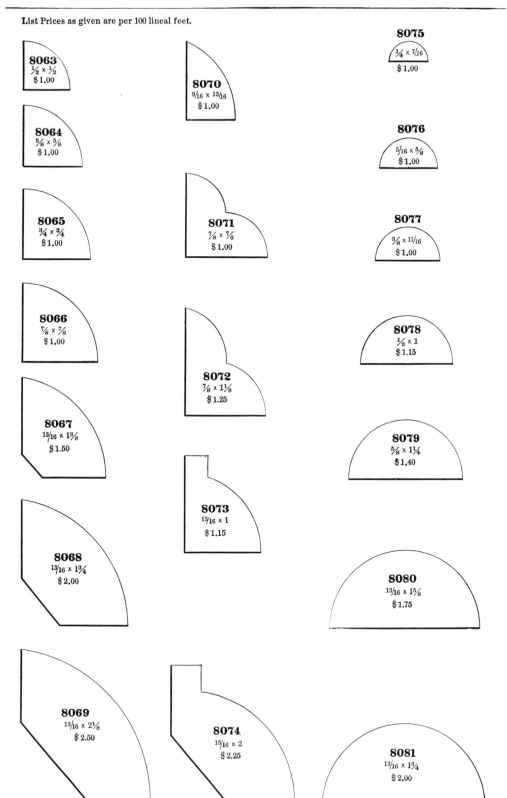

8063
½ × ½
$1.00

8064
⅝ × ⅝
$1.00

8065
¾ × ¾
$1.00

8066
⅞ × ⅞
$1.00

8067
13/16 × 1⅜
$1.50

8068
13/16 × 1¾
$2.00

8069
13/16 × 2⅛
$2.50

8070
9/16 × 13/16
$1.00

8071
⅞ × ⅞
$1.00

8072
⅞ × 1⅛
$1.25

8073
13/16 × 1
$1.15

8074
13/16 × 2
$2.25

8075
¼ × 7/16
$1.00

8076
5/16 × ⅝
$1.00

8077
⅜ × 11/16
$1.00

8078
½ × 1
$1.15

8079
⅝ × 1¼
$1.40

8080
13/16 × 1⅝
$1.75

8081
13/16 × 1¾
$2.00

O. G. STOPS.

List Prices as given are per 100 lineal feet.

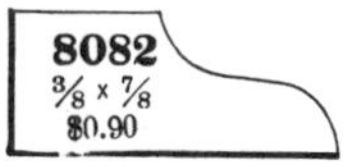

8082
⅜ x ⅞
$0.90

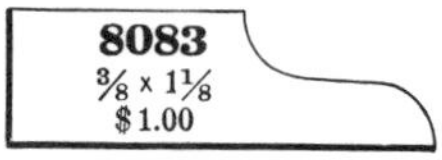

8083
⅜ x 1⅛
$1.00

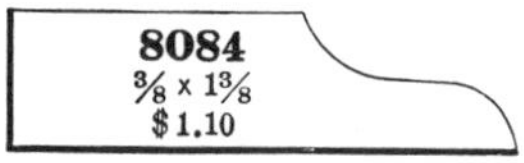

8084
⅜ x 1⅜
$1.10

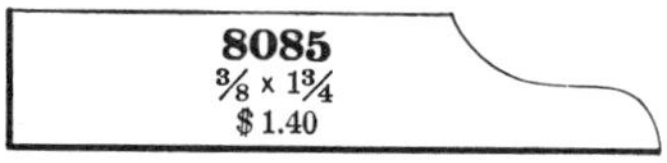

8085
⅜ x 1¾
$1.40

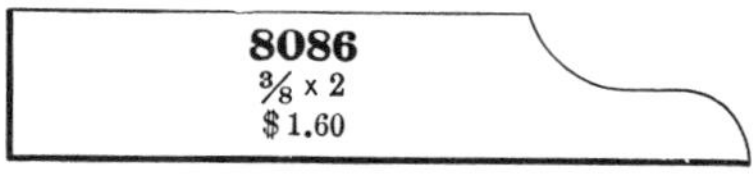

8086
⅜ x 2
$1.60

8087
⅜ x 2¼
$1.80

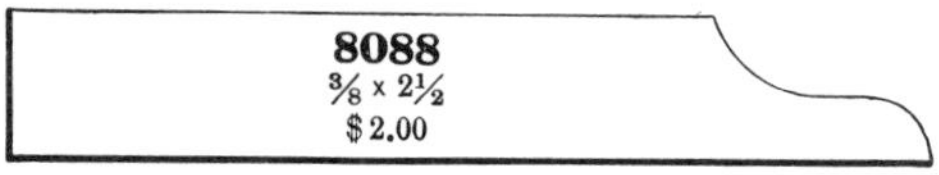

8088
⅜ x 2½
$2.00

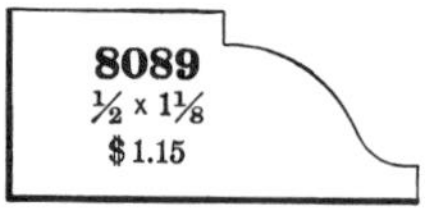

8089
½ x 1⅛
$1.15

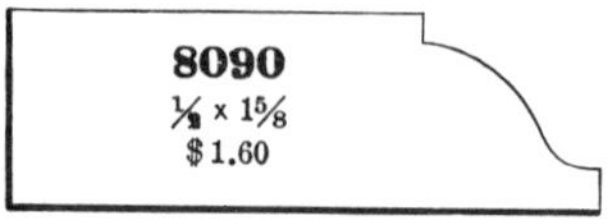

8090
½ x 1⅝
$1.60

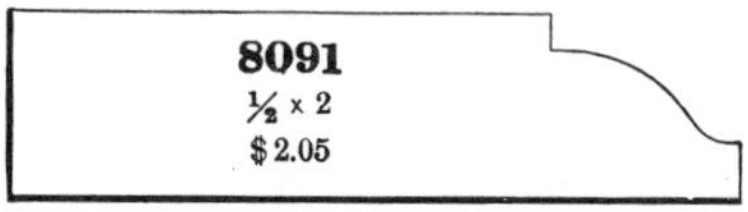

8091
½ x 2
$2.05

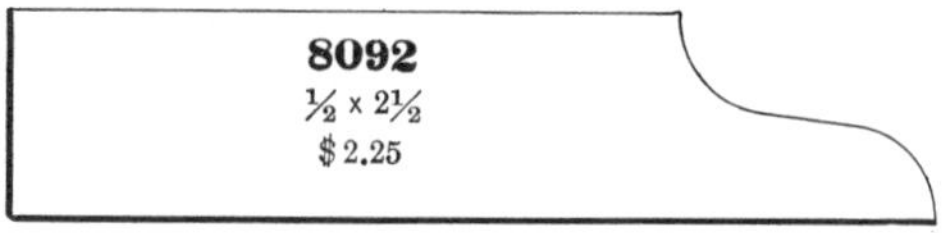

8092
½ x 2½
$ 2.25

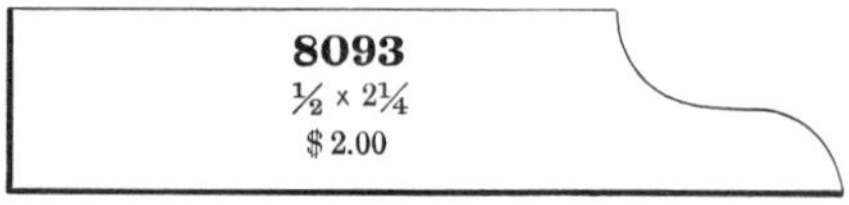

8093
½ x 2¼
$ 2.00

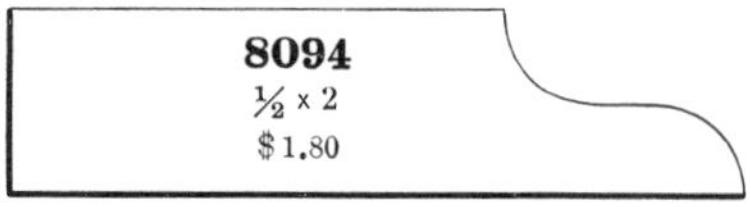

8094
½ x 2
$ 1.80

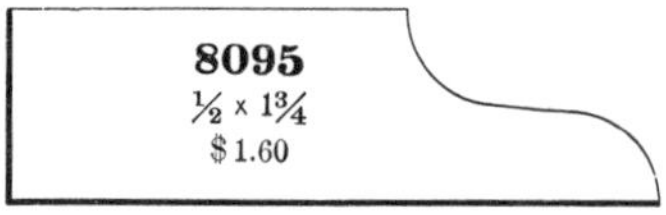

8095
½ x 1¾
$ 1.60

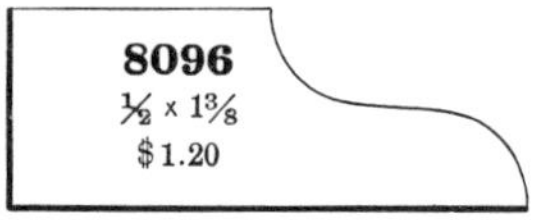

8096
½ x 1⅜
$ 1.20

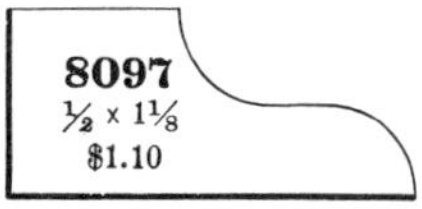

8097
½ x 1⅛
$1.10

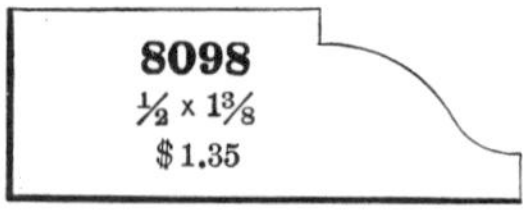

8098
½ x 1⅜
$ 1.35

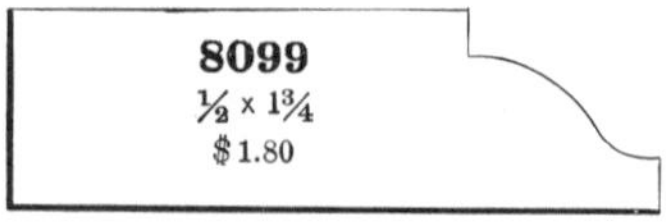

8099
½ x 1¾
$ 1.80

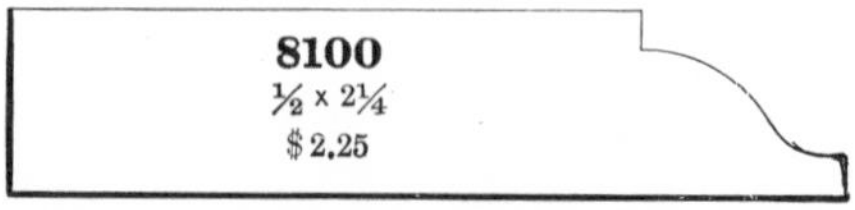

8100
½ x 2¼
$ 2.25

List Prices as given are per 100 lineal feet.

8101
3/8 x 1 1/8
$ 1.05

8112
1/2 x 2 1/2
$ 2.50

8102
3/8 x 1 3/8
$ 1.20

8113
1/2 x 2 1/4
$ 2.25

8103
3/8 x 1 3/4
$ 1.60

8114
1/2 x 2
$ 2.05

8104
3/8 x 2
$ 1.85

8115
1/2 x 1 3/4
$ 1.80

8105
3/8 x 2 1/4
$ 2.00

8116
1/2 x 1 3/8
$ 1.35

8106
3/8 x 2 1/2
$ 2.25

8117
1/2 x 1 1/8
$ 1.15

8107
3/8 x 2 1/4
$ 2.00

8118
1/2 x 1 1/8
$ 1.15

8108
3/8 x 2
$ 1.85

8119
1/2 x 1 3/8
$ 1.35

8109
3/8 x 1 3/4
$ 1.60

8120
1/2 x 1 3/4
$ 1.80

8110
3/8 x 1 3/8
$ 1.20

8121
1/2 x 2
$ 2.05

8111
3/8 x 1 1/8
$ 1.05

8122
1/2 x 2 1/4
$ 2.25

List Prices as given are per 100 lineal feet.

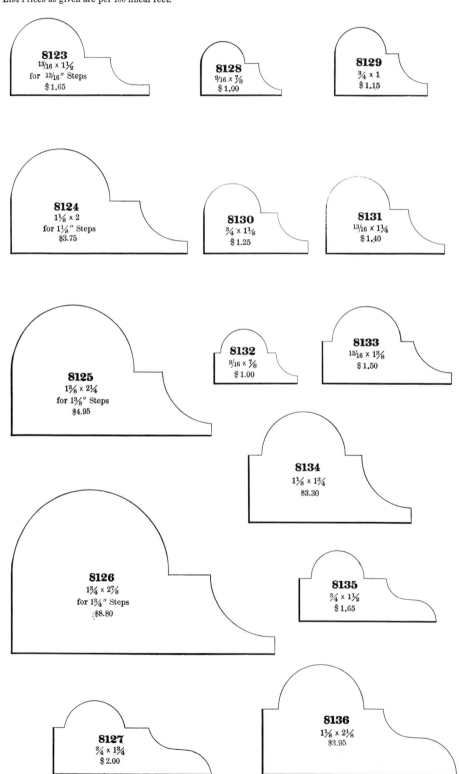

8123
13/16 x 1½
for 13/16″ Steps
$1.65

8128
9/16 x 7/8
$1.00

8129
¾ x 1
$1.15

8124
1⅛ x 2
for 1⅛″ Steps
$3.75

8130
¾ x 1⅛
$1.25

8131
13/16 x 1¼
$1.40

8125
1⅜ x 2¼
for 1⅜″ Steps
$4.95

8132
9/16 x 7/8
$1.00

8133
13/16 x 1⅜
$1.50

8134
1⅛ x 1¾
$3.30

8126
1¾ x 2⅞
for 1¾″ Steps
$8.80

8135
¾ x 1½
$1.65

8127
¾ x 1¾
$2.00

8136
1⅛ x 2⅛
$3.95

List Prices as given are per 100 lineal feet.

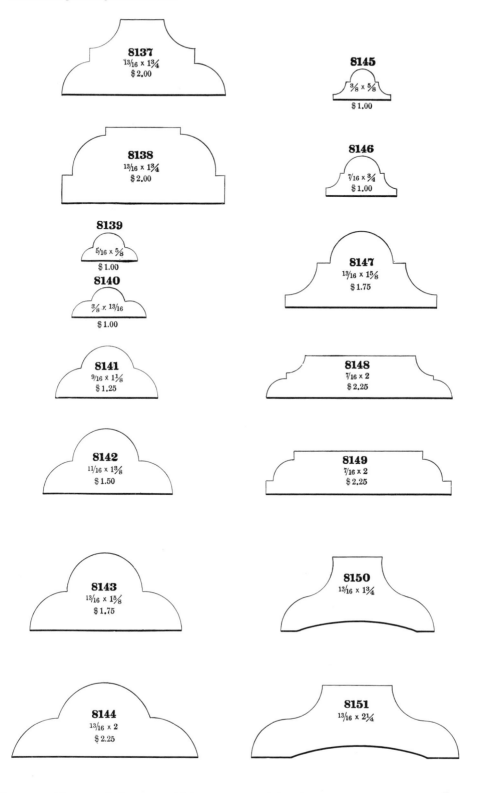

8137
$\frac{13}{16} \times 1\frac{3}{4}$
$ 2.00

8138
$\frac{13}{16} \times 1\frac{3}{4}$
$ 2.00

8139
$\frac{5}{16} \times \frac{5}{8}$
$ 1.00

8140
$\frac{3}{8} \times \frac{13}{16}$
$ 1.00

8141
$\frac{9}{16} \times 1\frac{1}{8}$
$ 1.25

8142
$\frac{11}{16} \times 1\frac{3}{8}$
$ 1.50

8143
$\frac{13}{16} \times 1\frac{5}{8}$
$ 1.75

8144
$\frac{13}{16} \times 2$
$ 2.25

8145
$\frac{3}{8} \times \frac{5}{8}$
$ 1.00

8146
$\frac{7}{16} \times \frac{3}{4}$
$ 1.00

8147
$\frac{13}{16} \times 1\frac{5}{8}$
$ 1.75

8148
$\frac{7}{16} \times 2$
$ 2.25

8149
$\frac{7}{16} \times 2$
$ 2.25

8150
$\frac{13}{16} \times 1\frac{3}{4}$

8151
$\frac{13}{16} \times 2\frac{1}{4}$

List Prices as given are per 100 lineal feet.

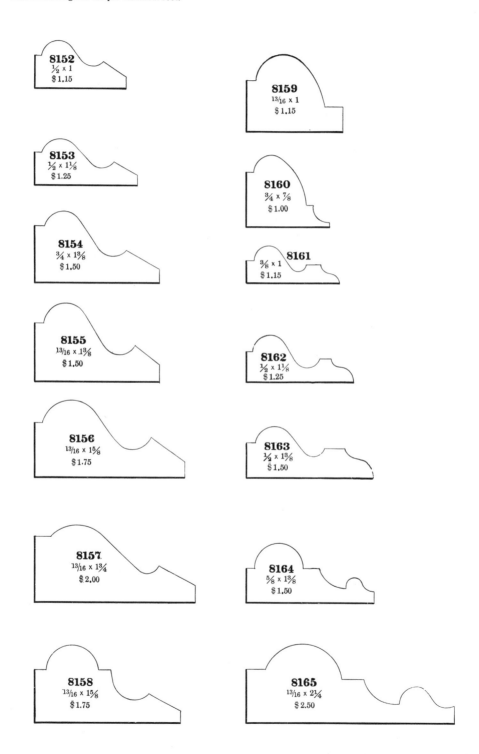

8152
½ x 1
$1.15

8153
½ x 1⅛
$1.25

8154
¾ x 1⅜
$1.50

8155
13⁄16 x 1⅜
$1.50

8156
13⁄16 x 1⅝
$1.75

8157
13⁄16 x 1¾
$2.00

8158
13⁄16 x 1⅝
$1.75

8159
13⁄16 x 1
$1.15

8160
¾ x ⅞
$1.00

8161
⅜ x 1
$1.15

8162
½ x 1⅛
$1.25

8163
½ x 1⅜
$1.50

8164
⅝ x 1⅜
$1.50

8165
13⁄16 x 2¼
$2.50

List Prices as given are per 100 lineal feet.

8166
⅝ x 1⅛
$1.25

8172
9/16 x 1¾
$2.00

8167
⅝ x 1¼
$1.40

8173
13/16 x 1¾
$2.00

8168
¾ x 1¾
$2.00

8174
¾ x 1⅝
$1.75

8169
¾ x 1¼
$1.40

8175
¾ x 1¾
$2.00

8170
13/16 x 1½
$1.65

8176
13/16 x 1¾
$2.00

8171
13/16 x 1¾
$2.00

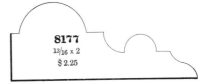

8177
13/16 x 2
$2.25

List Prices as given are per 100 lineal feet.

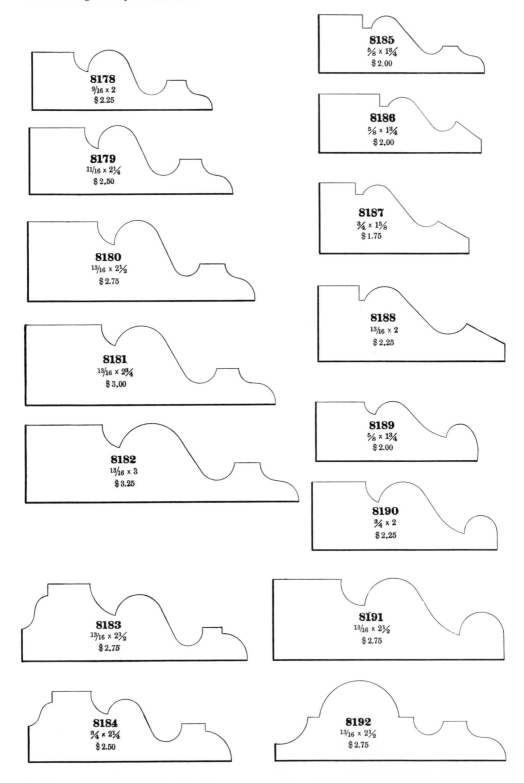

8178
9/16 x 2
$ 2.25

8179
11/16 x 2¼
$ 2.50

8180
13/16 x 2½
$ 2.75

8181
13/16 x 2¾
$ 3.00

8182
13/16 x 3
$ 3.25

8183
13/16 x 2½
$ 2.75

8184
¾ x 2¼
$ 2.50

8185
⅝ x 1¾
$ 2.00

8186
⅝ x 1¾
$ 2.00

8187
¾ x 1⅝
$ 1.75

8188
13/16 x 2
$ 2.25

8189
⅝ x 1¾
$ 2.00

8190
¾ x 2
$ 2.25

8191
13/16 x 2½
$ 2.75

8192
13/16 x 2½
$ 2.75

List Prices as given are per 100 lineal feet.

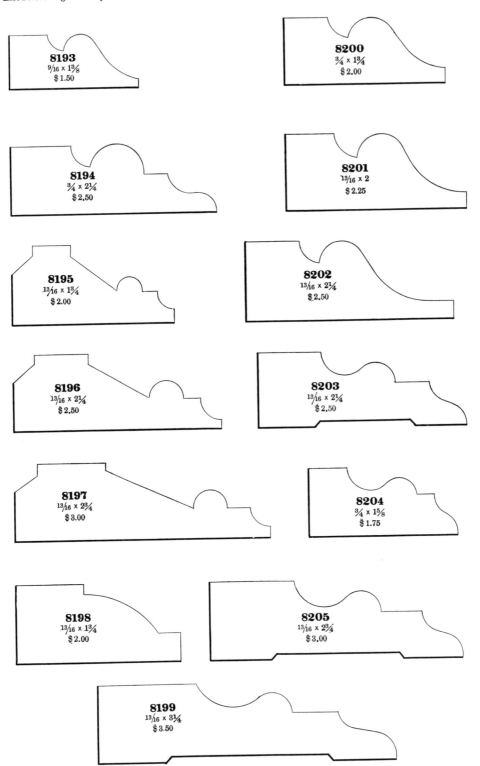

8193
9/16 x 1⅜
$ 1.50

8200
¾ x 1¾
$ 2.00

8194
¾ x 2¼
$ 2.50

8201
13/16 x 2
$ 2.25

8195
13/16 x 1¾
$ 2.00

8202
13/16 x 2¼
$ 2.50

8196
13/16 x 2¼
$ 2.50

8203
13/16 x 2¼
$ 2.50

8197
13/16 x 2¾
$ 3.00

8204
¾ x 1⅝
$ 1.75

8198
13/16 x 1¾
$ 2.00

8205
13/16 x 2¾
$ 3.00

8199
13/16 x 3¼
$ 3.50

List Prices as given are per 100 lineal feet.

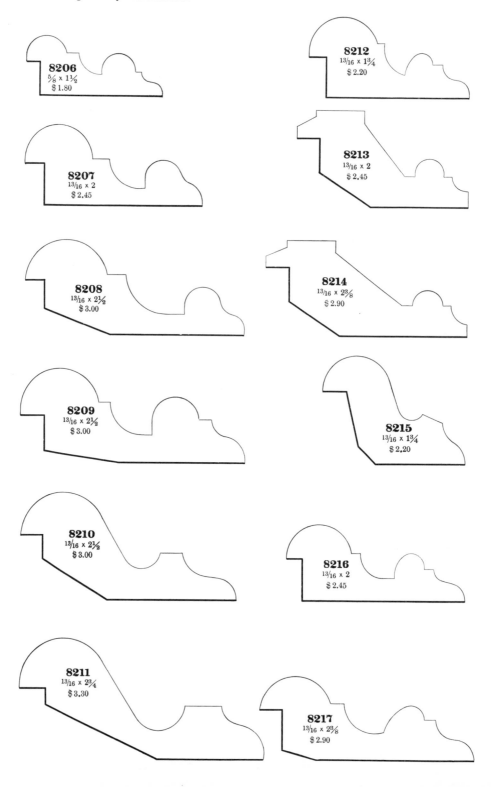

8206
5/8 x 1½
$ 1.80

8207
13/16 x 2
$ 2.45

8208
13/16 x 2½
$ 3.00

8209
13/16 x 2½
$ 3.00

8210
13/16 x 2½
$ 3.00

8211
13/16 x 2¾
$ 3.30

8212
13/16 x 1¾
$ 2.20

8213
13/16 x 2
$ 2.45

8214
13/16 x 2⅜
$ 2.90

8215
13/16 x 1¾
$ 2.20

8216
13/16 x 2
$ 2.45

8217
13/16 x 2⅜
$ 2.90

List Prices as given are per 100 lineal feet.

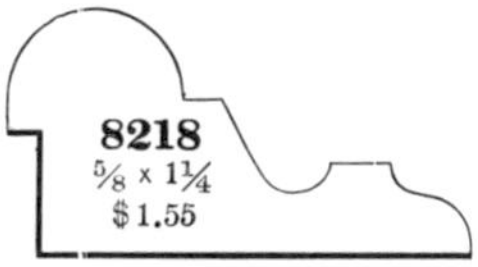

8218
5/8 x 1¼
$ 1.55

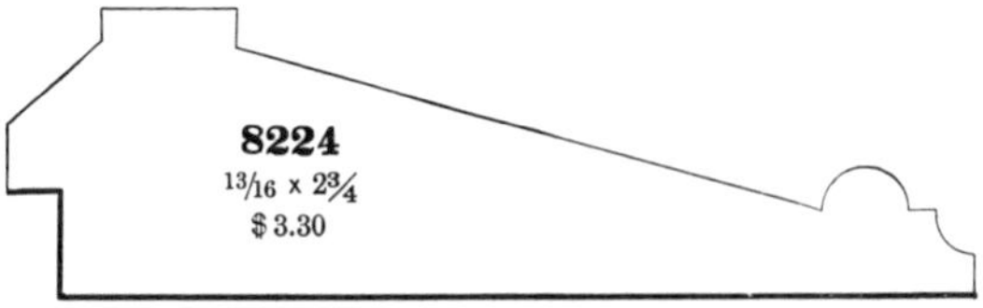

8224
13/16 x 2¾
$ 3.30

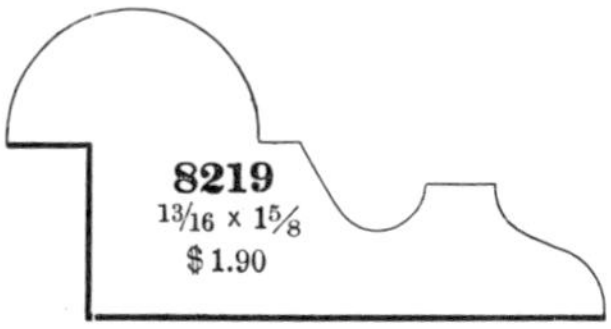

8219
13/16 x 1⅝
$ 1.90

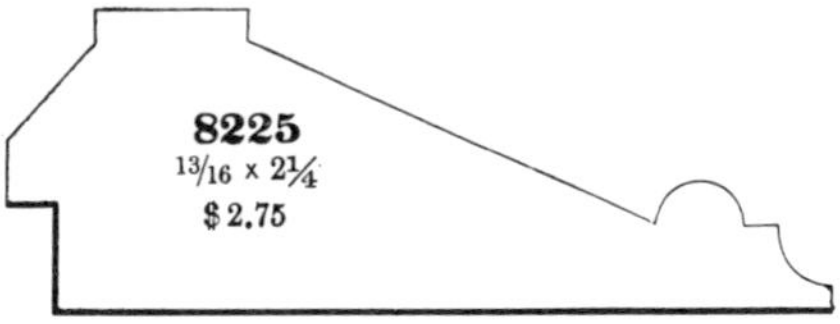

8225
13/16 x 2¼
$ 2.75

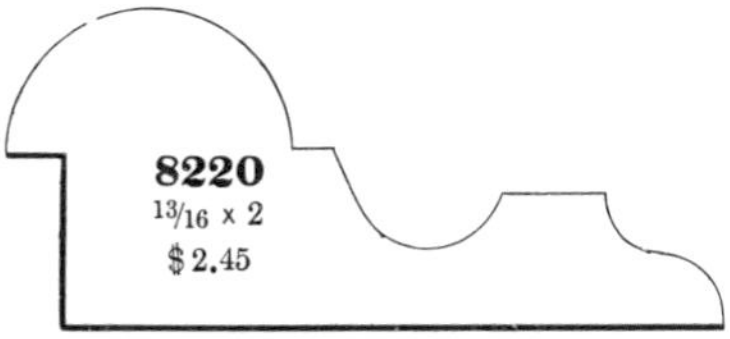

8220
13/16 x 2
$ 2.45

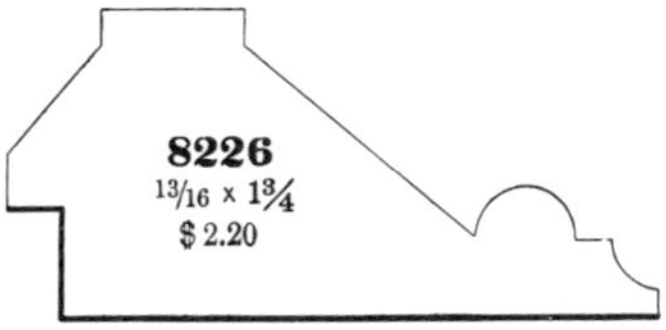

8226
13/16 x 1¾
$ 2.20

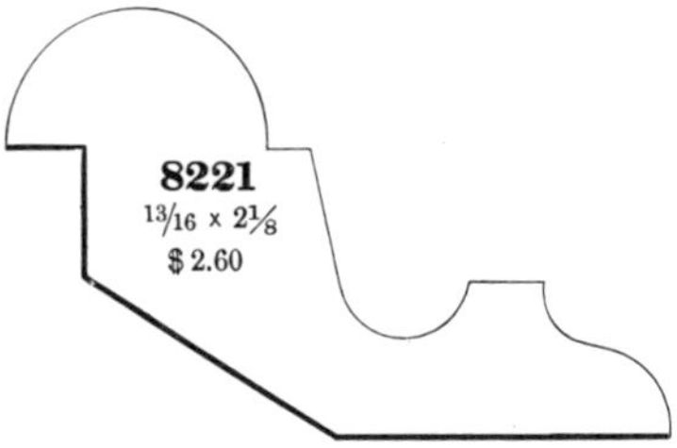

8221
13/16 x 2⅛
$ 2.60

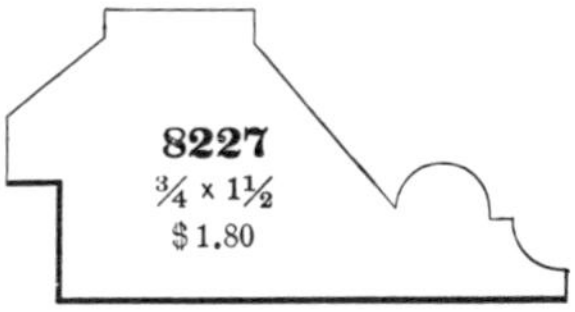

8227
¾ x 1½
$ 1.80

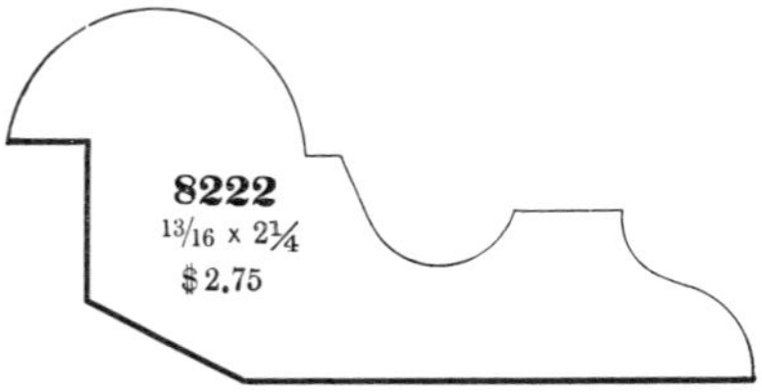

8222
13/16 x 2¼
$ 2.75

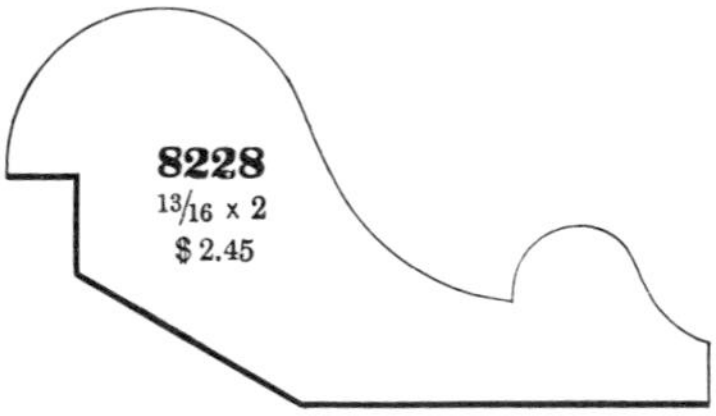

8228
13/16 x 2
$ 2.45

8223
13/16 x 2¾
$ 3.30

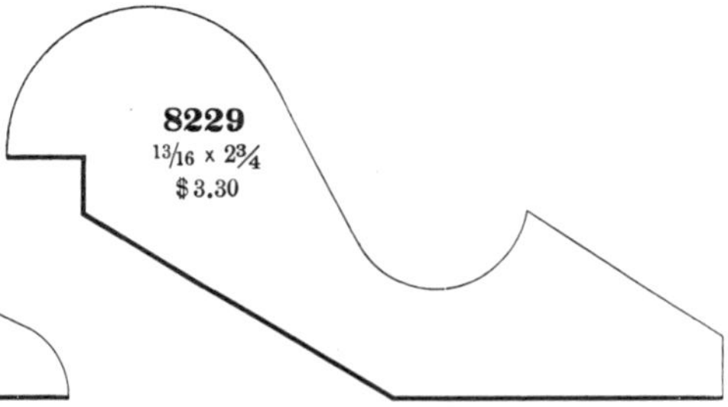

8229
13/16 x 2¾
$ 3.30

List Prices as given are per 100 lineal feet.

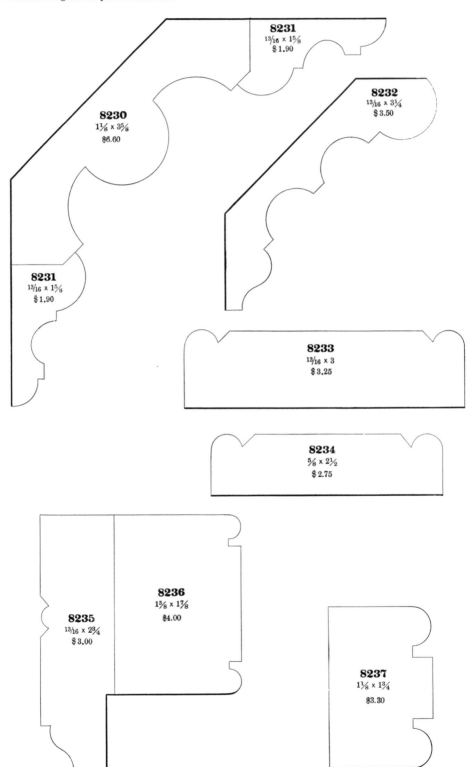

8231
$^{13}/_{16}$ x 1$^{5}/_{8}$
$ 1.90

8230
1$^{1}/_{8}$ x 3$^{5}/_{8}$
$6.60

8232
$^{13}/_{16}$ x 3$^{1}/_{4}$
$ 3.50

8231
$^{13}/_{16}$ x 1$^{5}/_{8}$
$ 1.90

8233
$^{13}/_{16}$ x 3
$ 3.25

8234
$^{5}/_{8}$ x 2$^{1}/_{2}$
$ 2.75

8236
1$^{3}/_{8}$ x 1$^{7}/_{8}$
$4.00

8235
$^{13}/_{16}$ x 2$^{3}/_{4}$
$ 3.00

8237
1$^{1}/_{8}$ x 1$^{3}/_{4}$
$3.30

List Prices as given are per 100 lineal feet.

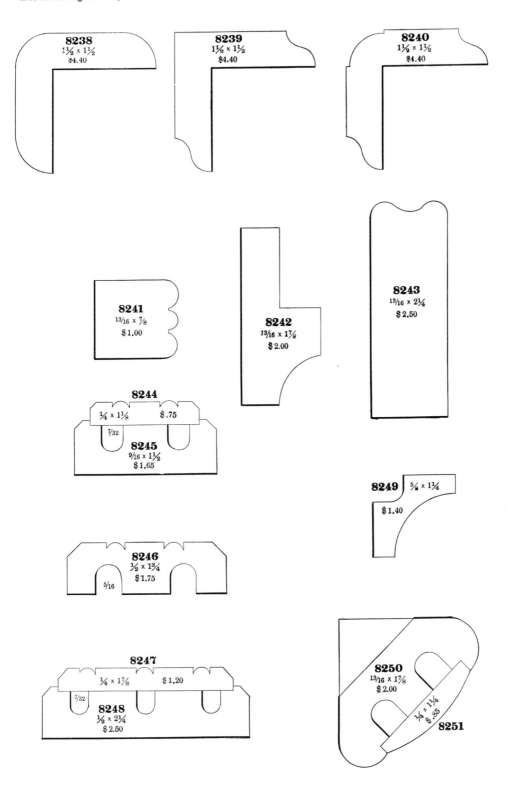

8238
1½ × 1½
$4.40

8239
1½ × 1½
$4.40

8240
1½ × 1½
$4.40

8241
13/16 × 7/8
$1.00

8242
13/16 × 1⅞
$2.00

8243
13/16 × 2¼
$2.50

8244
¼ × 1⅛ $.75
7/32

8245
9/16 × 1½
$1.65

8249   ⅝ × 1¼
$1.40

8246
½ × 1¾
$1.75
5/16

8247
¼ × 1⅞ $1.20
7/32

8248
½ × 2¼
$2.50

8250
13/16 × 1⅞
$2.00

¼ × 1¼
$.85

8251

List Prices as given are per 100 lineal feet.

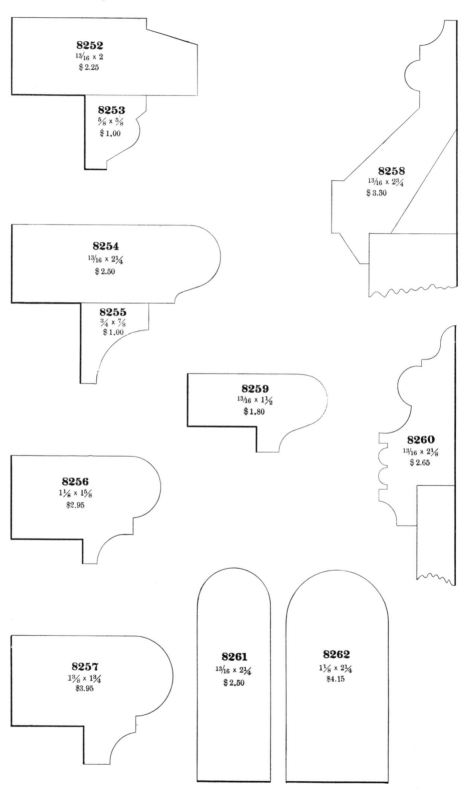

8252
13/16 x 2
$ 2.25

8253
5/8 x 5/8
$ 1.00

8258
13/16 x 2 3/4
$ 3.30

8254
13/16 x 2 1/4
$ 2.50

8255
3/4 x 7/8
$ 1.00

8259
13/16 x 1 1/2
$ 1.80

8260
13/16 x 2 1/8
$ 2.65

8256
1 1/8 x 1 5/8
$2.95

8257
1 3/8 x 1 3/4
$3.95

8261
13/16 x 2 1/4
$ 2.50

8262
1 1/8 x 2 1/4
$4.15

List Prices as given are per 100 lineal feet.

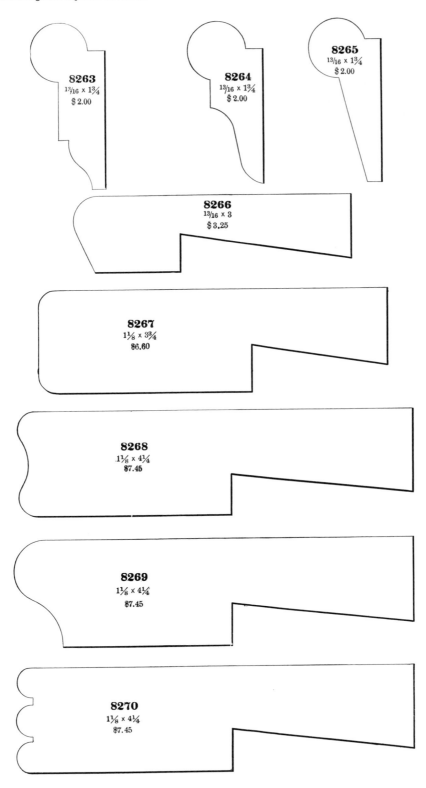

8263
13/16 x 13/4
$ 2.00

8264
13/16 x 13/4
$ 2.00

8265
13/16 x 13/4
$ 2.00

8266
13/16 x 3
$ 3.25

8267
1 1/8 x 3 3/4
$6.60

8268
1 1/8 x 4 1/4
$7.45

8269
1 1/8 x 4 1/4
$7.45

8270
1 1/8 x 4 1/4
$7.45

List Prices as given are per 100 lineal feet.

8271
$13/16 \times 1\frac{3}{4}$
$ 2.00

8272
$1\frac{1}{8} \times 2$
$3.75

8273
$13/16 \times 2\frac{1}{4}$
$ 2.50

8274
$13/16 \times 2\frac{1}{4}$
$ 2.50

8275
$1\frac{1}{8} \times 1\frac{5}{8}$
$2.95

8277
$\frac{1}{2} \times 3\frac{3}{4}$
$ 4.00

8276
$1\frac{3}{8} \times 1\frac{3}{4}$
$3.95

8278
$\frac{5}{8} \times 3\frac{3}{4}$
$ 4.00

8279
$\frac{5}{8} \times 4\frac{1}{4}$
$ 4.50

8280
$5/16 \times 1\frac{1}{8}$
$0.85

8281
$5/16 \times 1\frac{3}{8}$
$1.00

8282
$5/16 \times 1\frac{3}{4}$
$1.35

List Prices as given are per 100 lineal feet.

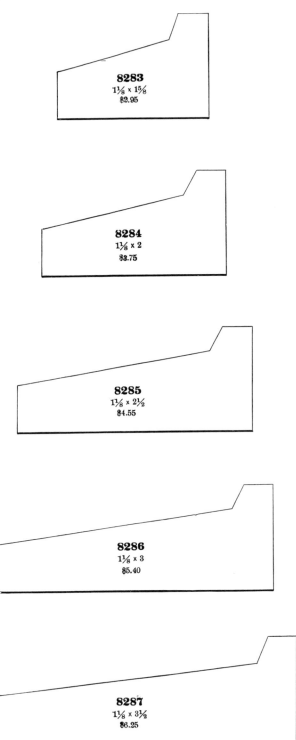

8283
1⅛ × 1⅝
$2.95

8284
1⅛ × 2
$3.75

8285
1⅛ × 2½
$4.55

8286
1⅛ × 3
$5.40

8287
1⅛ × 3½
$6.25

List Prices as given are per 100 lineal feet.

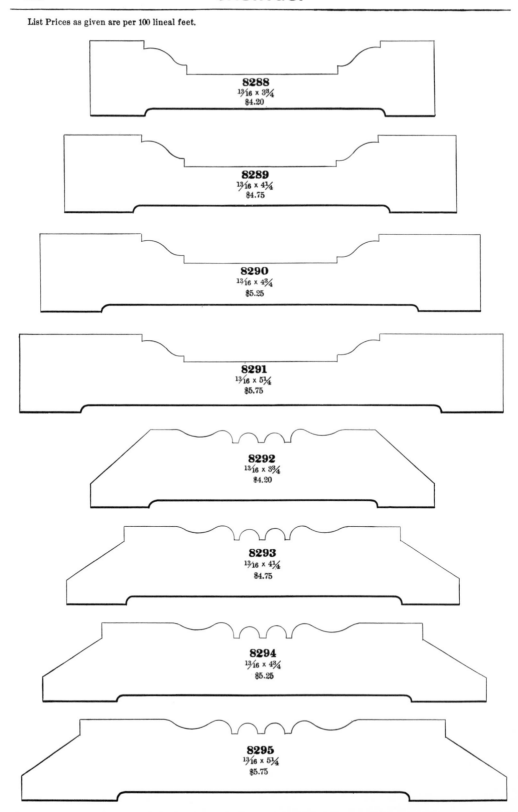

8288
13/16 x 3¾
$4.20

8289
13/16 x 4¼
$4.75

8290
13/16 x 4¾
$5.25

8291
13/16 x 5¼
$5.75

8292
13/16 x 3¾
$4.20

8293
13/16 x 4¼
$4.75

8294
13/16 x 4¾
$5.25

8295
13/16 x 5¼
$5.75

List Prices as given are per 100 lineal feet.

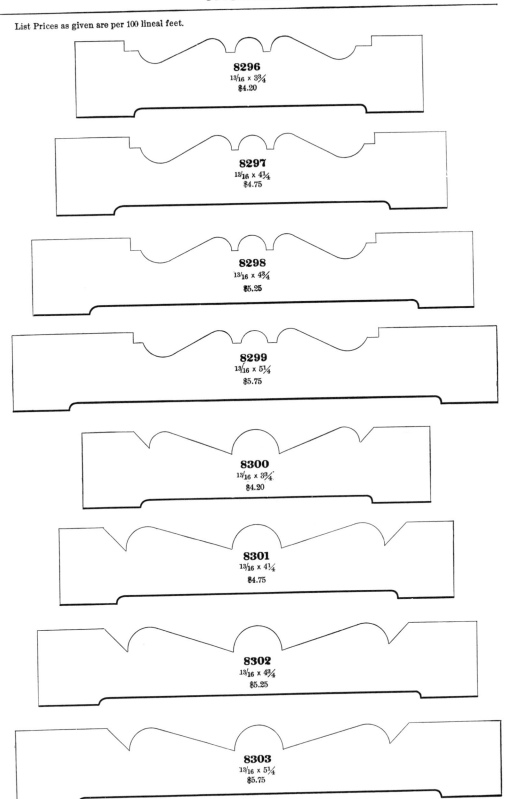

8296
13/16 x 3¾
$4.20

8297
13/16 x 4¼
$4.75

8298
13/16 x 4¾
$5.25

8299
13/16 x 5¼
$5.75

8300
13/16 x 3¾
$4.20

8301
13/16 x 4¼
$4.75

8302
13/16 x 4¾
$5.25

8303
13/16 x 5¼
$5.75

CASINGS.

List Prices as given are per 100 lineal feet.

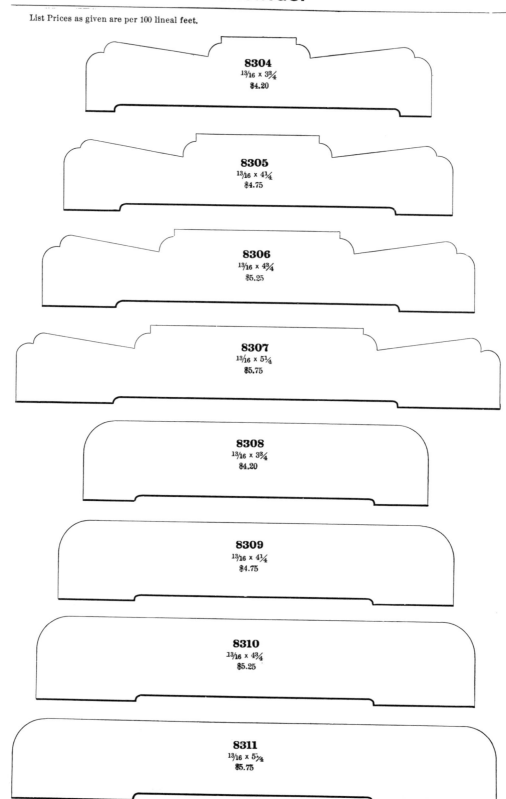

8304
$\frac{13}{16} \times 3\frac{3}{4}$
$4.20

8305
$\frac{13}{16} \times 4\frac{1}{4}$
$4.75

8306
$\frac{13}{16} \times 4\frac{3}{4}$
$5.25

8307
$\frac{13}{16} \times 5\frac{1}{4}$
$5.75

8308
$\frac{13}{16} \times 3\frac{3}{4}$
$4.20

8309
$\frac{13}{16} \times 4\frac{1}{4}$
$4.75

8310
$\frac{13}{16} \times 4\frac{3}{4}$
$5.25

8311
$\frac{13}{16} \times 5\frac{1}{4}$
$5.75

List Prices as given are per 100 lineal feet.

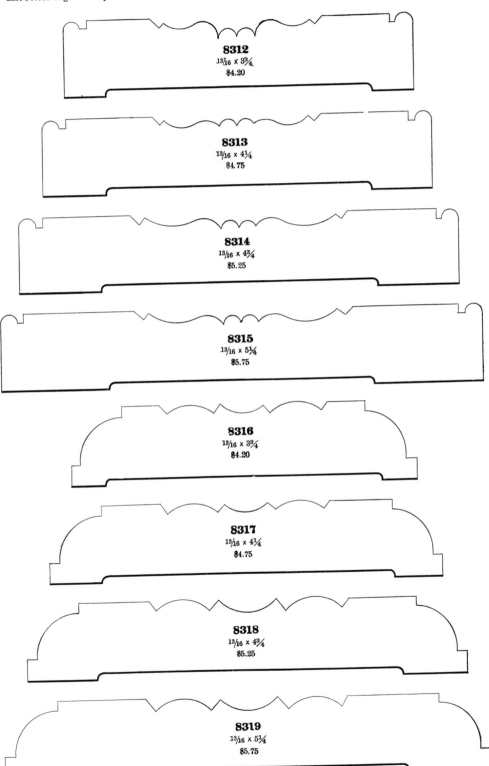

8312
$^{13}/_{16}$ x $3^{3}/_{4}$
$4.20

8313
$^{13}/_{16}$ x $4^{1}/_{4}$
$4.75

8314
$^{13}/_{16}$ x $4^{3}/_{4}$
$5.25

8315
$^{13}/_{16}$ x $5^{1}/_{4}$
$5.75

8316
$^{13}/_{16}$ x $3^{3}/_{4}$
$4.20

8317
$^{13}/_{16}$ x $4^{1}/_{4}$
$4.75

8318
$^{13}/_{16}$ x $4^{3}/_{4}$
$5.25

8319
$^{13}/_{16}$ x $5^{1}/_{4}$
$5.75

List Prices as given are per 100 lineal feet.

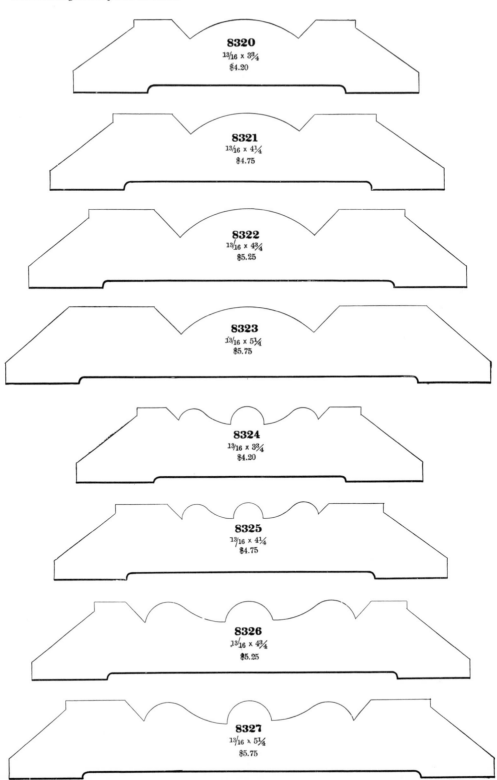

8320
$13/16 \times 3\frac{3}{4}$
$4.20

8321
$13/16 \times 4\frac{1}{4}$
$4.75

8322
$13/16 \times 4\frac{3}{4}$
$5.25

8323
$13/16 \times 5\frac{1}{4}$
$5.75

8324
$13/16 \times 3\frac{3}{4}$
$4.20

8325
$13/16 \times 4\frac{1}{4}$
$4.75

8326
$13/16 \times 4\frac{3}{4}$
$5.25

8327
$13/16 \times 5\frac{1}{4}$
$5.75

List Prices as given are per 100 lineal feet.

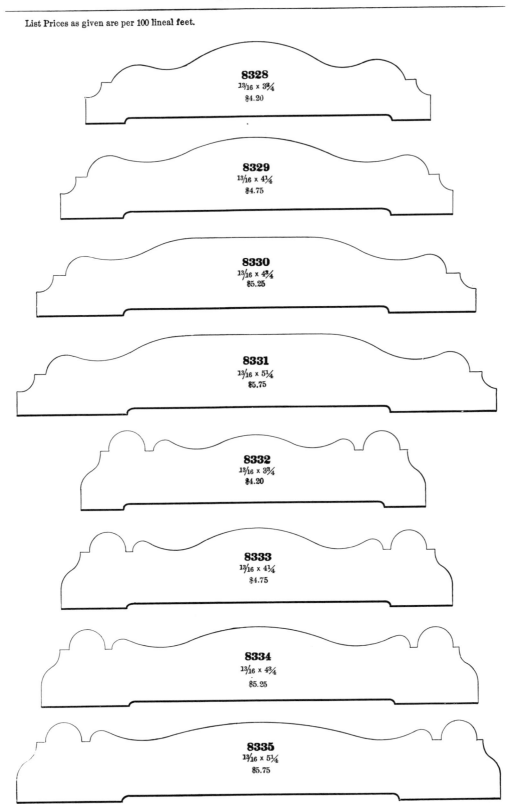

8328
$1\frac{3}{16} \times 3\frac{3}{4}$
$4.20

8329
$1\frac{3}{16} \times 4\frac{1}{4}$
$4.75

8330
$1\frac{3}{16} \times 4\frac{3}{4}$
$5.25

8331
$1\frac{3}{16} \times 5\frac{1}{4}$
$5.75

8332
$1\frac{3}{16} \times 3\frac{3}{4}$
$4.20

8333
$1\frac{3}{16} \times 4\frac{1}{4}$
$4.75

8334
$1\frac{3}{16} \times 4\frac{3}{4}$
$5.25

8335
$1\frac{3}{16} \times 5\frac{1}{4}$
$5.75

CASINGS.

List Prices as given are per 100 lineal feet.

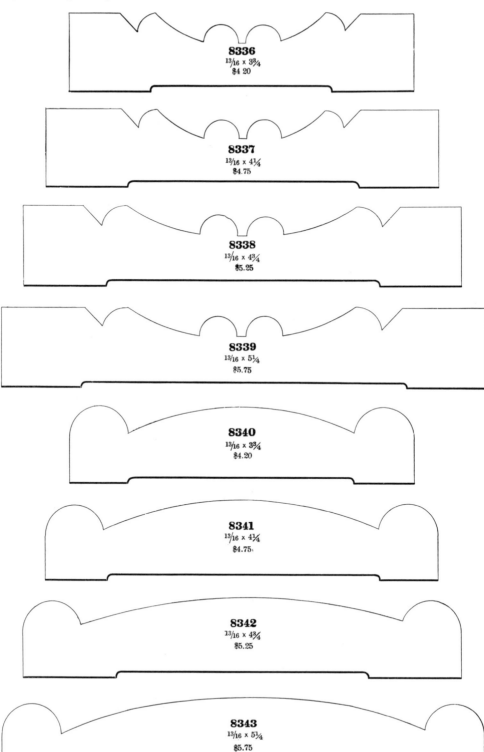

8336
13/16 x 3¾
$4 20

8337
13/16 x 4¼
$4.75

8338
13/16 x 4¾
$5.25

8339
13/16 x 5¼
$5.75

8340
13/16 x 3¾
$4.20

8341
13/16 x 4¼
$4.75

8342
13/16 x 4¾
$5.25

8343
13/16 x 5¼
$5.75

List Prices as given are per 100 lineal feet.

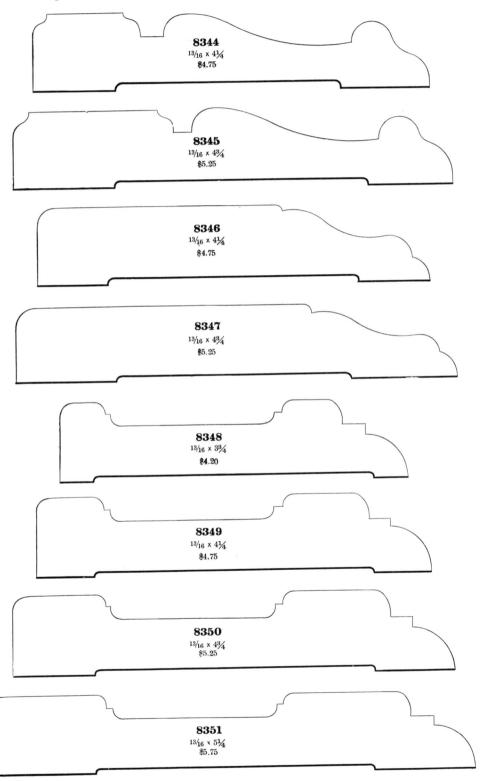

8344
$^{13}/_{16}$ x $4^{1}/_{4}$
$4.75

8345
$^{13}/_{16}$ x $4^{3}/_{4}$
$5.25

8346
$^{13}/_{16}$ x $4^{1}/_{4}$
$4.75

8347
$^{13}/_{16}$ x $4^{3}/_{4}$
$5.25

8348
$^{13}/_{16}$ x $3^{3}/_{4}$
$4.20

8349
$^{13}/_{16}$ x $4^{1}/_{4}$
$4.75

8350
$^{13}/_{16}$ x $4^{3}/_{4}$
$5.25

8351
$^{13}/_{16}$ x $5^{1}/_{4}$
$5.75

List Prices as given are per 100 lineal feet.

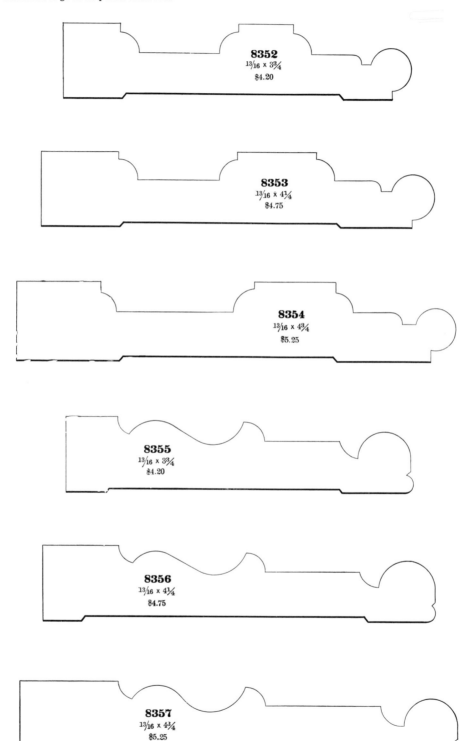

8352
13/16 x 3¾
$4.20

8353
13/16 x 4¼
$4.75

8354
13/16 x 4¾
$5.25

8355
13/16 x 3¾
$4.20

8356
13/16 x 4¼
$4.75

8357
13/16 x 4¾
$5.25

List Prices as given are per 100 lineal feet.

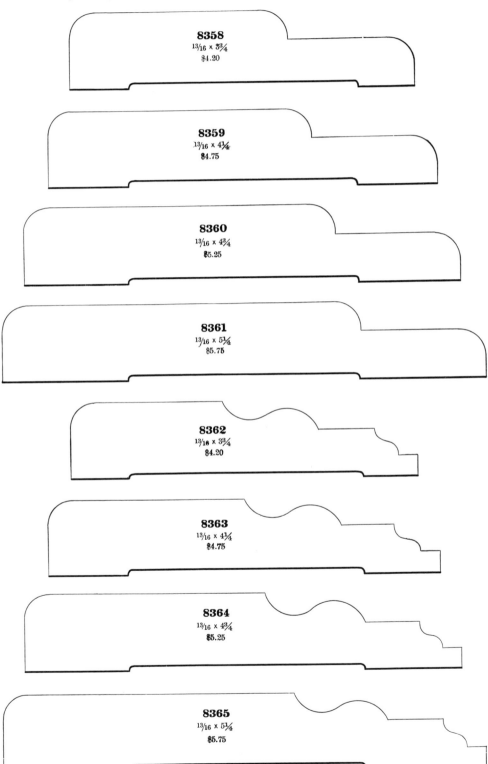

8358
13/16 × 3¾
$4.20

8359
13/16 × 4¼
$4.75

8360
13/16 × 4¾
$5.25

8361
13/16 × 5¼
$5.75

8362
13/16 × 3¾
$4.20

8363
13/16 × 4¼
$4.75

8364
13/16 × 4¾
$5.25

8365
13/16 × 5¼
$5.75

List Prices as given are per 100 lineal feet.

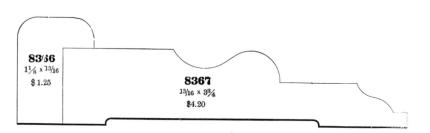

8366
1⅛ x 13/16
$ 1.25

8367
13/16 x 3¾
$4.20

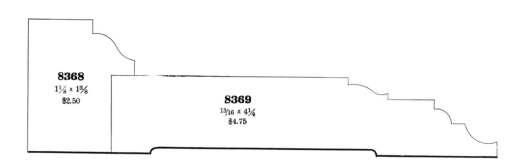

8368
1⅛ x 1⅜
$2.50

8369
13/16 x 4¼
$4.75

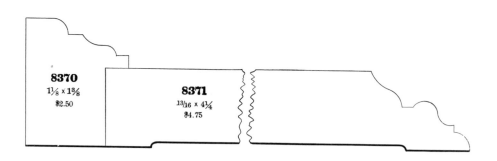

8370
1⅛ x 1⅜
$2.50

8371
13/16 x 4¼
$4.75

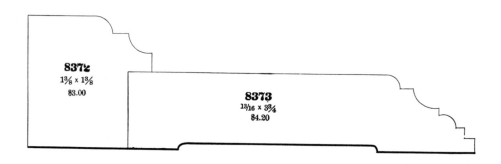

8372
1⅜ x 1⅜
$3.00

8373
13/16 x 3¾
$4.20

List Prices as given are per 100 lineal feet.

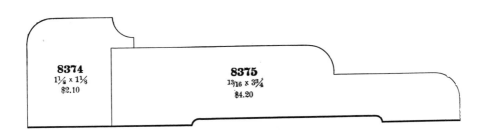

8374
1⅛ x 1⅛
$2.10

8375
13/16 x 3¾
$4.20

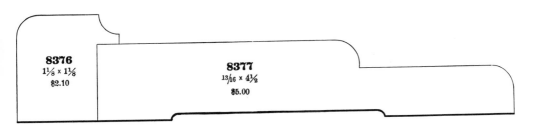

8376
1⅛ x 1⅛
$2.10

8377
13/16 x 4½
$5.00

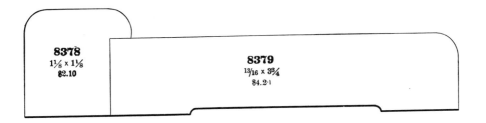

8378
1⅛ x 1⅛
$2.10

8379
13/16 x 3¾
$4.2·)

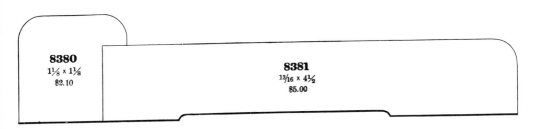

8380
1⅛ x 1⅛
$2.10

8381
13/16 x 4½
$5.00

List Prices as given are per 100 lineal feet.

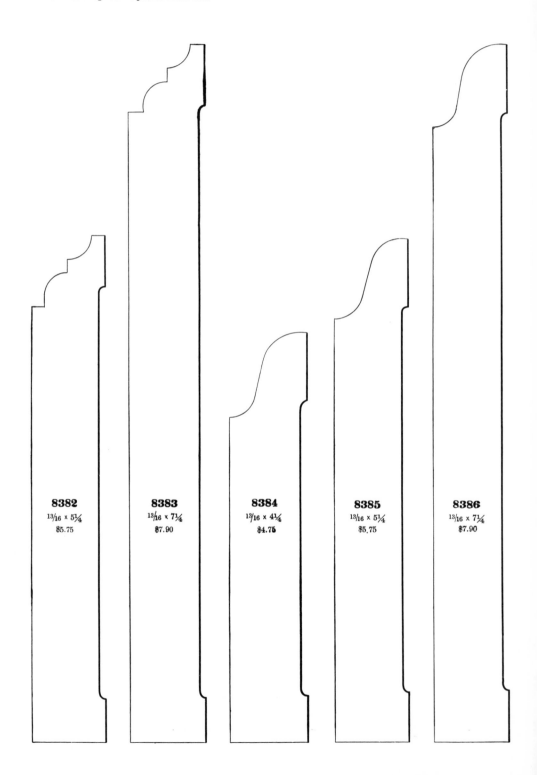

8382
13/16 x 5¼
$5.75

8383
13/16 x 7¼
$7.90

8384
13/16 x 4¼
$4.75

8385
13/16 x 5¼
$5.75

8386
13/16 x 7¼
$7.90

List Prices as given are per 100 lineal feet.

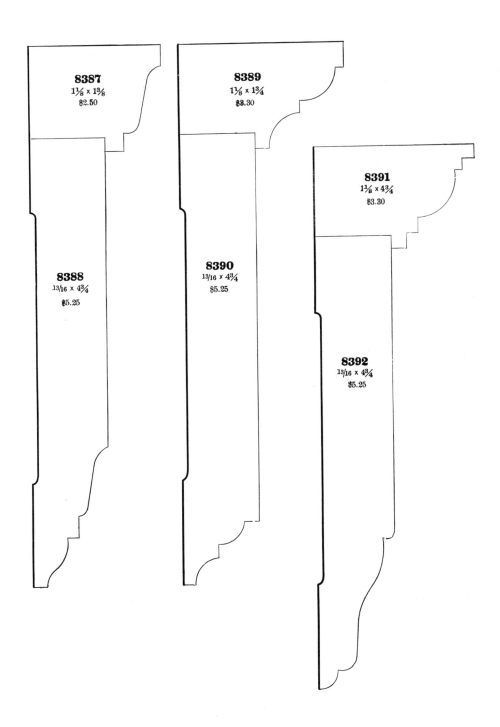

8387
1⅛ x 1⅛
$2.50

8389
1⅛ x 1¾
$3.30

8391
1⅛ x 4¾
$3.30

8388
13/16 x 4¾
$5.25

8390
13/16 x 4¾
$5.25

8392
13/16 x 4¾
$5.25

List Prices as given are per 100 lineal feet.

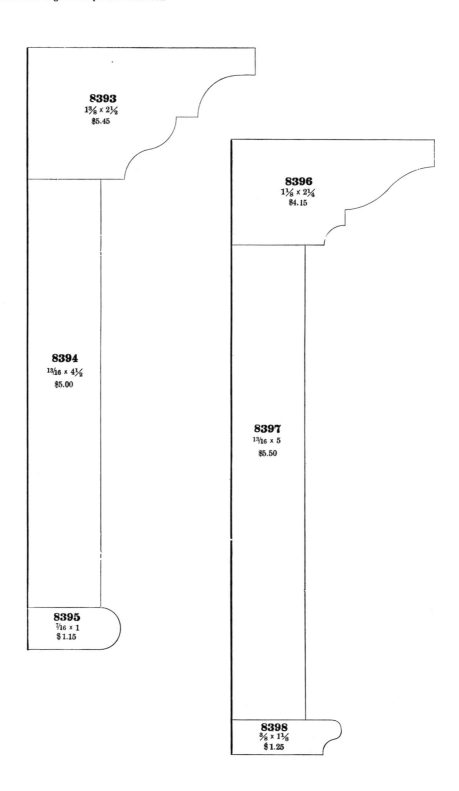

8393
1⅜ x 2½
$5.45

8396
1⅛ x 2¼
$4.15

8394
13⁄16 x 4½
$5.00

8397
13⁄16 x 5
$5.50

8395
7⁄16 x 1
$1.15

8398
⅜ x 1⅛
$1.25

List Prices as given are per 100 lineal feet.

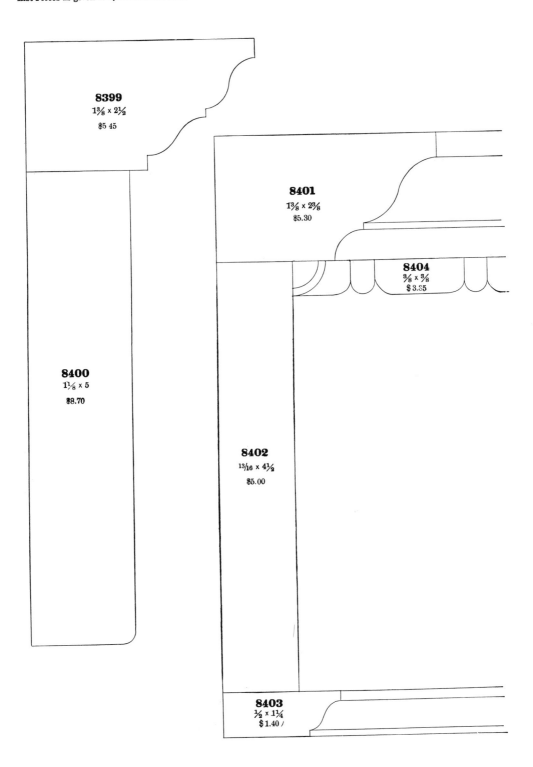

8399
1⅜ x 2½
$5.45

8401
1⅜ x 2⅜
$5.30

8404
⅜ x ⅜
$3.85

8400
1⅛ x 5
$8.70

8402
13⁄16 x 4½
$5.00

8403
½ x 1¼
$1.40

List Prices as given are per 100 lineal feet.

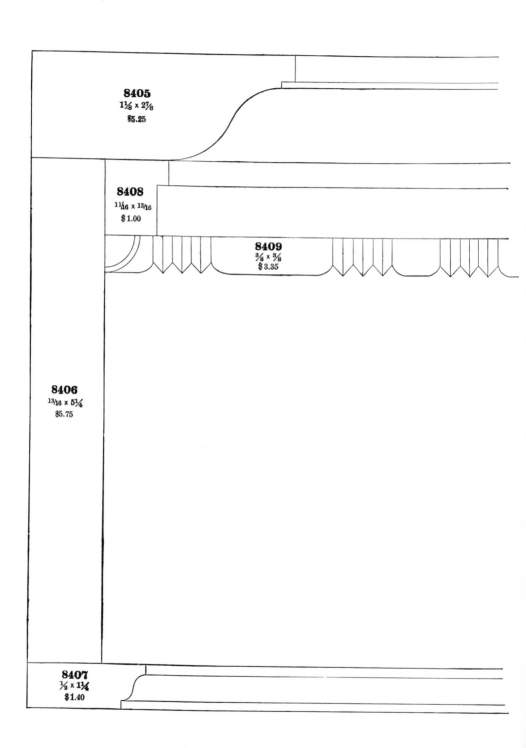

8405
1⅛ x 2⅞
$5.25

8408
11⁄16 x 13⁄16
$1.00

8409
⅜ x ⅜
$3.35

8406
13⁄16 x 5¼
$5.75

8407
½ x 1¼
$1.40

List Prices as given are per 100 lineal **feet.**

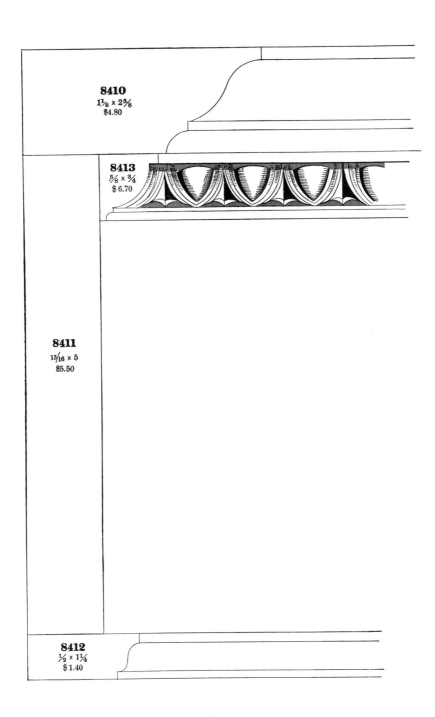

8410
1⅛ x 2⅝
$4.80

8413
⅝ x ¾
$ 6.70

8411
13⁄16 x 5
$5.50

8412
½ x 1¼
$ 1.40

List Prices as given are per 100 lineal feet.

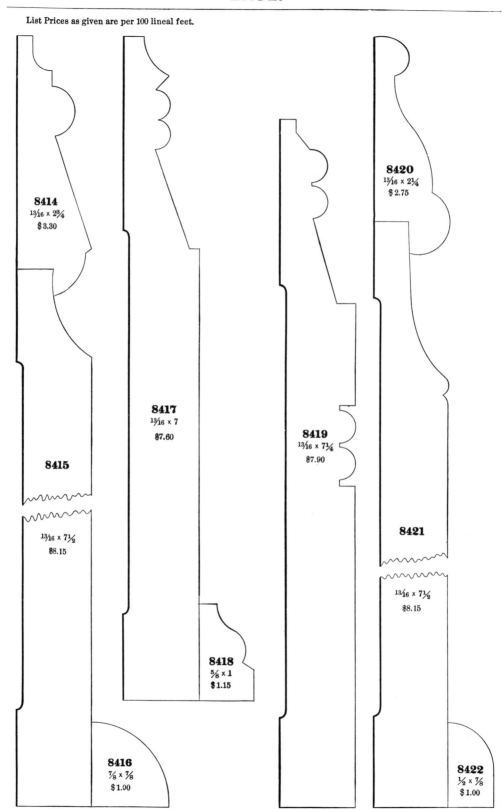

8414
13/16 x 2¾
$3.30

8415

13/16 x 7½
$8.15

8416
⅞ x ⅞
$1.00

8417
13/16 x 7
$7.60

8418
⅝ x 1
$1.15

8419
13/16 x 7¼
$7.90

8420
13/16 x 2¼
$2.75

8421

13/16 x 7½
$8.15

8422
½ x ⅞
$1.00

List Prices as given are per 100 lineal feet.

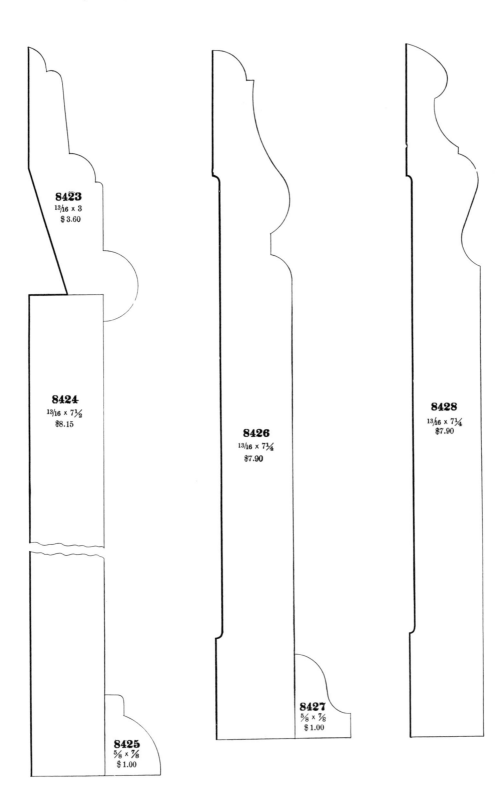

8423
13/16 x 3
$ 3.60

8424
13/16 x 7½
$8.15

8425
⅝ x ⅞
$ 1.00

8426
13/16 x 7¼
$7.90

8427
⅝ x ⅞
$ 1.00

8428
13/16 x 7¼
$7.90

List Prices as given are per 100 lineal feet.

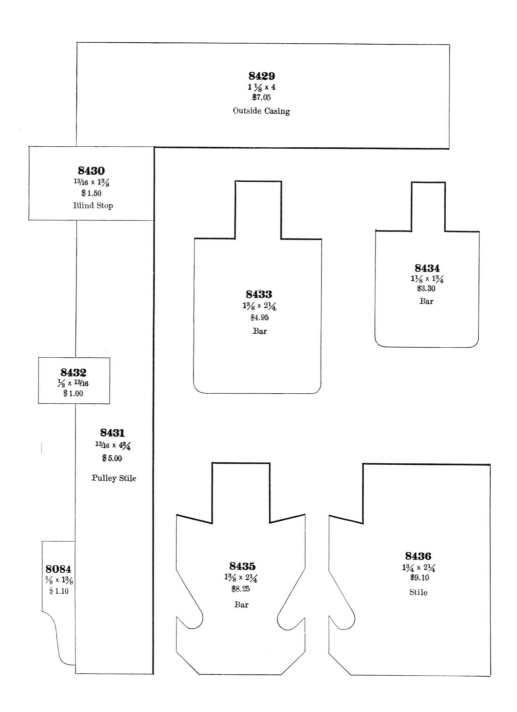

8429
1 ⅛ × 4
$7.05
Outside Casing

8430
13/16 × 1⅜
$1.50
Blind Stop

8433
1⅜ × 2¼
$4.95
Bar

8434
1⅛ × 1¾
$3.30
Bar

8432
½ × 13/16
$1.00

8431
13/16 × 4¾
$5.00
Pulley Stile

8084
⅜ × 1⅜
$1.10

8435
1⅜ × 2¼
$8.25
Bar

8436
1¾ × 2¼
$9.10
Stile

List Prices as given are per 100 lineal feet.

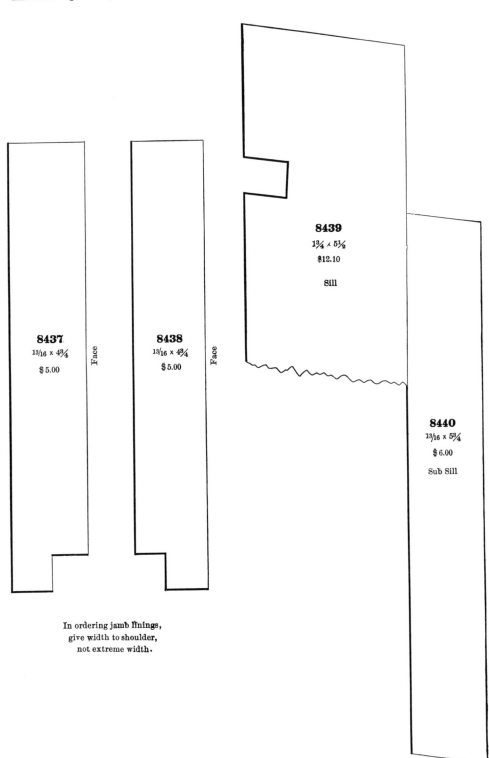

8439
1¾ × 5½
$12.10

Sill

8437
13/16 × 4¾
$ 5.00

Face

8438
13/16 × 4¾
$ 5.00

Face

8440
13/16 × 5¾
$ 6.00

Sub Sill

In ordering jamb linings,
give width to shoulder,
not extreme width.

List Prices as given are per 100 lineal feet.

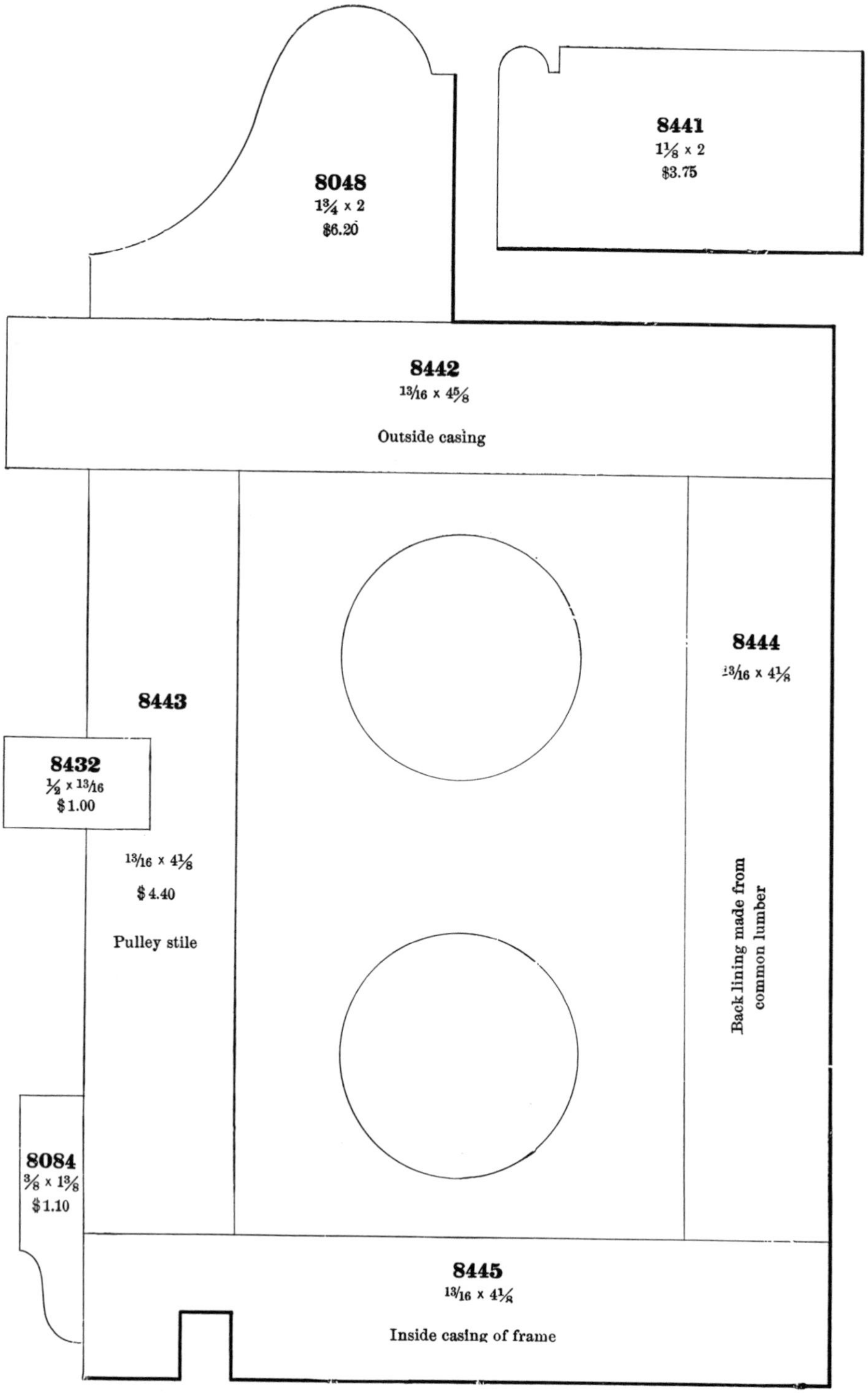
8048
1¾ x 2
$6.20
8441
1⅛ x 2
$3.75
8442
13/16 x 4⅝
Outside casing
8443
13/16 x 4⅛
$4.40
Pulley stile
8432
½ x 13/16
$1.00
8444
13/16 x 4⅛
Back lining made from common lumber
8084
⅜ x 1⅜
$1.10
8445
13/16 x 4⅛
Inside casing of frame

List Prices as given are per 100 lineal feet.

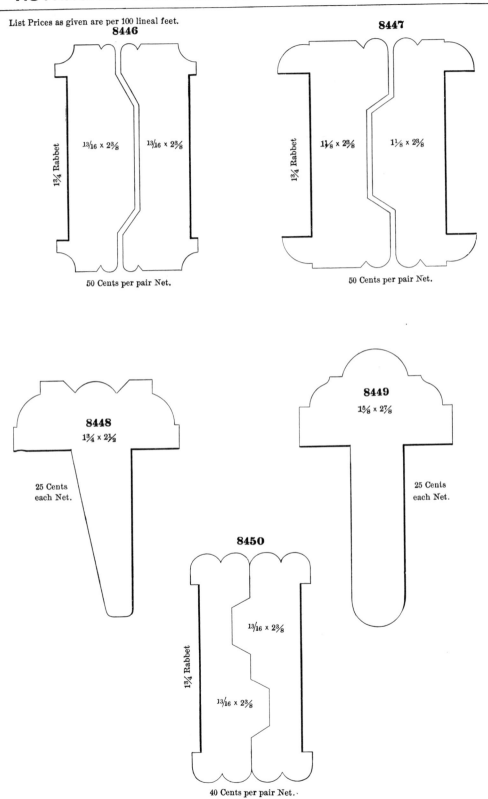

8446

$\frac{13}{4}$ Rabbet

$\frac{13}{16} \times 2\frac{3}{8}$ $\frac{13}{16} \times 2\frac{3}{8}$

50 Cents per pair Net.

8447

$\frac{13}{4}$ Rabbet

$1\frac{1}{8} \times 2\frac{3}{8}$ $1\frac{1}{8} \times 2\frac{3}{8}$

50 Cents per pair Net.

8448

$1\frac{3}{4} \times 2\frac{1}{2}$

25 Cents
each Net.

8449

$1\frac{5}{8} \times 2\frac{7}{8}$

25 Cents
each Net.

8450

$\frac{13}{4}$ Rabbet

$\frac{13}{16} \times 2\frac{3}{8}$

$\frac{13}{16} \times 2\frac{3}{8}$

40 Cents per pair Net.

PORCH RAILS.

List Prices as given are per 100 lineal feet.

8451
1¾ x 3

8452
1¾₁₆ x 3

8455
1¾ x 3

8453
1¾ x 2⅝

8454
2¾ x 2¾

8456
2¼ x 3¾

List Prices as given are per 100 lineal feet.

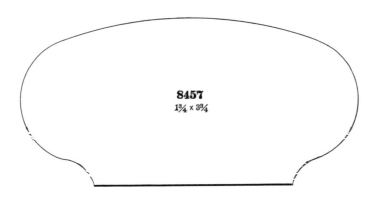

8457
1¾ x 3¾

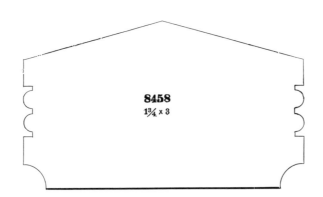

8458
1¾ x 3

8459
1¾ x 1¾

8460
1⅜ x 1⅜

LIST PRICE OF MOULDINGS.

PRICES GIVEN ARE PER 100 LINEAL FEET.

No.	Price	No.	Price	No.	Price	No.	Price	No.	Price
8000	$3.50	8054	$1.15	8108	$1.85	8162	$1.25	8216	$2.45
8001	6.00	8055	3.30	8109	1.60	8163	1.50	8217	2.90
8002	4.00	8056	4.85	8110	1.20	8164	1.50	8218	1.55
8003	3.00	8057	4.85	8111	1.05	8165	2.50	8219	1.90
8004	5.50	8058	1.00	8112	2.50	8166	1.25	8220	2.45
8005	5.00	8059	1.00	8113	2.25	8167	1.40	8221	2.60
8006	4.50	8060	1.00	8114	2.05	8168	2.00	8222	2.75
8007	2.00	8061	1.25	8115	1.80	8169	1.40	8223	3.30
8008	2.50	8062	2.00	8116	1.35	8170	1.65	8224	3.30
8009	4.00	8063	1.00	8117	1.15	8171	2.00	8225	2.75
8010	3.00	8064	1.00	8118	1.15	8172	2.00	8226	2.20
8011	2.50	8065	1.00	8119	1.35	8173	2.00	8227	1.80
8012	4.50	8066	1.00	8120	1.80	8174	1.75	8228	2.45
8013	5.00	8067	1.50	8121	2.05	8175	2.00	8229	3.30
8014	3.50	8068	2.00	8122	2.25	8176	2.00	8230	6.60
8015	1.15	8069	2.50	8123	1.65	8177	2.25	8231	1.90
8016	2.00	8070	1.00	8124	3.75	8178	2.25	8232	3.50
8017	1.65	8071	1.00	8125	4.95	8179	2.50	8233	3.25
8018	2.50	8072	1.25	8126	8.80	8180	2.75	8234	2.75
8019	3.00	8073	1.15	8127	2.00	8181	3.00	8235	3.00
8020	3.50	8074	2.25	8128	1.00	8182	3.25	8236	4.00
8021	4.50	8075	1.00	8129	1.15	8183	2.75	8237	3.30
8022	5.00	8076	1.00	8130	1.25	8184	2.50	8238	4.40
8023	4.00	8077	1.00	8131	1.40	8185	2.00	8239	4.40
8024	2.00	8078	1.15	8132	1.00	8186	2.00	8240	4.40
8025	2.50	8079	1.40	8133	1.50	8187	1.75	8241	1.00
8026	3.00	8080	1.75	8134	3.30	8188	2.25	8242	2.00
8027	4.50	8081	2.00	8135	1.65	8189	2.00	8243	2.50
8028	4.00	8082	90	8136	3.95	8190	2.25	8244	.75
8029	3.50	8083	1.00	8137	2.00	8191	2.75	8245	1.65
8030	2.50	8084	1.10	8138	2.00	8192	2.75	8246	1.75
8031	2.00	8085	1.40	8139	1.00	8193	1.50	8247	1.20
8032	2.25	8086	1.60	8140	1.00	8194	2.50	8248	2.50
8033	3.00	8087	1.80	8141	1.25	8195	2.00	8249	1.40
8034	3.50	8088	2.00	8142	1.50	8196	2.50	8250	2.00
8035	1.00	8089	1.15	8143	1.75	8197	3.00	8251	.85
8036	1.40	8090	1.60	8144	2.25	8198	2.00	8252	2.25
8037	2.50	8091	2.05	8145	1.00	8199	3.50	8253	1.00
8038	3.30	8092	2.25	8146	1.00	8200	2.00	8254	2.50
8039	5.50	8093	2.00	8147	1.75	8201	2.25	8255	1.00
8040	1.00	8094	1.80	8148	2.25	8202	2.50	8256	2.95
8041	1.25	8095	1.60	8149	2.25	8203	2.50	8257	3.95
8042	1.00	8096	1.20	8150		8204	1.75	8258	3.30
8043	1.00	8097	1.10	8151		8205	3.00	8259	1.80
8044	1.25	8098	1.35	8152	1.15	8206	1.80	8260	2.65
8045	1.65	8099	1.80	8153	1.25	8207	2.45	8261	2.50
8046	2.95	8100	2.25	8154	1.50	8208	3.00	8262	4.15
8047	3.45	8101	1.05	8155	1.50	8209	3.00	8263	2.00
8048	6.20	8102	1.20	8156	1.75	8210	3.00	8264	2.00
8049	4.85	8103	1.60	8157	2.00	8211	3.30	8265	2.00
8050	2.75	8104	1.85	8158	1.75	8212	2.20	8266	3.25
8051	1.70	8105	2.00	8159	1.15	8213	2.45	8267	6.60
8052	1.00	8106	2.25	8160	1.00	8214	2.90	8268	7.45
8053	1.00	8107	2.00	8161	1.15	8215	2.20	8269	7.45

PRICES GIVEN ARE PER 100 LINEAL FEET.

No.	PRICE	No.	PRICE	No.	PRICE	No.	PRICE	No.	PRICE
8270	$7.45	8309	$4.75	8348	$4.20	8387	$2.50	8426	$7.90
8271	2.00	8310	5.25	8349	4.75	8388	5.25	8427	1.00
8272	3.75	8311	5.75	8350	5.25	8389	3.30	8428	7.90
8273	2.50	8312	4.20	8351	5.75	8390	5.25	8429	7.05
8274	2.50	8313	4.75	8352	4.20	8391	3.30	8430	1.50
8275	2.95	8314	5.25	8353	4.75	8392	5.25	8431	5.00
8276	3.95	8315	5.75	8354	5.25	8393	5.45	8432	1.00
8277	4.00	8316	4.20	8355	4.20	8394	5.00	8433	4.95
8278	4.00	8317	4.75	8356	4.75	8395	1.15	8434	3.30
8279	4.50	8318	5.25	8357	5.25	8396	4.15	8435	8.25
8280	.85	8319	5.75	8358	4.20	8397	5.50	8436	9.10
8281	1.00	8320	4.20	8359	4.75	8398	1.25	8437	5.00
8282	1.35	8321	4.75	8360	5.25	8399	5.45	8438	5.00
8283	2.95	8322	5.25	8361	5.75	8400	8.70	8439	12.10
8284	3.75	8323	5.75	8362	4.20	8401	5.30	8440	6.00
8285	4.55	8324	4.20	8363	4.75	8402	5.00	8441	3.75
8286	5.40	8325	4.75	8364	5.25	8403	1.40	8442	....
8287	6.25	8326	5.25	8365	5.75	8404	3.35	8443	4.40
8288	4.20	8327	5.75	8366	1.25	8405	5.25	8444	....
8289	4.75	8328	4.20	8367	4.20	8406	5.75	8445	....
8290	5.25	8329	4.75	8368	2.50	8407	1.40	8446	....
8291	5.75	8330	5.25	8369	4.75	8408	1.00	8447	....
8292	4.20	8331	5.75	8370	2.50	8409	3.35	8448	....
8293	4.75	8332	4.20	8371	4.75	8410	4.80	8449	....
8294	5.25	8333	4.75	8372	3.00	8411	5.50	8450	....
8295	5.75	8334	5.25	8373	4.20	8412	1.40	8451	....
8296	4.20	8335	5.75	8374	2.10	8413	6.70	8452	....
8297	4.75	8336	4.20	8375	4.20	8414	3.30	8453	....
8298	5.25	8337	4.75	8376	2.10	8415	8.15	8454	....
8299	5.75	8338	5.25	8377	5.00	8416	1.00	8455	....
8300	4.20	8339	5.75	8378	2.10	8417	7.60	8456	....
8301	4.75	8340	4.20	8379	4.20	8418	1.15	8457	....
8302	5.25	8341	4.75	8380	2.10	8419	7.90	8458	....
8303	5.75	8342	5.25	8381	5.00	8420	2.75	8459	....
8304	4.20	8343	5.75	8382	5.75	8421	8.15	8460	....
8305	4.75	8344	4.75	8383	7.90	8422	1.00		....
8306	5.25	8345	5.25	8384	4.75	8423	3.60		....
8307	5.75	8346	4.75	8385	5.75	8424	8.15		....
8308	4.20	8347	5.25	8386	7.90	8425	1.00		....

IMPORTANT NOTICE.

When moulding is priced by the inch *it is in all cases understood* that the price is based on ripping width of lumber, that is: $\frac{1}{4}$ *of an inch wider than the finished size* of moulding. For example: A $\frac{7}{8}$ inch thick panel moulding, if made to finish $1\frac{3}{4}$ inch wide, would be charged as 2 inches (being ripping size); to finish full 2 inches, would be charged as $2\frac{1}{4}$ inch, etc.

Approximate weight of Mouldings, 1x1 inch per 100 lineal feet, 15 pounds.